Praise for *Black Lives Matter at School*

"The educators, students, and community activists whose stories are documented here are fighting for a transformative vision of what public schools can be, and the grassroots efforts we will need to get there. *Black Lives Matter at School* is an essential resource for all those seeking to build an antiracist school system."

—Ibram X. Kendi, National Book Award–winner
and #1 *New York Times* bestselling author

"We need this book right now. The shadow-loving fungus of white supremacy won't continue to send its spores to infect our children if we act now to bring the curative light of antiracist knowledge, compassion, and justice into their lives. Built upon the Black Lives Matter at School organization's Week of Action, this volume provides the adults in our educational institutions with inspiration, organizing principles, strategies, and examples to take 'bold action against anti-Blackness.' The authors—visionary educators of what is possible—call on all of us to radically reshape learning environments to make them safe, supportive, and transformative for all students (and teachers). Please read ASAP!"

—Lisa Delpit, executive director of the Center for Urban Education
and Innovation at Florida International University

"This book makes the strong case for why we need to elevate Black lives and people in our curriculum and pedagogy year-round. This book serves as a blueprint for achieving this honorable goal."

—José Luis Vilson, author, *This Is Not A Test,
A New Narrative on Race, Class, and Education*

"Toni Morrison reminds us: 'If you can't imagine it, you can't have it.' This book helps us to imagine Black lives mattering in schools. With accounts from teachers across the country doing the work, along with student interviews, poems, posters, and historical background, this is a primer for antiracist educators to see the way forward in terms of reshaping school curriculum, diversifying teacher hiring, and transforming school discipline."

—Jeanne Theoharis, author, *A More Beautiful and Terrible History:
The Uses and Misuses of Civil Rights History*

"There is no easy way to talk about the complexities of race facing our school system in America—but we have to talk about it if we are ever going to achieve the schools our children deserve. The Black Lives Matter at School movement has been disrupting the complacency of those who, for too long, have been comfortable not having these conversations about the impact of racism in the schools. *Black Lives Matter at School* is a playbook for undoing institutional racism in the education system.
—Michael Bennett, NFL defensive lineman, Super Bowl champion, and author, *Things That Make White People Uncomfortable*

"This book asserts that we are at a critical moment in time, where the racial uprisings emphasize the absolute need to transform education and its foundational practices. Black Lives Matter is a movement sweeping the globe and affirming that our babies' lives matter. It's time for educators to be bold, standing up for our students and communities. Our students are looking to us to lead the fight against injustice and dismantle systemic racism as we aspire to realize the schools our students deserve."
—Cecily Myart-Cruz, UTLA president, NEA Black Caucus chair

"*Black Lives Matter at School* centers the humanity of our children. It is a sharp rebuke of white supremacy—the very thing that interrupts the healthy development of Black youth. School communities must affirm Black lives. Educators have to dismantle systems of oppression—systems that we influence daily. We have to be radically different from the missionary educators depicted in popular culture. *Black Lives Matter at School* is essential. Period."
—Stacy Davis Gates, Chicago Teachers Union vice president

Black Lives Matter at School

An Uprising for Educational Justice

Edited by Denisha Jones and Jesse Hagopian

Foreword by Opal Tometi

Haymarket Books
Chicago, Illinois

Published in 2020 by
Haymarket Books
P.O. Box 180165
Chicago, IL 60618
773-583-7884
www.haymarketbooks.org
info@haymarketbooks.org

ISBN: 978-1-64259-389-1

Distributed to the trade in the US through Consortium Book Sales
and Distribution (www.cbsd.com) and internationally through Ingram
Publisher Services International (www.ingramcontent.com).

This book was published with the generous support of Lannan Foundation
and Wallace Action Fund.

Special discounts are available for bulk purchases by
organizations and institutions. Please call 773-583-7884
or email info@haymarketbooks.org for more information.

Cover artwork from *Rise*, 2020, by Ferrari Sheppard. Cover design by
Rachel Cohen.

Library of Congress Cataloging-in-Publication data is available.

*To the Black children of the future who will one day all be
taught the epic story of how Black people finally got free,
and who will grow up knowing that their lives matter at
school—and everywhere else.*

CONTENTS

Foreword

By Opal Tometi

Nearly every day in the United States we are bombarded with news stories illustrating the hardships that Black children face in their schools. Whether the headline is about a six-year-old girl being arrested by the police, a high school senior ineligible to graduate because of his hairstyle, or an eleven-year-old girl being assaulted by a school resource officer, the stories are outrageous, but their impact on the lives of Black students is real. Today, 1.7 million US children go to a school where a police officer stands guard yet no counselor is on staff—and some fourteen million students attend a school with a police officer and no counselor, nurse, psychologist, or social worker. It cannot be overstated: the United States is in the midst of an urgent moral and legal crisis over the safety, liberty, and well-being of Black young people.

As I write the foreword for this important and necessary book, I can't help but feel intimately committed to this project's central thesis. The issues this book grapples with are personal for me. They were the very concerns that led me, along with Alicia Garza and Patrisse Khan-Cullors, to found Black Lives Matter. As an educator, I've walked the halls of many campuses, and I've heard the concerns of students, parents, and teachers. And it feels like just yesterday that I, too, was a young person in school. The classroom was the site of my own formative understanding of my own value in the world and my sense of what was possible for me, a person of color. In fact, it was in school that I first became aware that some people took issue with my skin color.

I was in the first grade at my school in suburban Arizona and recess had just ended. Our teacher called our class to come inside, and some friends and I were scurrying to join the line of twenty or so first graders. I stumbled over a friend and accidentally kicked a boy's shoe. He looked at me and sneered, "Nigger." I had never heard the word before, nor did I have a clue what it meant. However, young Opal knew from his tone and stare that the word wasn't anything good. And in my bewilderment—mixed with shame at my failure to understand his outrage and why he had used this unique name for me and not the other girls—I knew intuitively that I couldn't share what had happened with my teacher. Thankfully, my parents overheard me telling my younger brother about the incident, and they took a stand for me. The very next day, they went to my classroom to discuss the episode with the teacher. While I never again heard that terrible work spoken in my class, I went on to have many other encounters over the years that left me feeling devalued and out of place. Still, it was that formative experience in first grade that helped me see that if we experience or witness injustice, we can speak up and change it.

It was in high school that I began to find my own unique voice. I joined a diversity and equality club and quickly assumed a leadership position as my passion and leadership skills became apparent. I was invited by our principal to join the district-wide diversity council. At age sixteen, I was the only Black person in that space, but I was emboldened by the acknowledgment of my voice and presence. At school, I worked to create programs, events, and opportunities for students of color that would reflect their beauty and ingenuity. I supported their visibility on campus by helping to usher in Diversity Week at my school. One of my most thrilling memories from that time was arranging to have some of our school's artistic Mexican students perform folkloric dance. Their vibrant, twirling skirts and dresses took up literal and figurative space in our school, ensuring that none could pass by the performance without being mesmerized and inspired.

I began to understand what it meant to create space for myself and others like me. During these same Diversity Weeks, I ensured that my Black step team, Dangerous, performed at my mostly white high school campus. Our step team was started by my dear friend Nicole West, who taught our team about Black culture and about the importance of coming together and expressing ourselves. From within our predominantly white high school campus, with its small enclaves of Latinx and Middle Eastern students, we spoke out. And we were loud—on purpose. We giggled; we were free; we figured out that we could learn new skills and be a joyful congregation of Black girls. Those experiences in school fueled my emotional well-being and created for me a powerful psychological safety net.

School is the place where this growth can happen or devastatingly fail to happen. It's the place where students of color can be empowered or left to struggle. When we look at the wide swath of research, the anecdotal evidence, and the rousing stories, it's abundantly clear that we must work to ensure that Black students' lives matter. And this work needs to happen in educational settings because when we create safe and affirming environments for young Black students, everyone benefits from the uplift.

My own process of awakening happened in suburbia, in predominantly white settings. It may come as a surprise to some readers that not once in my life did I have a Black educator. Not in elementary school, not in middle school, not in high school, and not in college. I can't stress this enough; not once did I receive an academic lesson from a Black teacher—unless you count Sunday school lessons at my church. In many ways, I was drawn to the work of finding my own voice and helping to usher in the most unapologetically Black movement in recent history because of the gaping void in my own background.

That educational deficit certainly isn't unique to me. Resonating throughout this volume and the lives of many of its contributors is this powerful truth: US schools need to hire more Black teachers. The reality is that many Black youth don't feel seen or supported in their classrooms, because of lack of representation. And we know that this challenge, along with other structural inequalities, causes extreme anxiety for students. There are myriad cases of high school students dropping out of school, not because of academic inability or due to problems at home, but because of the stress they experience within the school setting and in transit to school. One recent study found that under New York Mayor Michael Bloomberg's stop-and-frisk policy, higher numbers of students of color dropped out of school.[1]

Both within classrooms and outside the school grounds, Black lives are under threat. The events that led to the creation of Black Lives Matter—the murder in 2012 of Trayvon Martin and the acquittal of his killer—weren't isolated events. The culture of endangering Black lives is something students know well from inside their very own classrooms. It's a shameful fact that the United States is one of the very few countries in the world that conducts active policing of its children in schools. That fact is all the more alarming when you consider that many schools also fail to provide services to support comprehensive child development, positive discipline, and conflict resolution.

While I went on to co-found Black Lives Matter, what many people don't know is that I was a teacher in Arizona. That time in the classroom remains an all-time career highlight. I started as a long-term substitute teacher and fell in love with the profession and my students. And so, I quickly began working on my teaching certificate. My students were incredible, but they were the ones who were often labeled "lost causes." The classrooms I took over for months on end were those at alternative high schools and schools where English was a second language for most of my students. I had students who were experiencing hardship at home and some who had literally crossed the desert to travel to this country with their families.

As an important adult in their lives, I hoped to create a context where they could be inspired, find themselves in the material, and engage in deep learning. I was fortunate because I taught literature and history, and my assignments usually allowed my students to research little-known historical figures who came from their own culture or who participated in historical events in important but underappreciated ways. We pulled from a richly diverse canon of readings, and my once-failing students thrived. While other educators sometimes complained about the challenges of working with this student population, I fell in love.

What I learned during this period didn't just pertain to teaching. Some of my greatest challenges involved working with school administrators and fellow teachers. Teaching meant being a real advocate for students and doing what it took to let them flourish. At one of the schools where I taught there wasn't a library, so I partnered with Half Price Books to donate hundreds of used books so that my students could have books that would pique their interest in reading.

Every day, other teachers and students of color in wide-ranging educational settings are doing similar work to clear paths to learning and growth. In laying the foundation for this work, Alicia Garza, Patrisse Khan-Cullors, and I always hoped that people would apply these ideas to their respective contexts. We wanted people to feel a sense of ownership and authority over the thinking that drives this movement. We have been awestruck to see a growing movement across the United States and beyond these borders. Organizations such as the Advancement Project, Dignity in Schools, and youth-led groups like Students Deserve are calling for #PoliceFreeSchools.[2] These groups and others are documenting police assaults on youth of color across the United States and pushing a vision of school safety that is not reliant on policing.

Many other groups around the country and around the world are dedicated to transforming learning environments, as well, including the student-led Fees Must Fall movement in South Africa, the robust Black Lives Matter at School movement in Seattle, and the many students and educators who have participated in the week of action using lessons from the Black Lives Matter at School website.

Along with the other contributors to this volume, I believe that we need to radically transform our learning environments. Together with the thousands of educators and students in scores of cities who have participated in the Black Lives Matter at School Week of Action, we are driven by several key goals:

1. end zero tolerance discipline in school, and implement restorative justice
2. hire more Black teachers
3. mandate Black history and ethnic studies in K–12 curriculum
4. fund counselors, not cops

As you read this book, I hope you find inspiration and practical tools to help you embark on, or continue, working toward these goals in your own educational setting. It is imperative that we join the call, educate ourselves, and engage our students in equitable learning. Young people deserve safe, affirming environments where they know without a shadow of a doubt that their lives matter. The work that supporters of Black Lives Matter at School are doing is making this happen.

Introduction

CHAPTER 1

Making Black Lives Matter at School

By Jesse Hagopian

> *How do you make Black lives matter in schools when the whole system wasn't even built for us? I'll tell you how. You tear it down and you build it into something that is made for us. And so that's what we're doing. Step by step, policy by policy, person by person, we're tearing it down and rebuilding it into a system that is meant to make sure that Black lives matter in schools.*
>
> —Marshé Doss, member of Students
> Deserve, Los Angeles

This book is the story of how the "Black Lives Matter" cry for freedom hopped on the yellow bus, walked through the schoolhouse door, occupied the gymnasium, rallied in the auditorium, ripped up the textbooks, and took over the daily lesson plans.

The Black Lives Matter at School movement is the story of resistance to racist curriculums, educational practices, and policies. This is the

1

story of educators, students, parents, and community members defying the threats of violent white supremacists (as the account of the movement in Seattle will reveal in the pages to come) and the story of an uprising to uproot the racist policies and curriculum that are bound up in the American system of schooling. This is the story of how visionary educators in the Caucus of Working Educators took Seattle's action to a new level by transforming it from a single day into a week of action, and then launched a national movement. This is the story of students in Minneapolis who had been organizing for years, and then, in the wake of the horrific murder of George Floyd, organized a powerful campaign that resulted in the removal of police from the Minneapolis Public Schools.

This is the story of students in Vermont hoisting a Black Lives Matter flag on the school flagpole. This is the story of Boston Teachers Union leaders publicly defending their week of action against an attack by Boston police. This is the story of teachers creating antiracist lesson plans and wearing shirts that say "Black Lives Matter" as they lead students in discussions to affirm Black identity. This is the story of educator union activists organizing their unions to take up antiracist initiatives. It is the story of early childhood educators around the country bringing Black Lives Matter at School lessons to preschoolers and kindergartners so that conversations about race and skin color start at the beginning of a student's education. It is the story of parents, students, teachers, and community members rallying at school board meetings and city halls to demand Black studies, ethnic studies, and an end to racist schooling policies. In short, this is the story of bold action against anti-Blackness in elementary schools, junior highs, and high schools around the country.

Black Lives Matter at School began in 2016 in Seattle after John Muir Elementary School educators announced they would wear shirts that said "Black Lives Matter / We Stand Together / John Muir Elementary." In response, the school was targeted by a bomb threat from a white supremacist. That threat galvanized solidarity and resulted in some three thousand educators going to school wearing Black Lives Matter shirts the following month, with many of the shirts including the message "#SayHerName," a campaign to raise awareness about the often-unrecognized state violence against and assault of Black women in our country. This action attracted national news, helping it spread to Philadelphia and Rochester, New York.

Philadelphia's Caucus of Working Educators (WE) Racial Justice Committee moved Black Lives Matter at School in a bold new direction when they expanded the action to last an entire week and broke down the thirteen principles of the Black Lives Matter Global Network for each day of the week.[1] Philadelphia's week of action saw strong community engagement and widespread press coverage, emboldening organizers to begin strategizing for a nationally coordinated action. At the 2017 Free Minds, Free People conference in Baltimore, educators from the WE Racial Justice Committee and parent activists led a session on how to organize a Black Lives Matter Week of Action in your own city. The following year, organizers around the country took up Philadelphia's model for the week of action, elected a national steering committee, and grew the event into a national movement. Black Lives Matter at School also articulated four powerful demands for undoing instituitional racism in schools: end zero tolerance discipline and replace it with restorative justice; implement Black studies and ethnic studies (K–12); hire more Black teachers; and fund counselors, not cops.

The newly formed Black Lives Matter at School organization had important discussions about when to hold the week of action. Some argued it would be good to hold the week of action in September to send the message that Black students' lives should be centered from the start of the year. Others argued the week of action should begin later in the year to provide more time to coordinate all the activities. Ultimately, the proposal to hold the week of action during the first week of February won out because organizers knew that, sadly, in many places it would be challenging to openly declare that their Black students' lives had value and wage an all-out struggle against institutional racism in the schools. Because of this, educators reasoned, introducing Black Lives Matter at School during the already established Black History Month would give support to educators in more hostile conditions for challenging anti-Blackness. The Black Lives Matter at School Year of Purpose was launched, along with the week of action in February, at the beginning of the 2020–21 school year. The year of purpose would ask teachers to continually reflect on their teaching with regard to antiracist pedagogy and join in nationally coordinated actions one day every month of the year.

As of this writing, thousands of educators in scores of cities have participated in the week of action by teaching lessons, holding community events, and organizing rallies in defense of Black lives at school. As Brian Jones, education director for the Schomburg Center for Research in Black Culture, suggests in Chapter 2:

> The Black Lives Matter at School movement is a new phase of a long struggle to transform the conditions of teaching and learning for Black students in this country. Black parents, teachers, and students have not just been the object of historic educational battles (either wrongfully denied opportunities or grateful recipients of them), but have been leading this fight.

Every year since the movement erupted in Seattle, Philadelphia, and Rochester during the 2016–17 school year and subsequently was nationally coordinated for the 2017–18 year, "Black Lives Matter" T-shirts have been an important communication symbol. In school buildings and classrooms around the country, thousands of teachers during the first week of February stand before their students, sporting their T-shirts while facilitating lessons about intersectional Black identities, institutional racism, African diasporic histories and philosophies, and the contributions and struggles of Black people to the nation and the world.

This movement to value the lives of Black people and teach the truth about their place in history is a radical proposition only because the United States is a nation built on theft and deceit. It is a country made possible by the stolen land and lives of   and the stolen labor and lives of African people. And because those foundational transgressions have never been fully acknowledged and reckoned with, every era in American history has required its own rallying cry for racial justice. The long Black freedom struggle has gone by many names, including abolition, Reconstruction, the Civil Rights Movement, Black Power, and Black Lives Matter.

In every one of these stages in the struggle for human rights for Black folks, a corresponding impulse for liberatory education has emerged as a leading demand of the movement. Black people have always known that there is no liberation without education. Frederick Douglass knew it when he illegally taught himself how to read and write, forged his traveling pass, and escaped from the bondage of chattel slavery. The great educator and leader Septima Clark, called the "Queen Mother" of the civil rights movement, knew it when she established Citizenship

Schools across the Deep South to empower Black communities with literacy, an understanding of their rights, and a commitment to the struggle for social justice. The Black Panther Party knew it when its members founded Liberation Schools for youth and declared in point five of their ten-point program, "We want education for our people that exposes the true nature of this decadent American society. We want education that teaches us our true history and our role in the present day society."

Today, "Black Lives Matter" has become the rallying cry of a new generation who, again, have had to unlearn the deceptions drilled into them in school about the fundamental freedom of our nation. The word "freedom" rings hollow when we reflect on the fact that the United States is the world's biggest jailer. According to the Equal Justice Initiative, in 1972, there were only two hundred thousand people incarcerated in the United States. Today, the number of people in prison or jail has exploded to 2.2 million, so that even though this nation contains only 5 percent of the world's population, it accounts for nearly 25 percent of its incarcerated population.

The Movement for Black Lives has been galvanized by the extrajudicial executions of Black people, whether by the police or racist vigilantes. Seventeen-year-old Trayvon Martin was murdered by self-appointed neighborhood patroller George Zimmerman on the night of February 26, 2012, in Sanford, Florida, and the ensuing national protests showed the potential for the eruption of a social movement. Patrisse Khan-Cullors, Alicia Garza, and Opal Tometi, three Black women organizers, gave voice to this movement when they founded #BlackLivesMatter in the wake of Martin's murder. "As Khan-Cullors has said about the significance of the Black Lives Matter movement, Before BLM, there was a dormancy in our Black freedom movement. Obviously many of us were doing work, but we've been able to reignite a whole entire new generation, not just inside the US but across the globe, centering Black people and centering the fight against white supremacy."[2]

Scholar Barbara Ransby captured the magnitude of the political leap of the Black Lives Matter movement in her book *Making All Black Lives Matter* when she wrote,

> Black feminist politics and sensibilities have been the intellectual lifeblood of this movement and its practices. This is the first time in

the history of US social movements that Black feminist politics have defined the frame for a multi-issue, Black-led mass struggle that did not primarily or exclusively focus on women. I use the term *Black-led mass struggle* because it is decidedly not a Black-only struggle, and it is not only for Black liberation but rather contextualizes the oppression, exploitation, and liberation of Black poor and working-class people within the simple understanding, at least in the US context, that "once all Black people are free, all people will be free."[3]

The movement was catapulted to new heights in the wake of the 2014 police murder of Michael Brown in the streets of Ferguson, Missouri. Police left Brown's body in the street for hours, evoking the American legacy of racist lynchings designed to terrorize Black communities into submission. Yet instead of surrender, thousands of mostly Black residents of Ferguson poured into the streets, rebelling against not only this murder but the uniquely American ritual of police sacrificing Black bodies. The strength and courage of the Ferguson uprising inspired demonstrations in cities around the country, and #BlackLivesMatter became a mass phenomenon. When prosecutors failed to indict Michael Brown's killer, Officer Darren Wilson, #BlackLivesMatter erupted out of the internet and into the streets of American cities from coast to coast. Only a few months later, a New York prosecutor failed to indict the officer who strangled Eric Garner on camera while he gasped, "I can't breathe" eleven times before taking his last breath. Garner's death, captured on video, shocked millions around the world, confirming for many the American roots of anti-Blackness, while also dramatically accelerating the momentum of the movement for Black lives.

Since those early days of the movement, many other videos of police misconduct and murder have underscored the structural nature of racism in the United States. And yet, while those high-profile cases of Black boys and men were catalytic, many Black women have also suffered brutality and murder at the hands of the police, and their stories haven't garnered the same attention. In 2015, the African American Policy Forum (AAPF) launched the campaign #SayHerName to highlight the police killings of Black women—including Black queer and transgender women. The campaign took off after Sandra Bland died in jail after being detained by an officer for failure to signal a lane change. As the AAPF noted in their report *Say Her Name: Resisting Police Brutality against Black Women*:

As Mike Brown, Eric Garner, and Tamir Rice have become household names and faces, their stories have become an impetus for public policy debates on the future of policing in America. However, 2014 also marked the unjust police killings of a number of Black women, including Gabriella Nevarez, Aura Rosser, Michelle Cusseaux, and Tanisha Anderson. The body count of Black women killed by the police continued [to rise] in 2015 with the killings of Alexia Christian, Meagan Hockaday, Mya Hall, Janisha Fonville, and Natasha McKenna. The lack of meaningful accountability for the deaths of unarmed Black men also extended to deaths of unarmed Black women and girls in 2015. Just as the officers who killed Mike Brown and Eric Garner escaped punishment for these homicides, officers who killed Black women and girls were not held accountable for their actions.[4]

But it isn't only adults who are being killed by police—it is also children, including Aiyana Stanley-Jones (age seven), Tamir Rice (age twelve), Laquan McDonald (age seventeen), Jordan Edwards (age fifteen), Tyre King (age thirteen), and Darius Smith (age fifteen). These were children who were told that if they worked hard and got an education, the American promise was theirs, only to lose their lives to police violence, leaving behind grieving families, friends, and teachers.

Despite the many years of organizing to defend the humanity of Black people under the banner of Black Lives Matter, police violence toward Black adults and children, including Black LGBTQ+ people, has continued uninterrupted. Between 2015 and 2019, police killed about one thousand people a year; in 2019, Black people were nearly a quarter of those killed, despite making up only 13 percent of the population.[5]

The drive to stop police violence has long been a struggle, but Black Lives Matter activism erupted on May 25, 2020, with an unprecedented ferocity when Eric Garner's last words, "I can't breathe," were repeated by another Black man, George Floyd, at an intersection of East Thirty-Eighth Street and Chicago Avenue in the Powderhorn Park neighborhood of Minneapolis. Floyd was arrested for allegedly using a counterfeit bill at a nearby convenience story. Derek Chauvin, a white police officer, knelt on his neck for *eight minutes and forty-six seconds* while Floyd was handcuffed and lying facedown, begging for his life.

Floyd's murder followed other recent killings of unarmed Black people around the country. On February 23, 2020, Ahmaud Arbery was jogging in Glynn County, Georgia, when he was ambushed by a former police officer and his son, along with a third perpetrator, and shot down. On March 13, 2020, Breonna Taylor was gunned down in her home by Louisville Metro Police Department officers who were acting on a no-knock warrant to look for drugs that were not found. And, on May 27, 2020 (just two days after George Floyd was killed), Tony McDade, a 38-year-old Black transgender man, was killed by an officer of the Tallahassee Police Department.

The gruesome video of George Floyd's death kicked off a rebellion that the *Washington Post* characterized as "the broadest in US history."[6] The uprising began in Minneapolis—where protesters led a rebellion that burned down the Minneapolis Police Department's Third Precinct—and swept across the country. Tens of thousands of people took to the streets in all fifty states, and mass protests were organized in countries all around the world to express rage and grief over Floyd's murder and to demand changes to public safety and social inequality. Police responded with brutal force in city after city, and the National Guard was activated in thirty-one states.[7]

The protests dramatically changed the political climate and propelled the Black Lives Matter movement to a level of struggle not seen since perhaps the 1960s and 1970s. Despite fears about the possible impact of congregating during the global COVID-19 pandemic, massive demonstrations swept the country and prompted swift culture change and policy changes. The demand to "defund the police" became a rallying cry for large sections of the movement, who advocated for repurposing oversized policing budgets for social programs, affordable housing, healthcare, restorative justice programs, conflict de-escalation personnel, and social workers, with the goal of achieving a truly comprehensive approach to public safety. Other major demands included removing police from schools, freeing protesters arrested in the demonstrations, and firing and arresting killer cops in cities around the country.[8] The massive upheaval drew national attention to those advocating for the abolition of police and prisons, as well as the eradication of root causes of societal violence, including institutional racism and structural poverty. As prison and police abolitionist Mariame Kaba wrote in an op-ed for the *New York Times*, titled "Yes, We Mean Literally Abolish the Police:"

The surest way of reducing police violence is to reduce the power of the police, by cutting budgets and the number of officers. But don't get me wrong. We are not abandoning our communities to violence. We don't want to just close police departments. We want to make them obsolete. We should redirect the billions that now go to police departments toward providing healthcare, housing, education, and good jobs. If we did this, there would be less need for the police in the first place.[9]

The sudden change in the political climate was made possible by years of work put in by the many organizers in the struggle for racial justice and the groups involved in the Movement for Black Lives. Thanks to their efforts, just a few weeks into the uprising, organizers scored important victories. In Minneapolis, the city council voted to dismantle the police altogether, with city council member Jeremiah Ellison saying, "We are going to dismantle the Minneapolis Police Department. And when we're done, we're not simply gonna glue it back together. We are going to dramatically rethink how we approach public safety and emergency response. It's really past due."[10] In Los Angeles, Mayor Eric Garcetti committed to $150 million in cuts to the LAPD after the first few days of unrest there.[11] In Seattle, the city council voted to ban the use of all chemical weapons by police,[12] and the King County Labor Council voted to remove police from their association.[13] Confederate monuments—grotesque celebrations of genocide against Black people—have been torn down by protesters or removed in cities around the country, including Alexandria, Tuscaloosa, Richmond, Louisville, and Fredericksburg.[14] In Portland, protesters at Jefferson High School toppled a statute of Thomas Jefferson after spray-painting "slave owner" on it, a reference to the fact that Jefferson owned over six hundred Black people.[15]

In a resounding victory for the Black Lives Matter at School movement—and the many other groups working on this issue, including the Advancement Project and Dignity in Schools—police were expelled from the schools in Minneapolis, Portland, Charlottesville, Denver, Columbus, Rochester, St. Paul, Oakland, Seattle, and elsewhere.

It should be noted that Black Lives Matter at School is not formally affiliated with the Black Lives Matter Global Network or any other organization in the Movement for Black Lives, who have done so much important work toward ending police violence. But the educators who built

Black Lives Matter at School have relied on the momentum of those organizations and know that there can be no real education if students are not allowed to discuss police violence and other issues that matter most to them. Some educators have been accused of politicizing students by daring to hold discussions about institutional racism. But students are already having these conversations: in school hallways, on playgrounds, in lunchrooms, and online. Now more than ever students need to be encouraged to have these discussions in the classroom. Educators must ask themselves whether they will encourage open exchange about racial justice or if they would rather have school be a place that marginalizes the main concerns of their students' lives.

However, for some critics of Black Lives Matter at School, the idea of such conversations taking place in classrooms represents an unwelcome threat to the status quo. In an August 29, 2019, *New York Post* article, Peter Myers implies that allowing students to discuss attacks on Black people is a greater danger than the attacks themselves. Myers writes:

> In the BLM-inspired classroom, students will be catechized to deplore "the school-to-prison pipeline" and the "epidemic of police violence and mass incarceration" in America. [...]
>
> This teaching is both false and grossly irresponsible. Racism's wisest adversaries have always insisted, often under far more trying conditions than what prevails today, that in America there is always cause for hopefulness, and the key to liberty and happiness lies not in perpetuated opposition but in cultivating the virtues of mind, heart, and character.[16]

This patronizing counsel from a white writer on how to responsibly oppose racism is stomach turning. The suggestion that modern racism is a minor issue, incomparable to the injustices of past eras, is revisionist and ahistorical.[17] Likewise, the trivialization of the school-to-prison pipeline, police violence, hate crimes, and mass incarceration is openly racist and harmful to our students. The article goes on to attack the book *Teaching for Black Lives*, a volume that many educators in the Black Lives Matter at School movement have used (and one that I co-edited). Myers criticizes the book's references to the police murders of Black people, which, according to Myers, only have the effect of "stoking...students' fear and anger."

Myers seems to believe that attacks on the bodies and minds of Black students are not a real problem, at least not one that warrants "fear and anger." Yet hate crimes against Black people have increased in recent years under the Trump presidency. The president has personally incited racist violence by calling African nations and Haiti "shithole countries,"[18] declaring that the white supremacists who rallied in Charlottesville included "some very fine people,"[19] and retweeting a video of one of his supporters shouting "white power."[20]

Schools are not insulated from this climate of hate. Teaching Tolerance's report *Hate at School* had these findings about students' experiences of racism at school:

- More than two-thirds of the 2,776 educators who responded to [a] questionnaire witnessed a hate or bias incident in their school during the fall of 2018.
- Racism appears to be the motivation behind most hate and bias incidents in school, accounting for 63 percent of incidents reported in the news and 33 percent of incidents reported by teachers.
- Most of the hate and bias incidents witnessed by educators were not addressed by school leaders. No one was disciplined in 57 percent of them. Nine times out of ten, administrators failed to denounce the bias or reaffirm school values.[21]

In addition, there are abundant examples of the criminalization of Black students in school, including the episode of a ten-year-old boy who was charged with assault for playing dodgeball[22] or the many recent incidents of students being humiliated and penalized for wearing their hair in locs.[23] There have been a rash of cases involving police officers in schools abusing children,[24] such as the October 2019 episode caught on camera at a school in New Mexico, in which a white police officer threw an eleven-year-old girl into a wall and then wrestled her to the ground—all for the alleged crime of taking an extra carton of milk.[25]

And it's not only the physical attacks on students that must be acknowledged; it's also the curricular attacks. Much of the curriculum in US textbooks is Eurocentric and even overtly racist.[26] As an article in *Rethinking Schools* magazine maintains,

There is the daily curricular violence: the erasure and appropriation of Black struggle, as in the Lincoln-freed-the-slaves myth; the failure of the curriculum to account for the centrality of slavery and anti-Black racism in the shaping of US history, North, and South; teaching contempt for Black culture—including African American Vernacular English; and so much more.[27]

This Eurocentric, or "master narrative," approach to education permeates American schooling. The Black Lives Matter at School organization thus voted to adopt the global network's thirteen guiding principles as teaching points for the annual week of action:

Monday

> Restorative Justice: We intentionally build and nurture a beloved community that is bonded together through a beautiful struggle that is restorative, not depleting.
>
> Empathy: We practice empathy to connect with others by building relationships built on mutual trust and understanding.
>
> Loving Engagement: We embody and practice justice, liberation, and peace in our engagements with one another.

Tuesday

> Diversity: We acknowledge, respect, and celebrate differences and commonalities.
>
> Globalism: We see ourselves as part of the global Black family, and we are aware of the different ways we are impacted or privileged as Black people who exist in different parts of the world.

Wednesday

> Trans Affirming: We are self-reflexive and do the work required to dismantle cisgender privilege and uplift Black trans folk, especially Black trans women who continue to be dispropor-

tionately impacted by trans-antagonistic violence.

Queer Affirming: When we gather, we do so with the intention of freeing ourselves from the tight grip of heteronormative thinking, or rather, the belief that all in the world are heterosexual (unless s/he or they disclose otherwise).

Collective Value: We are guided by the fact that all Black lives matter, regardless of actual or perceived sexual identity, gender identity, gender expression, economic status, ability, disability, religious beliefs or disbeliefs, immigration status, or location.

Thursday

Intergenerational: We cultivate an intergenerational and communal network free from ageism. We believe that all people, regardless of age, show up with the capacity to lead and learn.

Black Families: We make our spaces family-friendly and enable parents to fully participate with their children. We dismantle the patriarchal practice that requires mothers to work "double shifts" so that they can mother in private even as they participate in public justice work.

Black Villages: We disrupt the Western-prescribed nuclear family structure requirement by supporting each other as extended families and "villages" that collectively care for one another, especially our children, to the degree that mothers, parents, and children are comfortable.

Friday

Black Women: We build a space that affirms Black women and is free from sexism, misogyny, and environments in which men are centered.

Unapologetically Black: We are unapologetically Black in our positioning. In affirming that Black lives matter, we need not qualify our position. To love and desire freedom and justice for ourselves is a prerequisite for wanting the same for others.

Over the past several years, the movement's curriculum committee has designed many lessons for each of these thirteen principles and for every grade level, available for free download at BlackLivesMatter-AtSchool.com. These principles and sample lessons have been used by thousands of educators to center intersectional Black experiences in the classroom for tens of thousands of students around the country. In Chapter 4, Philadelphia educator Christopher Rogers details the importance of each of these teaching themes and shows how Black Lives Matter at School organized to offer curricular support to teachers around each theme. What is so powerful about these principles is that they provide a framework for studying Blackness through an intersectional lens, which shows that in spite of the universality of racism against Black people, there isn't a singular "Black" experience and that Black people can face overlapping forms of oppression, such as racism, sexism, homophobia, and xenophobia.

Unsurprisingly, this effort to make the movement intersectional has powerful adversaries. During a February 2020 broadcast, Fox News co-host Laura Ingraham seethed with vitriol in her coverage of the Black Lives Matter at School curriculum, taking special offense at the Wednesday themes of trans affirming and queer affirming. The following is an excerpt from her show:

> Raymond Arroyo (co-host): This is part of a new curriculum the school announced based on the thirteen principles of the Movement for Black Lives—part of the Black Lives Matters movement—which calls for "Transgender Affirming"—
>
> Laura Ingraham (co-host): This is child abuse. Child abuse.[28]

In Ingraham's warped view, the real abuse Black children face from disproportionate discipline and police violence is not worth decrying, yet affirming a student's preferred gender identity is tantamount to corporal punishment. Ingraham has a long track record of bigoted commentary, so her homophobic and transphobic rant actually serves as endorsement of the Black Lives Matter at School movement to those engaged in the struggle for social justice.

Demanding change

Advocates for justice know that racism in the schools isn't only a product of openly racist and bigoted people. It is an institutional problem, rather than a merely individual one. As Black Lives Matter co-founder Opal Tometi has pointed out, "Anti-Black racism operates at a society-wide level and colludes in a seamless web of policies, practices, and beliefs to oppress and disempower Black communities."[29]

With this understanding, Black Lives Matter at School nationally has issued four core demands to disrupt this anti-Black web of policies, practices, and beliefs in the education system. *The first demand is to end "zero tolerance discipline" and replace it with restorative justice.* Black youth have been dramatically disproportionately suspended and expelled from school since the explosion of so-called zero tolerance policies modeled on the racist "war on drugs." As Michelle Alexander, author of *The New Jim Crow,* explained in an interview:

> Many people imagine that zero tolerance rhetoric emerged within the school environment, but it's not true. In fact, the Advancement Project published a report showing that one of the earliest examples of zero tolerance language in school discipline manuals was a cut-and-paste job from a US Drug Enforcement Administration manual. The wave of punitiveness that washed over the United States with the rise of the drug war and the get-tough movement really flooded our schools. Schools, caught up in this maelstrom, began viewing children as criminals or suspects, rather than as young people with an enormous amount of potential, struggling in their own ways and their own difficult contexts to make it and hopefully thrive. We began viewing the youth in schools as potential violators rather than as children needing our guidance.[30]

Today, Black students are suspended at four times the rate of white students nationally.[31] And as Monique Morris so powerfully illuminates in her book *Pushout*, Black girls are the most disproportionately suspended, at six times the rate of white girls. While Black girls make up only 16 percent of the female student population, they account for nearly one-third of all girls referred to law enforcement and more than one-third of all female school-based arrests.[32] Howard Zehr, a professor of restorative justice at Eastern Mennonite University, explains that punitive approaches to discipline, known as retributive justice, ask these questions:

- What rule has been broken?
- Who is to blame?
- What punishment do they deserve?[33]

By contrast, the Black Lives Matter at School movement has called for the funding and implementation of restorative justice practices to replace retributive and zero tolerance approaches. These restorative practices are used *proactively* in schools to build healthy relationships, not just *reactively* after a conflict arises. Some of these restorative practices include the use of peace circles, peer mediation, community conferencing, and trauma-informed approaches to teaching.

Zehr explains that when conflicts do arise, a restorative justice approach asks these questions:

- Who has been hurt and what are their needs?
- Who is obligated to address these needs?
- Who has a "stake" in this situation and what is the process of involving them in making things right and preventing future occurrences?[34]

Asking these questions holds the potential to build nurturing communities rather than to just react to disruptions of community and resort to punishment. And, increasingly, antiracist movements in education incorporate transformative justice. According to Zehr, a transformative approach to justice poses even more fundamental questions:

- What social circumstances produced the harmful behavior?
- What structures exist between this structure and others like it?
- What measures could prevent further occurrences?[35]

Asking these questions can transform the social conditions that produce harm and conflict in the first place and address the root causes of problems.

The other demands of the Black Lives Matter at School movement share the goal of determining root causes. *The second demand is to hire more Black teachers.* Nationally, around 80 percent of teachers are white.[36] Additionally, there has been a dramatic displacement of Black teachers in recent years. As an article in *Mother Jones* pointed out, since 2002, "26,000 Black teachers have disappeared from the nation's public schools—even as the overall teaching workforce has increased by 134,000. Countless Black principals, coaches, cafeteria workers, nurses, and counselors have also been displaced."[37]

The closing of schools in Black and Brown neighborhoods has been one of the biggest drivers in pushing out Black teachers, who are more likely to teach at those schools. In Chicago, for example, in 2013, then-mayor Rahm Emanuel led the effort to close nearly fifty schools where the vast majority of students were Black and Latinx. Chicago has also lost nearly half of all its Black teachers in the past fifteen years.[38]

The vital necessity of hiring more Black teachers was made clear in a 2017 study from American University, which found that "having just one Black teacher in third, fourth, or fifth grade reduced low-income Black boys' probability of dropping out of high school by 39 percent."[39]

The third demand of our movement is for Black history and ethnic studies to be mandated in every school, kindergarten through twelfth grade. Ethnic studies is a pedagogical approach fought for and won by students, beginning in the late 1960s. They centered the experiences of Black, Indigenous, and people of color (BIPOC) and demanded an end to Eurocentric and racist curricula that excluded the struggles and contributions of non-white people.

In 1968, students at San Francisco State College organized the Third World Liberation Front, a coalition of the Black Student Union, Latin American Student Organization, Asian American Political Alliance, Philippine American Collegiate Endeavor, and the Native American Student Union, to launch a victorious student strike for the establishment of a department of ethnic studies. The following year, students at the University of California at Berkley went on strike for an ethnic studies department and also won their struggle. Soon, all over the country, students were walking out and protesting for the right to learn about the many cultures, races, and ethnicities that had been excluded from the curriculum. Since those epic struggles in the 1960s and '70s, ethnic studies programs around the country have been underfunded and attacked, leaving young people increasingly vulnerable to corporate curriculums that minimize racism and Black history.

Take, for example, the textbook that fifteen-year-old Black student

Coby Burren exposed in the fall of 2015. Coby was in geography class at Pearland High School, near Houston, when he read an assigned page of his textbook and noticed something disturbing: a map of the United States with a caption claiming the Atlantic slave trade brought "millions of workers from Africa to the southern United States to work on agricultural plantations." Coby took a picture of his textbook and texted it to his mother, Roni Dean-Burren, adding, "We was real hard workers wasn't we," along with a sarcastic emoji. Not only had the McGraw-Hill textbook used the term "workers," instead of "enslaved African people," but they had placed the chapter on the enslavement of Africans within a section of the book entitled "Patterns of Immigration," as if Africans came to the United States looking for the American Dream, rather than in chains at the bottom of slave ships.

This is just one example of the humiliation and dehumanization that Black students experience from corporate curriculums on a daily basis. Another common problem is that Black history is often reduced to teaching primarily about slavery, as if the African American experience can be reduced to oppression. As Malcolm X once said: "When we send our children to school in this country they learn nothing about us other than that we used to be cotton pickers. Why, your grandfather was Nat Turner; your grandfather was Toussaint L'Ouverture; your grandfather was Hannibal." Echoing Malcolm's words, Black Lives Matter at School student organizer Israel Presley said in an interview about today's movement, "Why don't you ever teach me about our resistance, because I know our people are strong."[40]

The power of ethnic studies to transform education has been well documented. A 2016 study by researchers at Stanford University found strong positive associations with adding ethnic studies to the curriculum: students' GPAs improved on average by 1.4 grade points, attendance rose 21 percentage points, and class credits earned increased by twenty-three.[41] Bold educators and organizers around the country have revitalized the 1960s fight for ethnic studies courses.

Those three demands were issued during the first national Black Lives Matter at School Week of Action. Then, in the second year of the national week of action during the 2018–19 school year, organizers voted to add a fourth national demand: *Fund counselors, not cops.*

Security officers and cops outnumber counselors in three of the five biggest school districts in the United States.[42] Today, 1.7 million children go to a school in the United States where there is a police officer and no counselor[43]—and some 14 million students attend a school where there is a cop but no counselor, nurse, psychologist or social worker.[44]

Police are a huge drain on resources. When school districts fund police officers, they are choosing not to fund other vital support staff. According to an ACLU report, schools in Washington State pay on average $62,000—and as much as $125,000—per full-time equivalent officer per year. This is money that could be used to increase the number of school counselors, psychologists, teachers, and other student support services.[45] Or, for that matter, test for lead in the water fountains.

The use of police officers in schools has exploded across the country. In the past twenty years, their number has increased from only a handful to an estimated seventeen thousand police officers on school campuses nationwide.[46] And as the ACLU states, "The rise in school policing cannot be attributed to a rise in dangerous crime in schools. Particularly in Black and Brown communities, school police have historically gone well beyond addressing serious criminal activity, instead targeting perceived disorder or rowdiness." One of the reasons for the dramatic increase of police in schools is that from 1999 to 2005, "the federal COPS program awarded in excess of $753 million to schools and police departments to place police officers in schools."[47]

In terms of which students are being policed, students are not being targeted at random. A joint issue brief from the Advancement Project, the Alliance for Educational Justice, Dignity in Schools, and the NAACP Legal Defense and Educational Fund revealed, "Although students of color do not misbehave more than white students, they are disproportionately policed in schools: nationally, Black and Latinx youth made up over 58 percent of school-based arrests while representing only 40 percent of public school enrollment."[48] Despite these glaring inequalities, Education Secretary Betsy DeVos has rescinded the guidance issued by the Obama administration directing schools to reduce racial disparities in how they discipline students.[49]

Black high school graduate Marshé Doss describes in her interview (Chapter 23) the pain and humiliation of being targeted for a "random" search by the police in school:

They'll pull you out into the hallway and they'll ask you to empty your bags, but moving too slow causes them to rush you and dump it all out on the floor anyway. And then sometimes they'll briefly check through it after they dump everything on the floor, and then they'll be like, "Okay, pack up your things and go back to class." And for me, after they'd dumped everything, they took my hand sanitizer, and they were like, "You're going to use it to get high and sniff it." But I only had it because LAUSD is so underfunded that we don't have soap in our bathroom sometimes, and just for cleanliness and protecting yourself from germs and sickness, it's necessary to have hand sanitizer. But they told me that I was going to use it to get high and that they "knew my type."

Echoing Marshé's experience, a student in Washington State's King County stated, "School seems like a prison. You have police. You have all these security guards. There are security cameras everywhere you go, in your class and even outside the bathroom. They treat you like you're always about to do something. It feels like everyone has it out for you."[50]

Increasingly, school discipline issues that used to be handled by administration and parents are now being treated as criminal issues to be dealt with by police officers. Take the case of a high school student in Pierce County, Washington, who was sent by school police to the prosecuting attorney on suspected charges of assault in the fourth degree for pouring chocolate milk on another student in the school lunchroom (thankfully, the prosecutor declined to file charges in juvenile court).

The United States is one a few countries that stations police in schools, and the resulting arrests have terrible consequences for students. A first-time arrest doubles the odds that a student will drop out of high school, and a first-time court appearance quadruples the odds. Juvenile arrest also increases students' chances of future imprisonment.[51]

The four demands of Black Lives Matter at School expose the racist narrative that lower academic outcomes and graduation rates of Black students are due to lack of motivation or the dysfunction of Black families. The four demands also stand in stark contrast to the agenda of the massive corporate education reform effort led by billionaires who attempt to disrupt, dismantle, and profit from public education. These efforts—led most notably by Bill Gates, Eli Broad, and the Walton family (owners of Walmart)—have pursued a strategy for the schools consisting of ramping up the use of standardized testing, privatizing public education, closing schools serving Black and Brown students, and opposing teachers unions. Each of these efforts has only exacerbated the most entrenched aspects of institutional racism in the schools, and for all the money that they have poured into these initiatives, the major indicators for outcomes for Black students have not improved.

Meaningful education in times of crisis

As this book goes to press, schools around the United States and the world have been shut down due to the COVID-19 pandemic. Millions have been infected worldwide by the novel coronavirus, and hundreds of thousands have died. Millions of students are currently at home due to mass school closures, and a staggering number of their parents have lost their jobs. By April 2020, the US unemployment rate jumped to 14.7 percent, the highest level since the Great Depression, with some 20.5 million people out of work.[52]

These dire conditions provide a textbook example of what Naomi Klein calls the "shock doctrine," where the billionaire class seizes on times of crisis and uses them to push forward programs they have long sought in order to further their endless pursuit of profit.[53] Educational technology companies have long attempted to replace teachers with computers. Dubbed "personalized learning," the idea is that kids sit in front of computer screens in large classes, thereby reducing the need to pay for as many teachers and increasing expenditures on software. The corporations who advocate for these "improvements" also promote the expansion of remote online learning.

Now, in this time of physical distancing to stop the spread of COVID-19, online learning has become a necessity. It has also become a factor that compounds the opportunity gap, as many Black and Brown students, lacking access to high-speed internet and computers, are on the losing side of the digital divide. It's clear that any movement for educational justice must fully reject the idea that education can be done online. Meaningful education is a collaborative process that can only occur where strong relationships are built. That process cannot be done virtually. Additionally, as the COVID-19 crisis has revealed for many, schools are not just places where students receive academic instruction; they are places where students receive healthcare, two meals a day, special needs services, trauma counseling, and much more. The shutting down of schools, then, has had a dramatically disproportionate impact on Black, Brown, and Indigenous students, and students living in poverty.

The alternative to the shock doctrine educational model proposed by the powerful is that of social movements like Black Lives Matter at School and social justice unionism that can fight for a different vision of public school. For example, we have to demand that when schools finally reopen every school has a full-time nurse on staff. We have to make demands that prioritize the physical, social, and emotional well-being of our youth over the endless ranking and sorting of students with high-stakes standardized testing. As Jennifer Johnson explains in her interview (Chapter 6), this means building the struggle for community schools that "focus on culturally relevant pedagogy, effective teaching instead of high-stakes testing, restorative justice, wraparound services, cooperative decision making, and parent engagement."

The power of the Black Lives Matter at School Week of Action is its ability to shine a spotlight on initiatives that, if properly implemented, will have a transformative impact on Black students' lives. However, antiracist practices, pedagogy, and protest can't be confined to one week or one month if they are to be effective—they have to be integrated into the daily practice of educators and schools. The principles of Black Lives Matter at School must become part of the broader school culture and permeate all subjects—social studies, English language arts, math, science, music, art, world languages, theater, and beyond—if Black lives are to be truly valued in education.

It is essential to observe that, while Black educators are leading the Black Lives Matter at School movement, the vast majority of educators in the United States are white. These educators must join in this effort if we are going to achieve our demands. While BIPOC organizers should be centered in the movement, it is critical that white educators take the time to transform themselves into antiracist educators. They can do so by engaging in practices such as these:

- reflecting on their own racial identity
- identifying gaps in their knowledge of Black history, Black struggle, and Black contributions to the academic discipline that they teach

- engaging in study groups to cultivate a deeper understanding of how racial categories developed and became a defining aspect of US culture and capitalism, and how that history informs their own experience and the experience of their students
- reflecting on their pedagogy throughout the year and analyzing the degree to which antiracism is infused throughout the curriculum
- engaging in protests, organizing, and movement building for racial and social justice

As white educators Rosie Frascella, B. Kaiser, Brian Ford, and Jeff Stone write in Chapter 18,

> As white people, we cannot shy away from discussing the role of white people in the construction of this brutal, violent, and oppressive nation. When words or actions are racist, sexist, classist, heteronormative, or ableist, we must call them out. As Ibram X. Kendi explains, the term "racist" is not pejorative; it is an adjective that describes a behavior. If we do not name and identify racist behaviors when they occur, we cannot learn or grow from them. As educators, we challenge the idea of "neutrality" in the classroom. There is nothing neutral about a white person teaching a class almost entirely comprised of students of color.

Educators must also consider the proposition of Bettina L. Love that we become "abolitionist teachers." As she writes in Chapter 11, "Abolitionism is not a social-justice trend. It is a way of life defined by commitment to working toward a humanity where no one is disposable, prisons no longer exist, being Black is not a crime, teachers have high expectations for Black and Brown children, and joy is seen as a foundation of learning."

While the movement for Black lives in schools is on the rise, readers of this book could be forgiven for wondering whether advocates for change will really achieve their goals. Will Black lives ever truly matter in the education system? The answer to that question will not be determined by political elites or billionaire corporate education reformers. In 1857, the great abolitionist Frederick Douglass made the observation that we must remember today if we are to achieve an emancipatory education system: "Who would be free, themselves must strike the blow... The limits of tyrants are prescribed by the endurance of those whom they oppress."[54] The answer, then, to whether we will someday see a school system worthy of Black students lies in the hearts of educators, students, parents, and antiracist organizers everywhere who tire of inequality and rise up to strike the blow for freedom.

Poster for Black Lives Matter at School Week of Action, created by Caryn Davidson.

CHAPTER 2

Black Lives Matter at School

Historical Perspectives

By Brian Jones

The Black Lives Matter at School movement is a new phase of a long struggle to transform the conditions of teaching and learning for Black students in this country. Black parents, teachers, and students have not just been the object of historic educational battles (either wrongfully denied opportunities or grateful recipients of them) but have been leading the fight. By entering this struggle, you are joining a stream of historic activism and advocacy, led by Black people, for justice in schooling. All the moralizing about whether Black people "value" education falls apart in the face of their unwavering, hundreds-years-long effort to get it. No other people in this land have fought so hard for so long for access to and justice in schooling.[1]

Each of the week of action's four demands (end zero tolerance, mandate Black history and ethnic studies, hire more Black teachers, and fund counselors, not cops) has echoes, precedents, and activist ancestors to call upon. While the heroes and sheroes of this long struggle are mostly unknown to history, some, like Carter G. Woodson and Mary McLeod Bethune, are better remembered. The struggles of other groups, including

Indigenous people, people from Latin America, and people from Asia, are related to and connected to the history of Black people's struggles for education, but they are not the focus of this chapter. What follows is an attempt to provide a quick overview of a story that could easily fill books, bookshelves, and libraries. Its purpose is to give you a sense of how the present movement fits into past patterns and inspire you to read on, to keep pushing and learning more.

Mandate Black history and ethnic studies

In the late twentieth century, Black college students rose up all over the United States, demanding the formation of Black studies and ethnic studies departments on their campuses. From historically Black colleges like Tuskegee Institute in Alabama to Ivy League institutions like Brown University, students in the 1960s and '70s protested, sat in, occupied buildings, and more, with a wide range of demands that almost always included the teaching of Black history and the mandating of Black studies in some form. When a majority of the students at San Francisco State College went on strike in 1968, they won the formation of the nation's first Black studies department as part of a new School of Ethnic Studies.[2]

Public schools were a major battleground in the US civil rights movement, but Black parents and activists often had to create their own schools from scratch. Some, like Septima Clark's Citizenship Schools, were created by the movement, for the movement. In hundreds of Citizenship Schools spread across the US South, students of all ages could acquire the rudiments of literacy, increase their knowledge of political processes, and gain exposure to highlights from Black history.[3] Another type of self-organized Black schools were the Freedom Schools, created by civil rights activists to supplement inadequately funded and often degrading schooling provided by the state, and to raise political consciousness. The first Freedom School was organized in Mississippi in the summer of 1964, and the idea spread nationwide (and continues today).[4]

Building on the energy of the movements of the 1960s, Black parents, educators, and activists developed regional and national networks of independent Black schools in the 1970s that put Black studies at the core of their mission.[5] Foremost among these was the popular and successful independent school created in Oakland by the Black Panther

Party, where reclaiming Black history also meant learning African history. "We knew the map of Africa," one former student recalled, "just as well as we knew the United States."[6]

But many decades before these uprisings, Black educators and activists collected and curated books and other materials related to Black history and disseminated Black history curricula to schoolteachers nationwide. In Harlem, Black working-class intellectuals like Arturo Schomburg and Hubert Harrison built impressive personal Black history libraries and lectured widely in the 1920s and '30s. Black scholar and educator Carter G. Woodson started the Association for the Study of African American Life and History in Chicago in 1915 and launched a Negro History Week initiative in 1926.[7] Like the Black Lives Matter at School Week of Action, Negro History Week was a do-it-yourself, grassroots effort. Woodson produced the *Negro History Bulletin*, a periodical that aimed to provide accessible stories and ideas about Black history for teachers to use in their classrooms. As an annual event in February, Negro History Week spread to a few cities in its first years but did not become codified as Black History Month until the 1970s. One bulletin in 1938 emphasized that the point of studying Black history is not to elevate Black people above any other people but to serve as a corrective to racist history. "The fact is…that one race has not accomplished any more good than any other race," an article titled "History Is Truth" explained, "for it would be contrary to the laws of nature to have one race inferior to the other. But if you leave it to the one to set forth his special virtues while disparaging those of others, it will not require many generations before all credit for human achievements will be ascribed to one particular stock. Such is the history taught the youth today."[8]

The *Negro History Bulletin* was just one part of the broader landscape of efforts by social justice–minded Black (mostly female) educators nationwide to raise Black pride and consciousness inside of the classroom and beyond. Negro History Week was an occasion for self-organized community marches, Black history lectures, musical concerts, and singing the Black national anthem, "Lift Every Voice and Sing."[9]

We can trace the impulse to demand instruction in Black history even earlier. In the late nineteenth century, after the abolition of slavery, Black people seized every opportunity to acquire literacy and to create for themselves and their children a new narrative about their place in the nation and the world.[10] Black people were so determined that they actually became more literate than white people in the US South during this period.[11] Young and old alike grabbed any spelling book they could get hold of and learned side by side. While some of these booklets produced by white missionary societies were condescending in tone, literate free Black people in northern states also produced materials to send south.[12] These resources narrated Black history as a story of heroic rebellion, from Toussaint L'Ouverture (leader of the Haitian Revolution) to Nat Turner (leader of a revolt in Virginia in 1831). One such journal, the *Freedman's Torchlight*, was the first curriculum published by Black people for Black students. It aimed to teach the alphabet, phonemes, and rudiments of grammar and literacy, along with passages for the newly literate to read aloud. The first issue from 1866 promised that "[h]istory will tell you about the different nations, and great cities that ever have been. It will tell you who first came to this country, and all about the Colored people and every people. It is delightful to read history. As soon as you can read all in this little paper, called *The Torchlight*, you will be able to read history."[13]

End zero tolerance and fund counselors, not cops

Sending their children to school for the first time in the aftermath of abolition, some of the freed people and, to their credit, some of their new teachers were opposed to corporal punishment for students because it was too reminiscent of the violence of slavery.[14] There doesn't seem to be evidence of widespread corporal punishment in the late nineteenth-century schools that Black students attended or widespread opposition to it where it took place.[15] The demand to stop over-punishing Black students may date back to the Great Migration in the early twentieth century, when millions of Black people fled Jim Crow terrorism in the South and relocated in northern and western states during the twentieth century. Fleeing rural terrorism and poverty for new political and economic opportunities, they found themselves in an urban landscape defined by racism and segregation. Northern white teachers and administrators almost universally viewed Black students as inherently (or, at best, culturally) inferior.[16] Some organizations of radical white teachers were important exceptions to this pattern.

In 1936, a fourteen-year-old Black student, Robert Shelton, was involved in a disturbance in the hallway of his sister's Harlem elementary school, PS5. He was brought to Gustav Schoenchen, the white principal, who beat him. Two doctors determined that Shelton had contusions on his arms, traumatic injuries to the muscles in his ribs, and injuries on his scalp.[17] Black parents immediately organized to demand Schoenchen's removal as principal. Their organization, the Committee for Better Schools in Harlem, received assistance from educator and activist Ella Baker, as well as from an organized group of mostly white teachers. New York City's teachers during this period had two competing trade unions: the Teachers Guild and the Teachers Union. The Teachers Union was led by members of the Communist Party, and so they were deeply committed to antiracism. They challenged racism in the city's curriculum and fought for the inclusion of Black history lessons, protested segregation and overcrowding in schools that served mostly Black and Brown students, and joined the Harlem parents on picket lines to demand Schoenchen's removal from PS 5. Unfortunately, the Teachers Union was red-baited out of existence during the McCarthy anti-communist purges, when many radical teachers were fired.[18] The Teachers Guild, which supported these purges, went on to organize all of New York City's teachers and is known today as the United Federation of Teachers. Tragically, the UFT, like most teachers unions in cities with large populations of Black and Brown students, has a history of supporting provisions that strengthen the ability of teachers to remove "disruptive" children from the classroom.[19]

The term "zero tolerance" comes from the US Customs Service's antidrug program in the 1980s, but police began patrolling the hallways of schools for Black and Latinx students as early as the 1940s. Over the next several decades, municipal leaders in urban school districts increasingly turned to police to control young Black, Indigenous, and people of color (BIPOC). As they moved through their school day, by 1972 such students in at least forty states did so under the watch of police.[20]

The presence of uniformed police officers in public schools emerged as a national policy priority in the 1990s after a wave of suburban school shootings. Ironically, although these shootings most often involved white students, it was predominantly schools serving Black and Brown students that saw police departments move in and take over the functions of school safety agents. In 1998, the New York City Police Department took over school safety in the city's public education system (the nation's largest), starting with 1,500 officers.[21] By 2008, the number had jumped to more than 5,000. Meanwhile New York City's 1.1 million public school students only had 3,000 guidance counselors.[22] Police in schools quickly became normalized in many large urban school districts, but student activists have been at the forefront of calling this priority into question.

Hire more Black teachers

In the twenty-first century, the demand to hire more Black teachers has emerged from two historic waves of mass firing of Black teachers. The first large-scale attack on Black teachers occurred after the famous *Brown v. Board of Education* Supreme Court decision. Ironically, this great victory for Black educators and activists was experienced as a calamity for many Black communities. Black teachers and administrators prepared for desegregation by drawing up plans for the best way to approach the transition. All over the United States, Black educators worked out careful plans to have some Black administrators and teachers change schools along with Black students, so that the educators could help their white colleagues get to know the new students. Tragically, white politicians and school leaders did not think that desegregation should mean shared power with Black educators or parents. Rather, they drew up desegregation plans that almost always required Black students to travel to attend previously all-white schools, and never the reverse. White administrators were reluctant to hire Black teachers, and so one of the perverse results of the *Brown* decision was mass closure of previously all-Black schools and mass unemployment for Black educators. Between 1954 and 1965, approximately 50 percent of black teachers and 90 percent of Black principals lost their jobs.[23] Speaking to the all-Black Georgia Teachers and Education Association in 1967, Dr. Martin Luther King Jr. said, "Integration doesn't mean the liquidation of everything started and developed by Negroes." Rather, he continued, real integration meant shared power. "And I am not one that will integrate myself out of power."[24]

The second wave of destroying Black teaching jobs has taken place as a result of the recent neoliberal push for the privatization of public schools.[25] Once again, apparent victories for Black parents and students—in this case the bipartisan consensus in support of charter schools, Common Core standards, and Common Core–aligned standardized testing, as well as the weakening of teacher unions—amounted to a loss for Black teachers. The double irony is that unions have been a principal lever of social mobility for Black people, and the test-and-punish regime that has come to dominate the contemporary approach to public education has primarily targeted schools where Black teachers work, leading to school closures and the pushing of large numbers of Black teachers out of the profession. Black teachers are only about 7 percent of the nation's teaching force but tend to be concentrated in areas with large populations of Black students. In New York City, for example, 20 percent of public school teachers are Black. Chicago and New Orleans are two of the most extreme examples; from 1995 onward, the percentage of Black teachers in Chicago has dropped from 45 percent to 25 percent. Before Hurricane Katrina hit New Orleans in 2005, 73 percent of its teachers were Black. After the storm, which city leaders used as an excuse to close public schools and bring in charter schools staffed with Teach for America members, only 49 percent of the teachers were Black.[26]

What both historic waves of attacks on Black teachers have in common is the attempt to carry out programs of racial justice for people, instead of with them. Black teachers, parents, and administrators greeted the *Brown* decision with a mixture of enthusiasm and dread. But in many cities around the country, Black educators drew up plans for the integration of schools. These plans were ignored. Likewise, the opening of gleaming new hedge fund–backed charter school facilities in places like Harlem was greeted with an initial wave of enthusiasm. But there, too, it eventually became clear to parents and students that grinding through successive waves of brand-new teachers semester after semester provided no miracles, and many students moved from charter schools back to public schools, where they could find a stable community of educators (and a higher percentage of Black educators) to care for and instruct them.

In four hundred years on this land, Black people have waged an uninterrupted battle for education. The equally persistent and ongoing resistance to their demands for reform should give us all pause. To get some small measure of access, they have had to draw up petitions and make demands of existing institutions. At the same time, they have developed and built their own resources and institutions, creating their own curricular materials and even their own schools. The Black Lives Matter at School movement shares these aims. It calls upon you, the reader of this chapter, to join in demanding more from our schools and applying pressure to school and political officials. But it is a grassroots initiative created, conceived, and coordinated by parents, teachers, and students nationwide—not by officials. Not unlike the early development of Negro History Week, the Black Lives Matter at School Week of Action is, at heart, a DIY movement, inviting you to take action now, teach Black history now, affirm Black students now, regardless of whether the demands are met.

The Black Lives Matter movement (initiated by Alicia Garza, Patrisse Khan-Cullors, and Opal Tometi in 2013 after George Zimmerman was acquitted for the murder of Trayvon Martin in Florida) has sparked a wide range of initiatives and organizations. Because schools are so central to modern life—as community centers, as workplaces, and as crucial sites of making and remaking ideas—it is not surprising that the Black Lives Matter movement has found a durable form of organization in the form of the Black Lives Matter at School Week of Action. Our public schools touch nearly every person in one way or another, and as the week of action spreads from school to school, we are putting down roots for one of the most important new social movements of our time.

How One Elementary School Sparked a Movement to Make Black Students' Lives Matter

By Wayne Au and Jesse Hagopian

Teachers at one Seattle school show the important role that educators have to play in the Movement for Black Lives, in part by creating a Black Lives Matter at School day, leading to some three thousand teachers wearing #BlackLivesMatter T-shirts to school, and responding together to events like the death of Charleena Lyles. This article was originally published in the fall 2017 issue of *Rethinking Schools*.

It was the morning of September 16, 2016, and a conscious party of resistance, courage, and community uplift was happening on the sidewalk in front of John Muir Elementary in Seattle. Dozens of Black men were lined up from the street to the school doorway, giving high fives and praise to all the students who entered as part of a locally organized event called Black Men Uniting to Change the Narrative. African American drummers pounded defiant rhythms. Students smiled and laughed as they made their way to the entrance. Teachers and parents milled about in #BlackLivesMatter T-shirts, developed and worn in solidarity with the movement to make Black lives matter at John Muir Elementary.

You never would have known that just hours before, the school was closed and emptied as bomb-sniffing dogs scoured the building looking for explosives.

That September morning was the culmination of purposeful conversations among John Muir administration and staff, as well as activism and media attention. John Muir Elementary sits in Seattle's Rainier Valley, and its student population reflects the community: 68 percent of Muir's roughly 400 students qualify for free or reduced lunch; 33 percent are officially designated transition bilingual; 10 percent are Hispanic; 11 percent are Asian American; 11 percent identify as multiracial; and almost 50 percent are African American—mostly a mix of East African immigrants and families from this historically Black neighborhood.

By that autumn, John Muir Elementary had been actively working on issues of race equity, with special attention to Black students, for months. The previous year, Muir's staff began a deliberate process of examining privilege and the politics of race. With the support of both the school and the parent–teacher association, Ruby Bridges—who as a child famously desegregated the all-white William Frantz Elementary School in New Orleans in 1960—had also visited Muir as part of a longer discussion of racism in education among staff and students. During end-of-the-summer professional development, with the support of administration and in the aftermath of the police killings of Alton Sterling and Philando Castile, school staff read and discussed an article on #BlackLivesMatter and renewed their commitment to working for racial justice at Muir.

As part of these efforts, an African American male student support worker, DeShawn Jackson, organized the Black Men

Uniting to Change the Narrative event for that September morning, and, in solidarity, school staff decided to wear T-shirts that read "Black Lives Matter / We Stand Together / John Muir Elementary," designed by the school's art teacher.

A local TV station reported on the teachers wearing #BlackLivesMatter T-shirts, and as the story went public, political tensions exploded. Soon *Breitbart*, the white supremacist, hate group–fueled news source, picked up the story, and the right-wing police support group Blue Lives Matter publicly denounced the effort. Hateful emails and phone calls began to flood the John Muir administration and the Seattle School Board. And then the horrifying happened: someone made a bomb threat against the school. Even though the threat was deemed not very credible by authorities, Seattle Schools officially canceled the Black Men Uniting to Change the Narrative event at Muir out of extreme caution.

All of this made that September morning all the more powerful. The bomb-sniffing dogs found nothing and school was kept open that day. The drummers drummed and the crowd cheered every child coming through the doors of John Muir Elementary. Everyone was there in celebration, loudly proclaiming that yes, despite the racist and right-wing attacks, despite the official cancellation, and despite the bomb threat, the community of John Muir Elementary would not be cowed by hate and fear. Black men showed up to change the narrative around education and race. School staff wore their #BlackLivesMatter T-shirts and devoted the day's teaching to issues of racial justice. All involved were bravely and proudly celebrating their power. In the process, this single South Seattle elementary school galvanized a growing citywide movement to make Black lives matter in Seattle schools.

Organizing across the district

Inspired by that bold action, members of the Social Equity Educators (SEE), a rank-and-file organization of union educators, invited a few John Muir staff to a meeting to offer support and learn more about their efforts. The Muir educators' story explaining how and why they organized for Black lives moved everyone in attendance, and the SEE members began discussing taking the action citywide.

Everyone agreed that there were potential pitfalls of doing a citywide Black Students' Lives Matter event. The John Muir teachers had a race and equity team as well as dedicated time for professional development from the previous year that they had used to discuss institutional racism, and they had collectively come to the decision as a school to support the action and wear the shirts. But what would it mean, at a different school, if some teachers wore the shirts and taught antiracist lessons and others didn't? What if only a few dozen teachers across Seattle wore the shirts? Would that send the wrong message? What if other schools received threats? What if those threats materialized?

These and other questions fueled an important discussion and debate among SEE members and highlighted the need to educate our communities about why this action was urgently needed. However, with the videos of police killing Philando Castile and Alton Sterling fresh in the minds of SEE members, the group decided that to fail to boldly declare that Black lives matter would be a statement in and of itself.

It wasn't just the police murder of Black people that motivated SEE to organize action across the school system. It was also the institutional racism infecting Seattle Public Schools. Seattle has an alarming pattern of segregation both between and within schools, with intensely tracked advanced classes overwhelmingly populated with white students. Moreover, the Department of Education's 2013 investigation found that Seattle Schools suspended Black students at about four times the rate of white students for the same infractions.

SEE members decided that on October 19, 2016, they would all wear #BlackLivesMatter shirts to school and voted to create a second T-shirt design that included "#SayHerName." The African American Policy Forum created this hashtag in the wake of the death of Sandra Bland while in the custody of Waller County, Texas, police, to raise awareness about police violence against Black women, especially Black queer women and Black transgender women.

As part of this action, SEE also developed a three-point policy proposal that would serve as an ongoing campaign to support Black Lives Matter in schools and aid in the struggle against institutional racism:

1. support ethnic studies in all schools
2. replace zero-tolerance discipline with restorative justice practices
3. de-track classes within the schools to undo the racial segregation that is reinforced by tracking

In addition, SEE voted to bring a resolution to the Seattle Education Association (SEA), the union representing Seattle's educators, to publicly declare support for the action of the John Muir teachers and community, and to call on all teachers across the district to actively support the October 19 action.

At the September SEA Representative Assembly, SEE member Sarah Arvey, a white special education teacher, brought forward the following resolution:

> Whereas the SEA promotes equity and supports antiracist work in our schools; and, Whereas we want to act in solidarity with our members and the community at John Muir who received threats based on their decision to wear Black Lives Matter T-shirts as part of an event with "Black Men Uniting to Change the Narrative"; and, Whereas the SEA and SPS promote Race and Equity teams to address institutionalized racism in our schools and offer a space for dialogue among school staff; and, Therefore be it resolved that the SEA Representative Assembly endorse and participate in an action wearing Black Lives Matter T-shirts on Wednesday, October 19, 2016, with the intent of showing solidarity, promoting antiracist practices in our schools, and creating dialogue in our schools and communities.

SEE members expected a difficult debate at the SEA Representative Assembly, and many didn't think the resolution would pass. But they underestimated the impact of the ongoing protests against police brutality and racism that were sweeping school campuses. Inspired by San Francisco 49ers quarterback Colin Kaepernick, the Garfield High School football team captured headlines around the city and nation when every single player and coach took a knee during the national anthem—and maintained that action for the entire season. The protest spread to the girls' volleyball team, the marching band, the cheerleaders, and many other high school sports teams across Seattle. When it came time for the SEA vote, the resolution to support Black Lives Matter at School day passed unanimously.

As word got out about the SEA Representative Assembly vote, and in reaction to the threats against John Muir Elementary earlier in the month, allies also began to step forward in support of making Black students' lives matter. The Seattle NAACP quickly endorsed the event and lent its support. Soup for Teachers, a local parent organizing group formed to support the 2015 SEA strike, as well as the executive board of the Seattle Council Parent Teacher Student Association, also endorsed the action and joined in solidarity.

SEE helped gather representatives from these organizations for an October 2016 press conference to explain why parents, educators, and racial justice advocates united to declare Black lives matter at school. Predictably, news outlets repeatedly asked teachers if they thought they were politicizing the classroom by wearing BLM shirts to school. NAACP education chair Rita Green responded directly, saying: "We're here to support families. We're here to support students. When Black lives matter, all lives matter."

Sarah Arvey, of SEE, told reporters: "It's important for us to know the history of racial justice and racial injustice in our country and in our world…in order for us to address it. When we're silent, we close off dialogue, and we close the opportunity to learn and grow from each other." Other teachers pointed out that students were already having discussions in the halls, during sports practice, and outside of school about racism, police violence, and the Black Lives Matter movement. A better question to ask, teachers asserted, would be "Is school going to be relevant to the issues that our students are discussing every day?"

In an effort to build greater solidarity for Seattle educators taking part in the Black Lives Matter at School day, one of us—Wayne—organized a national letter for professors to sign in an effort to build support for the action. After only a few days, close to 250 professors, many of them well-recognized scholars in educational research locally and nationally, had signed on. Another letter of support was signed by luminaries such as dissident scholar Noam Chomsky, former MSNBC anchor Melissa Harris-Perry, 1968 bronze medalist and activist John Carlos, Black Lives Matter co-founder Opal Tometi, noted education author Jonathan Kozol, and Pulitzer Prize–winning journalist Jose Antonio Vargas.

As support for Seattle's Black Lives Matter at School action swelled, in a surprising move, the Seattle school district's administration officially endorsed the event with no formal provocation from activists or the school board. An October 8, 2016, memo read:

> During our #CloseTheGaps kick-off week, Seattle Education Association is promoting October 19 as a day of solidarity to bring focus to racial equity and affirming the lives of our students—specifically our students of color.
>
> In support of this focus, members are choosing to wear Black Lives Matter T-shirts, stickers, or other symbols of their commitment to students in a coordinated effort. SEA is leading this effort and working to promote transformational conversations with staff, families, and students on this issue.
>
> We invite you to join us in our commitment to eliminate opportunity gaps and accelerate learning for each and every student.

At that point, we in Seattle felt that we had accomplished something historic, because for perhaps the first time in the city's history, teachers and the teachers union, parents and the PTSA, and students and the Seattle School District administration had all reached a consensus support for a very politicized action for racial justice in education.

As the October 19 Black Lives Matter at School day approached, orders for #BlackLivesMatter T-shirts soared. John Muir set up a site that allowed T-shirt purchases to directly benefit the school's racial justice work. SEE's online T-shirt site received some two thousand orders for the BLM shirts, with proceeds going to support racial justice campaigns and a portion going to John Muir. Other schools created their own T-shirt designs specific to their schools. The Seattle schools were now poised for unprecedented mass action for racial justice.

Black Lives Matter at School Day

As October 19 arrived, Garfield High School senior Bailey Adams felt waves of disbelief. She told Seattle's *KING 5 News*: "There was a moment of like, is this really going to happen? Are teachers actually going to wear these shirts? All of my years I've been in school, this has never been talked about. Teachers have never said anything where they're going to back their students of color."

But sure enough, every school across the city had educators come to school wearing the shirts. Hundreds of teachers took advantage of the day to teach lessons and lead discussions about institutional racism. SEE and Soup for Teachers partnered to make a handout called "Teaching and Mentoring for Racial Justice" that suggested BLM resources for both teachers and parents. The SEA also emailed suggested resources to teachers.

Some schools changed their reader boards to declare "Black Lives Matter." Parents at some elementary schools set up tables by the front entrance with books and resources to help other parents talk to their kids about racism. Many schools coordinated plans for teaching about Black lives, including lessons about movements for racial justice and lessons about the way racism impacts the school system today. Several teachers across the district showed the film *Stay Woke*, about the origins of the Black Lives Matter movement, and held class discussions afterward. Some educators used the opportunity to discuss intersectional identities and highlighted how Black and queer women had first launched the #BlackLivesMatter hashtag.

Schools such as Chief Sealth International High School and Garfield High School put up Black Lives Matter posters / graffiti walls, which quickly filled up with antiracist affirmations from students and educators. A teacher at Dearborn Park International Elementary built a lesson plan from a photo of Colin Kaepernick kneeling. To capture the power of the day, educators from most of the schools around the district took group photos wearing the BLM shirts and sent them to the union for publication.

During lunchtime, the Garfield faculty, staff, and students rallied on the front steps of the school. In one of the most moving and powerful moments of the day, Black special education teacher Janett Du Bois decided she finally had to tell everyone a secret she had been quietly suffering with. In front of all the assembled school community and media she revealed that the police had murdered her son several years ago—and this had happened after he had been failed by the education system and pushed out of school. Fighting through tears, Du Bois said, "When our kids are failed, they have to go to alternative places and end up with their lives hanging in the balance because someone does not care."

To cap off the extraordinary and powerful day, SEE organized a community celebration, forum, and talent showcase that evening that drew hundreds of people. The event was emceed by educator, organizer, poet, attorney, and soon-to-be Seattle mayoral candidate Nikkita Oliver. Spoken word poets, musicians, and the Northwest Tap Connection (made up of predominantly Black youth performers) delighted and inspired the audience. Black youth activists from middle schools and high schools engaged in an onstage discussion about their experience of racism in school and what changes they wanted made that would result in the education system truly valuing their lives. Seahawks Pro Bowl defensive end Michael Bennett came to the event and pledged his support for the movement, saying, "Some people believe the change has to come from the government, but I believe it has to be organic and come from the bottom."[1]

By the end of the day, thousands of educators had reached tens of thousands of Seattle students and parents with a message of support for Black students and opposition to anti-Black racism—with local and national media projecting the message even further. While the educators who launched this movement were quite aware that the institutions of racism remained intact, they also knew that those same institutions had been shaken.

Lessons learned

In many ways we had a successful campaign around making Black lives matter in Seattle schools, and, from an organizing perspective, we learned several important lessons. To begin, we learned that one school can make a big difference: a single elementary school bravely took a stand that prompted an already-simmering citywide movement and influenced national discussions, as educators in Philadelphia and Rochester followed suit that school year with similar Black Lives Matter actions. It was particularly inspiring that year to see Philadelphia's Caucus of Working Educators expand the action to last an entire week as they broke down the thirteen principles of the Black Lives Matter Global Network into teaching points for each day of the week.

We also learned that acting in the context of a broader social movement was critical. The police killings of Philando Castile and Alton Sterling in the summer of 2016, as part of the long-standing pattern of Black death at the hands of police, ensured that there were ongoing protests and conversations associated with #BlackLivesMatter. This broader movement created the political space we needed and helped garner support for the actions of both John Muir Elementary specifically, and Seattle Public Schools more generally.

In addition, we learned that sometimes when white supremacists, the "alt-right," and right-wing conservatives attack, it can make our organizing stronger and more powerful. In the case of Seattle, it was the avalanche of hateful emails and phone calls, the right-wing media stories, and the bomb threat against John Muir Elementary that ultimately galvanized teachers and parents across the city.

We also learned that developing a broad base of support was essential to the success of the campaign to make Black student lives matter in Seattle Schools. Garnering the official support of the teachers union, the executive board of the Seattle Council PTSA, and even the Seattle Public Schools, combined with acts of solidarity from scholars and others, helped build a protective web of political support to shield Seattle educators as they moved forward with their action.

In the end, we also learned that with more time and resources we could have done better organizing. For instance, we had to grapple with the fact that when the John Muir Elementary staff made the decision to wear their #BlackLivesMatter T-shirts, that decision came on the heels of years of sustained discussion and professional development. Not all schools were in the same position. Ideally, all schools should have a foundation of discussion and learning so that when the time comes for action, staff members have a strong understanding of racial justice to guide their decisions.

Another improvement would have been to be able to offer a clearer vision of curriculum across the district for the Black Lives Matter at School day. Despite the strength of the "Teaching and Mentoring for Racial Justice" resource handout developed by SEE and Soup for Teachers, the quality and depth of what children at different schools learned on the day of the districtwide event varied widely from school to school. With more time and resources, we could have provided teachers with a cluster of grade-level-appropriate teaching activities that they could have used on that day. In particular, that is something that might have helped teachers around the district who wanted to support the action but struggled with ways to explicitly make Black lives matter in their own classroom curriculum.

It wasn't until the end of the school year that we learned two more lessons. The first was that, despite widespread community support for the Black Lives Matter at School day, the passive-aggressive racism of some of Seattle's notoriously liberal, white parents had been lurking all along. In a June 2017 story, local news radio station KUOW reported on a series of emails from white parents who live in the more affluent north end of Seattle. According to the story, white parents complained not just about the perceived militancy and politics of the Black Lives Matter at School day in Seattle but that children couldn't handle talking about racism and that we should be colorblind because "all lives matter." Unsurprisingly, many of these parents openly questioned the existence of racial inequality in Seattle's schools.

The second lesson we learned well after the Black Lives Matter at School day was that our action helped strengthen the political groundwork for a continued focus on racial justice in Seattle schools. On July 5, 2017, the Seattle School Board unanimously passed a resolution in support of ethnic studies in Seattle schools in response to a yearlong campaign from the NAACP, SEE, and other social justice groups, including formal endorsement from the Seattle Education Association. While this policy shift happened on the strength of the community organizing for ethnic studies specifically, Seattle's movement to make Black lives matter at school demonstrated to the district that there was significant public support for racial justice initiatives in Seattle schools, effectively increasing the official space for other initiatives like ethnic studies to take hold.

Putting the shirts back on

After these gains, the school year ended with a horrific reminder of why we must continue to declare the value of Black lives. On Sunday, June 18, 2017, Seattle police shot and killed Charleena Lyles, a pregnant mother of four, in her own apartment after she called them in fear that her home was being burglarized. She was shot down in a hail of bullets in front of three of her kids, two of whom attended public elementary schools in Seattle. The immediate media narrative of her death dehumanized her by focusing on the facts that the police alleged Charleena was wielding a kitchen knife, that she had a history of mental illness, and that she had a criminal background. This was the usual strategy of killing the person and then assassinating their character in an attempt to turn public opinion in support of the police.

But in Seattle, there were the countervailing forces of Charleena's organized family, community activists, and Seattle educators who forced a different public discussion about the value of Black lives and their callous disregard by unaccountable police. SEE and the SEA immediately put out a call for teachers to put their #BlackLivesMatter shirts back on—many of which also featured #SayHerName—for a school district–wide action in solidarity with Charleena and her family on June 20. Within three days of Charleena's death, hundreds of teachers came to school wearing their heartbreak, rage, and solidarity in the form of their #BlackLivesMatter T-shirts—with shirt sales this time going to Charleena's family.

A couple hundred educators swelled the ranks of the after-school rally that day as Charleena's family and hundreds of other supporters gathered at the apartment complex where she had been killed. With educators and others from across the district rallying to Charleena's side, the press was compelled to run stories about her as woman, as a parent of Seattle schoolchildren, and as a person with talents and struggles like everyone else.

Seattle's Black Lives Matter at School day was only a beginning. Having nearly three thousand teachers wear T-shirts to school one day doesn't magically end anti-Black racism or white supremacy. If that were the case, then perhaps Charleena Lyles would still be alive today to drop her kids off at school, chat with other parents on the playground, and watch the children play. But something powerful and important did happen in Seattle. At John Muir Elementary, the school staff and community stood strong against white supremacist hate, and across Seattle Schools, teachers and parents found ways to stand in solidarity with Black students and their families. In the process, the public dialogue about institutionalized racism in Seattle schools was pushed forward in concrete ways. And while we have so much more work to do, in the end, what happened in Seattle showed that educators have an important role to play in the movement for Black lives. When they rise up across the country to join this movement—both inside the school building and outside on the streets—racist institutions can be challenged in the search for solidarity, healing, and justice.

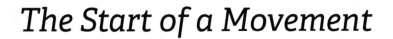
The Start of a Movement

CHAPTER 3

From Philly with Love

Black Lives Matter at School Goes National

By Tamara Anderson

W e live in a society that dispossesses Black and Brown communities, and our schools are the front lines in the struggle between oppression and empowerment. "My history classes in high school...taught me early on that my Black life didn't matter," recalls Keziah Ridgeway, a history teacher in Philadelphia. "As a result, I decided to become a history teacher and participate in Black Lives Matter week so that the children that I educate will understand the value of their life and history."[1] Those of us who share this goal know that our work won't end as long we are operating within a broken system. Along the way, we need to check in, evaluate, restrategize, move forward, recover, and start again. It is vital that we continue to transform our words into powerful actions. In the words of James Baldwin, "Any real change implies the breakup of the world as one has always known it, the loss of all that gave one identity, the end of safety." Only when we embrace risk can the system be rebuilt rather than simply being reformed to repeat the errors of the past.

A few years ago, educators in Philadelphia began contributing to this spirit of change. Inspired by the Black Lives Matter at School action carried out by educators in Seattle in the fall of 2016, the Caucus of Working Educators Racial Justice Organizing Committee (RJOC) sat down to figure out what a similar action should look like in Philadelphia. I came into this work when I started writing a column on educational policy for *Examiner*, a former online publication. This journalism work brought me to the caucus and the Teacher Action Group as I covered many of their events and actions. I was also an avid writer for the former School Reform Commission. I joined the caucus in 2015 and was elected as a steering committee member; that same year, I co-founded the RJOC with Ismael Jimenez.

Shaw MacQueen, Ismael Jimenez, Christopher Rogers, Charlie McGeehan, Kristin Luebbert, Shira Cohen, myself, and other members of the RJOC decided that the events we were planning should last a week and be centered on the thirteen guiding principles developed by the original organizers of Black Lives Matter. There wasn't a specific event in Philadelphia public schools that prompted our action. Rather, we were responding to ongoing adverse conditions. School funding was lacking, school control was draconian, and these problems disproportionately affected the district's African American and Latinx populations. It was vital to start shining a light on the systemic racism and austerity that resulted in our children receiving less, year after year, stripping them of the education they deserved.

It was vital to us that the week feel inclusive and not be limited to schools or educational settings and issues. The action needed to speak to connective issues like poverty, housing, and a living wage in order for the collective action to result in actual change. As a parent organizer, former steering committee member of the Caucus of Working Educators, and core member of the RJOC, I supported the decision that any action we took should be in partnership with parents, educators, higher education faculty, and organizers local to Philadelphia who had been working on racial justice issues that plagued the city and schools. We chose a name that would encompass a wide range of participants and settings—one that would encourage solidarity and bridge the gap between communities and schools: Black Lives Matter Week of Action.

In January 2017, the week of action came to Philadelphia. Right away, we received some pushback. Some school administrators did not allow their teachers to participate. Some schools received threats or racist calls before and during the week. A group of parents suggested holding an "All Lives Matter" day because they believed the week's focus to be anti-police. The Philadelphia Federation of Teachers (PFT) did not publicly support us during the first year. Finally, some of our own caucus members did not fully embrace or understand the need for the week, believing that the rhetoric of the action was inflammatory.

We responded to this pushback by re-centering the narrative on the truth of the Black Lives Matter movement, a grassroots movement for "freedom, liberation, and justice." We also faced fear with truth by using the blueprint of Black Lives Matter's thirteen guiding principles, which emphasize inclusive values, including restorative justice, globalism, trans affirming, and, the power that resides in being unapologetically Black and no longer silent or invisible. The thirteen principles laid the groundwork for our planning and curriculum, and, eventually, for the week going national.

During the first week, I was invited several times to interview with a local conservative reporter, Dom Giordano, and the conversation always veered to the anti-police rhetoric that swirled around the Black Lives Matter movement. We fully anticipated the negative response, which is why we prepared an FAQ for educators, parents, families, and schools to share. It provided talking points for teachers and letters detailing the curriculum and its purpose. The week brought to the forefront the importance of Black lives and how this movement is *the* movement of our time. It included a robust curriculum connected to the African American studies high school requirement and in-school and community events scheduled during the day and evenings. We also provided detailed descriptions of the thirteen guiding principles. Each day had two or three principles as a theme (e.g., Black women, Black families, trans affirming). This resource offered some leverage for educators to get buy-in from their school administrators.

After introducing the week of action, another major milestone came in July of 2017 when members of the RJOC spoke at the Free Minds, Free People conference in Baltimore and gave a presentation about the Black Lives Matter Week of Action. This opportunity to discuss the work we were doing in Philadelphia resulted in over twenty cities expressing interest in getting involved in organizing this effort around the country, and with that the national Black Lives Matter Week at School was birthed.

In 2018, the National Black Lives Matter Week at Schools committee decided on three new demands: ending zero tolerance discipline for students; hiring and retaining Black teachers, and offering antiracist training; and including Black studies and ethnic studies in the curriculum. In 2019, a fourth demand was added to the list: fund counselors, not cops, to encourage the presence of counselors and social workers in all schools.

In Philadelphia, we made a decision to focus on the demand for antiracist training for all educators and staff for all Philadelphia public schools. We wrestled with the question of how the Caucus of Working Educators could maintain a purpose aligned with racial and social justice. Specifically, how could a predominately white educator caucus continue to purposefully recruit educators of color and also not lose them? This question led to the creation of affinity groups that include some members of Working Educators who were also a part of the RJOC. An example of one such affinity group, Building Antiracist White Educators (BARWE), was created for district and charter school educators who identify as white. It is a space where white educators can work with their peers to develop antiracist identities and practices. BARWE's vital and necessary work has been recognized by Teaching Tolerance with the Award for Excellence in Teaching, given to Charlie McGeehan and Rebecca Coven for their leadership.

Another affinity group, Melanated Educators Collective (MEC) began in 2018, to provide a space for educators who identify as Black / African American / Caribbean American / Afro-Latinx / POC to have conversations about teaching, learning, and building community without the presence of white gaze. MEC has hosted two annual conferences since its inception, featuring keynote speakers Bettina L. Love and Dana King and workshops led by educators and community leaders.

In Philadelphia, members of the RJOC, BARWE, and MEC (of which I am also a member) decided to develop an antiracist training for administrators in the district. It was imperative that the training be created in house, by educators, and not farmed out to the School District of Philadelphia. The material needed to have an antiracist approach steeped in critical race theory and intersectionality, and not simply an "improving diversity" focus. We developed a plan of action during several planning meetings beginning in September of 2018. We decided that the first step in creating the training should be to collect data on racial incidents in Philadelphia public schools. We conducted an informal qualitative study of teachers and students, inviting them to recount their experiences within the school setting. The survey results came back with some of the following comments:

- "White teacher at my school said to [a] Black student (sixth grade), 'Do I look like one of your n*ggas?'"
- "All of the students with an Emotional Support designation on their IEP [individualized education plan] are Black boys. Every last one of them. Since our school has an ES [Emotional Support] room, white teachers are constantly trying to shoehorn more Black boys into that room. 'Least restrictive' and FAPE [Free and Appropriate Public Education] be damned. It is MADDENING."
- "When I was teaching at a K–8 school (majority African American), we had a pair of young, white teachers designate their lines and classroom groups using 'cute' animal names. Several more experienced teachers heard them use 'monkey' as one of the names. We had a visceral negative reaction to this and let the teachers know the historical and racial issues with using the term 'monkey' to refer to Black children. Our experience and knowledge [were] disregarded and 'pooh-pooh-ed'—the younger teachers said it was no big deal and the students did not mind. We emphasized that [kindergarten and first grade] students may be too young to mind, but that it still was inappropriate. We were ignored. About a week later, a Black staff member heard the students referred to as 'monkeys' and went straight to the principal to complain about the inappropriate racial language. If the teachers had wanted to learn, that step could have been avoided and they would be serving their students better."
- "I feel like my voice does not matter at all because I am too 'young' and it's apparently [an] 'adult' thing. Anything I say is invalid because I am either too young or my skin is too dark."
- "[It was hard] being the only Black student in a class and nobody wanted to communicate with me."

These are just a few examples of the comments that were submitted by educators and students in response to the survey. These case studies provided a baseline for thinking about the training. What should be included? How long should the training last? What core materials will guide the work? What are the core issues that need to be addressed? The results also confirmed just how unsafe and toxic the school environments are for Black and Brown youth and teens. These questions and concerns became the core agenda topics at every monthly RJOC meeting from September of 2018 to spring of 2019.

Finally, after much deliberation and collection of data, materials, and more case studies, we decided that *Stamped from the Beginning*, by Ibram X. Kendi, would be the core text to guide our educational materials. In addition, we gathered an impressive collection of videos, articles, quotes, books, and studies that informed our training. By now our curriculum had turned into a comprehensive, twenty-hour antiracist and bias training that includes the following subject areas: history of race; understanding antiracism; privilege, bias, and white supremacy; intersectionality (Black feminism and queer racism); and creating an antiracist action plan or approach for your school or organization.

In the spring of 2019, two members of the RJOC, Clarice Brazas and Blair Downie, curated a shorter, ninety-minute professional development training from the twenty-hour antiracist training and were selected to present it at two public high schools on "Tune-Up Tuesday," a citywide opportunity for teachers to facilitate professional development for their peers on a variety of topics through the School District of Philadelphia. They conducted two sessions, which had over thirty participants each. The questions and comments shared during the trainings were recorded and shared with the larger organizing committee, and they made us realize that conversations centered on antiracism and bias are lacking for Philadelphia educators. Many asked when we would be doing another training and suggested that their own schools would benefit from the opportunity to learn.

After this successful reception, the same training material was presented as a part of the School District of Philadelphia New Hire Orientation in August of 2019. A sixteen-hour version was also shared at the Caucus of Working Educators' annual summer institute as a part of a larger training. The feedback we received following these events informed changes, edits, and additions to the material. Utilizing tools like "White

Supremacy Culture," by Tema Okun, and the "Racial Justice Organization Assessment," created by the Western States Center, provided space for necessary conversation and debate.

The Caucus of Working Educators also needed to shine a critical light on itself, we realized. An ongoing challenge of the caucus and the RJOC has been to recognize, question, and challenge our own internalized structures. In 2019, approximately seven hundred individuals participated in Black Lives Matter Week of Action via events, classrooms, and public actions, and 60 percent of the organizers were African American. Yet, the number of African American caucus members is far fewer. In light of that discrepancy, we need to find sustainable solutions and engage in necessary, uncomfortable conversations. We looked at case studies of racialized incidents from within the caucus and other organizations. The ongoing reflection supported our conviction that the training needed to be called "antiracist." The term "racism" was necessary, as opposed to terms like "implicit bias," "social justice," or even "racial justice," in order to keep from sanitizing the truth. The antiracist training we developed has since been conducted at other locations, such as West Chester University and Baltimore Teachers Union, and this work continues in the absence of support from the PFT.

As we ensure that teachers receive effective training, we continue to strengthen and seek out support for student education. Each year in Philadelphia, the RJOC of the Caucus of Working Educators promotes the robust curriculum of the national Black Lives Matter at School coalition. This ensures that the work doesn't start and end with just the yearly week of action but is part of a larger African American history curriculum, which is a required high school graduation credit in Philadelphia public schools. The board of the School District of Philadelphia has given verbal support in the press for the curriculum and started including it with its social studies and African American studies curriculum in February of 2020. Black Lives Matter Philly continues to support the week and has developed, in partnership with MEC Black Educator Fellowship that provides small grants for Black educators and support staff for their classroom. The Philadelphia City Council, led by Councilmember Helen Gym, voted unanimously that the first week of February is Black Lives Matter Week of Action at Schools in 2019 and 2020.

In addition, we have advocated for a more robust curriculum that demands the inclusion of Indigenous voices and histories, reflecting the need for ethnic studies in schools. The One Book, One Philadelphia program, sponsored by the Free Library, supports this expanded lens. In addition, our growing partnerships in addressing issues like housing, gun violence, and trauma extends this work into the very communities plagued with these problems. Today, the RJOC hosts meetings with community organizers and educators regarding gun violence and trauma. During the COVID-19 crisis, we have hosted virtual reading groups about abolitionist educators, special education, queer and trans educators, and more so that the work continues to have purpose and sustainability.

We have also created a COVID-19 resource guide with information regarding housing, mental health, utilities, healthcare, and more for educators and families. Additionally, the higher education community in and around Philadelphia has their own unique events for Black Lives Matter Week of Action at Schools that are geared toward supporting students and faculty. These educational partnerships provide additional spaces for introspection, scholarship, and racial justice goals to be realized.

The goal of all these efforts is to push the movement beyond a single week and beyond even Black History Month to a year-round movement. The work of antiracist education and uplift needs to continue away from the cameras and be directly infused into the lifeblood of public education and the surrounding communities. This work continues to be important because in many corners of society the question is still being asked if Black lives matter. Until we eradicate white supremacy and the social constructs that support it, it is vital that we make space for conversations and debate about racial justice. In Philadelphia, the poverty rate ranks number one among the top ten cities; school budgets are constantly slashed; toxic, unsafe school conditions are rampant. These inequalities should be seen for what they are—racialized attacks against Black and Brown students. However, we now have an opportunity as students, teachers, parents, and community organizations to develop an antiracist approach to learning and reach for sustainable solutions, not only in Philadelphia but in public education across the globe.

CHAPTER 4

Organizing the National Curriculum

By Christopher Rogers

> *Listening to, analyzing, creating, and disseminating stories, and doing so with courage, keenness, skill, and cunning, with the clear purpose of changing human consciousness in the direction of choosing justice—this is what organizing is all about.*
>
> —**Aurora Levins Morales**

When Philadelphia teachers affiliated with the Racial Justice Organizing Committee of the Caucus of Working Educators first began planning for the 2017 Black Lives Matter Week of Action, I was deeply excited to participate in the curriculum building. As a teacher at an independent school in Northwest Philadelphia and curriculum contributor for Teacher Action Group in Philadelphia, I was well aware of the need for a solid set of resources to help teachers transform their classrooms into insurgent on-ramps for antiracist struggle.

Charlie McGeehan of the Caucus of Working Educators reached

out to me to see if I had ideas for the week, and I began to put together materials. For those of us involved in shaping the teaching materials that would be used in pre-K–12 public schools throughout Philadelphia, there was no shortage of inspirational wells to draw from. As I thought about helping students see themselves as part of a worldwide cause, I looked at intersectional justice principles from the Black Lives Matter Global Network, including the network's statement on diversity and globalism, which declares, "We see ourselves as part of the global Black family, and we are aware of the different ways we are impacted or privileged as Black people who exist in different parts of the world."[1]

It was important to me to show students how Black people are being targeted, harmed, and criminalized within the current white supremacy-laced anti-immigration movement, so I looked to the work of Black Alliance for Just Immigration, the organization where BLM co-founder Opal Tometi worked at the time. I also drew on the cultural organizing project Until We Are Free, a set of online resources especially useful for middle schoolers.[2]

The Until We Are Free website features a call to action penned by NoViolet Bulawayo entitled "Migrant Rights Meets Social Justice: A Declaration of Unity." Made available in six languages, the piece beautifully proclaims its purpose:

> We call for innocent Black–Brown children who are the apple of the world's eye. Who grow and live to the fullest because their lives are so sacred that nothing, no police weapon, will dare try to kill them before they grow. Who strive and win because they have food, shelter, healthcare, education, chances, love, beauty, and everything that holds them to the sun. Because their proud parents are not behind bars but at home being parents. Because they live in a world that does not fight them but fights for them.
>
> Because oppression stops here, Because dignity starts here.

The educational resources that I and others developed in 2017 were grounded in a belief that centering the words and deeds of Black freedom fighters in the classroom would have a liberatory potential for all involved. In that initial year, we were able to set up a framework that performed what Barbara Ransby calls "political quilting"—bridging movement work across time and place, and nurturing relationships and mass awareness. We learned that by recognizing the inherent intellectual practice in diverse organizing traditions, we were building a rich repository to reimagine the purpose of education toward a praxis of liberation.[3]

When the Black Lives Matter at School Week of Action went national after the Free Minds, Free People conference in 2017, I evolved from local Philadelphia curriculum contributor to chair of the National Curriculum Committee. We built a listserv of more than thirty-five educators from across the country working at various levels, from early childhood to higher education, to serve in the continued curation and creation of educational resources to shape what intersectional justice may look like in the classroom. In the process, our curriculum has continued to grow and deepen. By drawing on primary and secondary sources from Black-led justice movements from all around the world, we strive to see the classroom as space where, as Django Paris and H. Samy Alim suggest, we can recover and envision new community-rooted forms of teaching and learning that de-center whiteness and aspire toward social transformation for oppressed peoples.[4]

Our organizing during the week of action follows in principle a call to action led by Noah De Lissovoy, who suggested the tactic of a "curricular strike," whereby educators and community members refuse the high-stakes, neoliberal, corporate curriculum for a set period in order to create space for educational activities answerable to the freedom dreams of communities of color.[5] I cherish my role as curriculum chair because I believe that this shared, collective, reiterative process of curricular organizing pushes us to "reimagine everything," in the words of Grace Lee Boggs, as we (re)center the purpose of education and the co-constitutive work of educators and families toward the honoring of community knowledges, (her)stories, and cultural imaginaries that build collective power and seek to (re)imagine the world *otherwise*.[6] As Ashon Crawley offers, the only way to practice the alternative worldmaking that is *otherwise possibility* is to, indeed, practice *otherwise*.[7] We do that by accessibly curating, archiving, attributing, and spreading educational resources that show students and teachers alike that another world is possible and we have nothing to lose but our chains.[8] Alongside recent collaborative digital syllabi like the #FergusonSyllabus,[9] #CharlestonSyllabus,[10] and the Prison Abolition Syllabus,[11] we offer this collection of resources (the Black Lives Matter at School curriculum) freely to anyone, through our

Google Drive, for people to adapt and remix for their learning spaces. (I should note that we debate every year about whether we should move to a new platform due to our wish not to endorse Google, but we've stuck with this platform due to its ease of use. Definitely hit us up if you have ideas!)

While the technology is new, it is important for us to remind ourselves that this radical, collaborative work is not without historic precedent. Educational historians like Vanessa Siddle Walker, Heather Andrea Williams, and Jarvis Givens have documented the ways in which African American educators have creatively and subversively deployed radical Black historical narratives to stretch students' imaginations about the possibilities for social transformation, refusing the unjust educational policies of their time.[12] Students have also been at the front and center of these movements to reimagine schooling in service of social transformation, such as the envisioning of Third World studies during the San Francisco State College strike of 1968.[13] The multiracial coalition of college students at the center of the Third World Liberation Front (TWLF) updated the language first offered by the Black Student Union to call for the creation of a school of Third World studies, which sought to amplify the insurgent lessons from antiracist, anti-imperialist social movements contesting power throughout the world. Their example is instructive as the students sought something beyond just the mere inclusion of their cultural histories within the official curriculum. They proposed the establishment of a Third World College that would be "deliberately designed to focus on solving problems that have victimized Third World people and Third World communities."[14] As Robin D. G. Kelley writes, while we can't expect educational institutions themselves to be "engines of social transformation," they remain crucial sites of political struggle.[15]

The oft-erased work of the TWLF in jump-starting ethnic studies and the words of Kelley challenge us to not save or amend the colonial project of schooling through the addition of multicultural representation but to truly imagine otherwise by embracing the subversive space of thinking, planning, and gathering that Stefano Harney and Fred Moten call "the undercommons."[16] This work of reimagining has the potential to incite collectives of change agents, insurgents, and revolutionaries who see public schools as but one site where one can enter into radical study for social transformation.[17] The horizon of our struggle is not for Black students to behold the achievement of more advanced degrees, nor to pursue the privileges of white, cis, heteronormative, middle-class-dom, but—to return to NoViolet Bulawayo—the creation of a world where "justice comes to our neighborhoods. And the world at last guarantees our living. Because [we] are not free until all of us are free."[18]

How to browse the Black Lives Matter at School curriculum

You can browse all the resources from Black Lives Matter at School at bit.ly/blmweekcurriculum, or find the curriculum linked at our website, blacklivesmatteratschool.com.

How to get involved in the Black Lives Matter at School Curriculum Committee

For the past two years, the National Steering Committee of Black Lives Matter has created open-invite national work committees during planning season (October–January), including for curriculum development. During this open-invite session, students, parents, and educators can submit their emails and experiences to be included in the Curriculum Committee planning sessions. In committee, we break into five grade groups: early childhood, elementary, middle, high school, and postsecondary/higher education. Each section curates and offers resources in advance of the curriculum launch, which has for the past two years occurred on Martin Luther King Jr. Day. Join our mailing list to be in the know and to contribute to this ongoing, critical work. It is through the recovery of rebellious histories worldwide and their spread among the masses, in traditional and makeshift classrooms, that we build the road to another world.

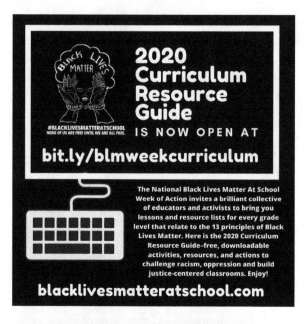

Curriculum Resource Guide flyers, created by Christopher Rogers.

CHAPTER 5

MapSO Freedom School and the Statewide and National Black Lives Matter at School Week of Action Organizing

By Awo Okaikor Aryee-Price

I still hear my brother crying—"I can't breathe"
Now I'm in the struggle singing—"I can't leave"
We calling out the violence of these racist police
And we ain't gonna stop [clap, clap] 'til our people are free!
—Ellisha and Steven Flagg

The roots of MapSO Freedom School

The atmosphere is dark and suffocating. It's the kind of dark, suffocating mist that leaves those of us in the African diaspora collectively gasping for air in a united utterance of "I can't breathe." We are the song of the canaries.

MAPSO Freedom School logo, created by MapSO Freedom School co-founder Ikechukwu Onyema in 2016.

"I can't breathe" echoes in our very existence. "I can't breathe" was the dark mist that I witnessed early in the mythical end-of-the-world films that my childhood church would show each year (I am convinced these films were their Christian version of *Scared Straight*, meant to ensure that all of us wayward Brick City ghetto children traveled the straight and narrow path toward white righteousness).

But this new suffocation isn't happening in my old church. It's taking place in my living room on the evening of August 14, 2017. And while it isn't the apocalypse, the situation feels dire, like I'm headed down a new road to perdition.

White nationalists are staging deadly protests in the Charlottesville, Virginia, in the wake of the decision to remove a Confederate statue. The nation is divided; some are still in a state of shock after the election of an openly and unapologetically racist, anti-Semitic, xenophobic, sexist, misogynist, ableist, homoantagonist brute; others were in a state of jubilee. One by one, an international wave of openly fascist national leaders is being "elected" and assuming positions of leadership (read: stealing elections and manipulating the levers of power).

And here we are, a nation in the "free" world, displaying our perverted "exceptionalism" for the entire world to see.

Tonight, like most nights since the year began, I choose to enter an early slumber at night, resting with the TV still on. Maybe falling asleep early will allow me to remain in the company of dreams and imaginations a little bit longer. But, seemingly betrayed, I wake to the televised chants of white nationalists. (At one level or another, we all collectively awakened to the chants of white supremacists staking their claim in a country and land that was never theirs.) On the screen, white nationalist "torchbearers" are drowning out the airwaves with their hate: "White lives matter!" they cry. "Blood and soil! You will not replace us! Jews will not replace us!"

The chants continue, echoing in my room. I see their violence: faces red with the collective anger of their ancestors. They want blood: "White lives matter! Blood and soil! You will not replace us! Jews will not replace us!"

I mute the TV. Unmute. Mute. Unmute. I need to hear what they're saying, but I want just a moment of peace.

Ding!

I hear my iPhone go off, but I don't want to answer.

Ding!

I bury my head in the pillow. I cannot help but wonder if this what it felt like to live in the world of my grandmother and mother. Here I am, their progeny, living in a reincarnation of their nightmare—my reality.

Ding!

I do not want to always be "on." I want to rest, at least for a moment, but the precarity of being Black in America means even our rest is under attack by white supremacy.[1]

Ding!

At last, I look. It's a text from my friend Melissa Katz, a local education organizer. Mel is also bearing witness to the violence and hate in Charlottesville. We text back and forth for a while, and then she has this to say:

Also this is incredibly random, but I was reading a bunch of different things on twitter last night and something I kept seeing were people encouraging teach ins about Charlottesville. I know we're really close to the start of the school year, but I was thinking how powerful it would be if there was a teach in for the beginning of the year about addressing not only Charlottesville but also sustained dialogue anti-racist/ anti-oppression curriculum. Maybe this is happening already?!

Text message from Melissa Katz to Awo Okaikor Aryee-Price, August 14, 2017.

The conversation that ensued marked the start of New Jersey–area organizing and the creation of MapSO (which stands for the Maplewood–South Orange district) Freedom School, a force for statewide organizing behind the Black Lives Matter at School Week of Action.

Founding a force for change

Formed in the summer of 2016, MapSO Freedom School was created and nurtured by a multi-ethnoracial group of New Jersey educators. We shared the goals of putting a stop to the racial profiling of Black students within New Jersey schools and providing empowerment programming and antiracist training for students, parents, and teachers alike. The founding group of MapSO organizers included Awo Okaikor Aryee-Price, Jacob Chaffin, Melissa "Mel" Katz, Ikechukwu Onyema, Stephanie Rivera, Jacob Willy Sumner, Greg Tuttle, and Thomas "T. J." Whitaker.

Together, we organized and spearheaded a teach-in about the events in Charlottesville for educators in the New Jersey area. Our flyers for the event circulated widely, attracting the attention of the organizers of the Philadelphia Caucus of Working Educators, which led to a collaborative planning call that included WE organizers Ismael Jimenez, Shira Cohen, Christopher Rogers, Charlie McGeehan, Hanako Franz, and Kelley Collings. It was then that we decided, with WE, to not only plan parallel events but to reconvene for a recap of what we'd learned from these events and a conversation about how our organizations could collaborate on a much larger national project to bring Black Lives Matter at School Week of Action to communities across the nation. Although I (Okaikor), had attended Free Minds, Free People in 2017, where the WE organizers proposed the idea for the national education project, it was the Charlottesville teach-in that connected us and drew us together.

The BLM at School Week of Action was grounded in the organizing work that WE started the year before, in January 2017. At the suggestion of Philadelphia educator and advocate Tamara Anderson, the week of action centered on the guiding principles of the Black Lives Matter Global Network, whose commitment to Black liberation, including the liberation of the Black LGBTQIA+ community, aligned with MapSO's politics. We became one of the first groups to lead the national and statewide BLM at School Week of Action. Initially, our organizing work focused mostly in northern New Jersey, but we knew we needed to expand our reach throughout the entire state.

MapSO's organizing strategy for New Jersey

MapSO's plan was to serve as a central organization for other people and organizations throughout New Jersey to help create space for us all to share ideas, organize our own local week of actions, create a network of New Jersey BLM at School Week of Action organizers, and to develop and strengthen relationships. As organizers, we felt a clear need to organize locally in our own communities as well as to create a space for other organizers to share and build together.

Our strategy allowed potential organizers in New Jersey to connect with others through monthly and bimonthly video conference calls. In the first two years, the initial calls were planned by MapSO co-founders, but those calls were planned, facilitated, and documented by New Jersey organizers associated with other organizations. This system allowed those organizers to share power and assume ownership in the planning process. This was not a MapSO endeavor; it was an "us" endeavor, and we just happened to be the vehicle for organizing. In our first year, we were able to organize educators and community organizers from Collingswood, Newark, Bayonne, East Orange, Trenton, Pennsauken, New Brunswick, South Orange–Maplewood, and Montclair, including Montclair State University. In the second year, we were able to add Cherry Hill and Camden.

Although MapSO's statewide New Jersey organizing has been slow, we are growing in ways that are not always easy to quantify. The New Jersey Education Association (NJEA) funds BLM at School events, which offers us both tangible and intangible support and has helped spread word about our own efforts into areas that we would not have otherwise been able to reach. Those of us involved with MapSO Freedom School know that our strongest resources are community members, board members, students, and the local education association. These relationships have made it possible to get free meeting spaces, food for our events, as well as small honoraria for our guests.

Drawing on the BLM guiding principles, we have centered a radical Black feminist framework, which has made our organizing efforts purposeful and intentional. The events we've sponsored throughout New Jersey have all prioritized the voices of Black queer, trans, and gender nonconforming folx, such as our event focused on community and school policing dialogue using the Advancement Project's report *We Came to Learn: A Call to Action for Police-Free Schools*.[2] To facilitate the organizing of BLM at School, MapSO hosted film and documentary screenings, book talks like the ones we had with Mama Africa, from the group MOVE, and Shani Robinson, a former Atlanta teacher and a critic of the racist policies behind education "reform." We also hosted open mics, community conversations, and panel discussions uplifting Black educators.

In the first year, MapSO received almost-immediate backing and support from Newark Education Workers (NEW) Caucus—a small yet more radical arm of the Newark Teachers Union (NTU), an affiliate of the American Federation of Teachers (AFT)—and the often more progressive South Orange–Maplewood Education Association, an affiliate of the NJEA and the National Education Association (NEA). The effort to get the backing of the NTU was spearheaded by the organizing work of NEW caucus members Yvette Jordan and Al Moussab, both classroom teachers in Newark. In fact, the NTU was the very first union in New Jersey to officially endorse BLM at School organizing and state events, and one of the first nationally. That alone was motivation for those of us affiliated with the NJEA/NEA to move forward with getting our local associations on board. As the New Jersey folks at the national level, we organized statewide calls to report back what was happening nationally. These calls were the bursts of motivation we all needed to organize to get the NJEA to formally endorse the week of action.

Since not all the organizers on the calls were Delegate Assembly (DA) members, we knew that the only way that we (the BLM state organizing team) could get the endorsement was if a DA member presented the idea. Twanda Taylor from the Trenton Education Association (TEA) proposed the idea and stated that we could bring a new business item (NBI) to the DA. We raised that idea on our next call.

Melissa Tomlinson, a DA member for the NJEA, volunteered to draft and present an NBI in preparation for the next NJEA DA meeting in January of 2018. In the NBI, drafted by Melissa and edited by the rest of the organizers, we asked the DA to endorse BLM at School Week of Action through the following actions: (1) publishing support for the NBI on the NJEA website; (2) fully supporting and advocating for the Amistad Curriculum (a New Jersey K–12 Black and African studies curriculum) through research and implementation; and (3) advocating for research on charter schools and their impact on communities, and the pushout of teachers of color.

Even though the NJEA endorsed the NBI, it was by no means a smooth endorsement. As Melissa Tomlinson stood at the microphone, others looked on in anticipation. Two members of our organizing team, Fatimah Hayes and Mel Katz, sat in the crowd, unsure of the outcome but there to bear witness and document the final results. Melissa read each word of the NBI, the intensity building with each word. Christine Sampson-Clark, a Mercer County DA member, seconded the NBI. Marie Blistan, the president, then explained that she believed the NBI would accrue a financial expense, but she could not state exactly what it would be. She asked Melissa if she would like to speak to that point, and

Melissa responded by underscoring the importance of this action and how it would move in the same social justice direction that the organization already appears to be heading.

We could have heard a pin drop.

Without much fanfare, Marie called for the voice vote after Melissa finished her presentation, prompting the delegates to vocalize their support with a "yay" or their disapproval with a "nay." The cacophony of voices reverberating throughout the room, and the vote could not be called; Marie Blistan declared the voice vote inconclusive. All was not lost yet. "Would you like to call for a stand vote?" she asked, and Melissa responded, "Yes!"

"All in favor, stand. And remain standing, please." People slowly, one by one, stood up in support. In the silence, you could hear, "Don't be racist! Stand up!" coming from one delegate. An NJEA staff member counted the delegates who were proudly standing. The number was recorded.

"All who vote no, stand." People, slowly, one by one, stood up in opposition to declare they could not support the NBI. The designated NJEA staff member counted the numbers. It was a narrow margin, and had it not been for the people who outright abstained from voting, the NBI might not have passed. It was a win, not because the majority of delegates believed Black lives matter in their schools but because the vast majority either could not decide if they mattered, did not care enough to take a stand, or did not want to be on record as voting on the wrong side of history. Either way, their inaction and silence amounted to an act of violence and complicity within a white supremacist ideology that holds to the conviction that Black lives do not, in fact, matter. We, however, accomplished a small win, with or without their support. Black lives still matter even without their validation.

Part of this work means that educators—because of what bell hooks calls "imperialist white supremacist capitalist patriarchy"—will face pushback and resistance as they try organize against power and privilege.[3] For one of our organizers, pushback meant having their superintendent threaten their job—not because they were a negligent educator, but because they were calling for the district to adopt the demands of Black Lives Matter at School Week of Action: (1) hire more Black teachers; (2) end zero tolerance policies and replace them with restorative practices; (3) teach Black and other ethnic studies; and (4) fund counselors, not cops. The problem didn't lie with these demands; it lay in the ways that anti-Blackness and misogynoir have been internalized by a society firmly situated in white supremacy, anti-Blackness, and anti-Indigeneity. The superintendent was merely a product and tool of such a society.

As educators and organizers engage in this critical antiracist work, it is imperative that we band together in community and foster relationships to strengthen and sustain our work. Our belief in the necessity for dialogue has shaped the organizing and event planning we do through MapSO, as well as our work to ensure institutional support for the work of BLM at School. As we move forward, we must be unapologetic, disciplined, and committed to centering Black, queer, and trans womxn in order to actualize the world we want to see.

With thanks to Melissa Katz, Ikechukwu Onyema, Jacob Willy Sumner, Greg Tuttle, and Thomas "T. J." Whitaker, who generously offered their feedback toward the development of this chapter. Their insights, wisdom, and experiences helped shape the account I have presented here.

Letter in Solidarity with Black Lives Matter at School

In the run-up to the first national Black Lives Matter at School Week of Action, organizers reached out to prominent educators, authors, activists, and artists to see if they would support the movement.

Black Lives Matter at School organizers knew that in some places wearing a shirt to school that said, "Black Lives Matter" and teaching antiracist lessons could prompt a backlash, and they hoped to preempt attacks on the movement by showing the widespread support it had.

What follows is a letter of solidarity signed by many social justice luminaries around the country who helped encourage the Black Lives Matter at School movement in its early stages.

> We, the undersigned, are writing in support of a new uprising for racial justice that is being organized by educators around the country who have declared February 5–9, 2018, "Black Lives Matter at School Week." Many thousands of educators will be wearing shirts to school that say "Black Lives Matter at School" and will teach lessons about structural racism,

intersectional Black identities, and Black history in cities all across the country.

At a time when the president makes openly racist statements about Africa, Haiti, and El Salvador, it is more important than ever to support antiracist pedagogy and support Black students. In addition, in this era of mass incarceration, there is a school-to-prison-pipeline system that is more invested in locking up youth than unlocking their minds. That system uses harsh discipline policies that push Black students out of schools at disproportionate rates; denies students the right to learn about their own cultures and whitewashes the curriculum to exclude many of the struggles and contributions of Black people and other people of color; and is pushing out Black teachers from the schools in cities around the country. That is why we support the three demands issued by the Black Lives Matter at School movement:

1. End zero tolerance discipline, and implement restorative justice
2. Hire more Black teachers
3. Mandate Black history / ethnic studies, K–12

Show your solidarity during this week of struggle by wearing your Black Lives Matter shirt to school or to work.

Signed,

Opal Tometi
Co-founder of #BlackLivesMatter, Executive Director of the Black Alliance for Just Immigration (BAJI)

Keeanga-Yamahtta Taylor
Assistant Professor of African American Studies at Princeton University

Curtis Acosta
Former Mexican American Studies Teacher; Assistant Professor, Language and Culture in Education, University of Arizona South

Sam Anderson
Co-organizer, National Black Education Agenda; retired

Professor of Math and Black History, Medgar Evers College of the City University of New York

Jose Antonio Vargas
Pulitzer Prize–winning journalist; filmmaker; founder/CEO of Define American

Wayne Au
Professor, School of Educational Studies, University of Washington Bothell

Bill Ayers
Distinguished Professor of Education (retired), University of Illinois at Chicago

Michael Bennett
Pro Bowl defensive end, Seattle Seahawks

Bill Bigelow
Curriculum Editor, *Rethinking Schools* magazine

Judith Browne Dianis
Executive Director, Advancement Project, National Office

Alex Caputo-Pearl
President, United Teachers of Los Angeles (UTLA)

John Carlos
Bronze–medal winner in the 200 meters at the 1968 Summer Olympics

Nancy Carlsson-Paige
Professor Emerita, Lesley University; Senior Advisor, Defending the Early Years

Linda Christensen
Oregon Writing Project

Noura Erakat
Human Rights Attorney; Assistant Professor, George Mason University

Eve L. Ewing
Assistant Professor, University of Chicago School of Social Service Administration

Kevin James
Emcee, Son of Nun; former Baltimore City high school teacher

Brian Jones
City University of New York Graduate Center

Ibram X. Kendi
Director, the Antiracist Research and Policy Center, American University; National Book Award–winning author of *Stamped from the Beginning: The Definitive History of Racist Ideas in America*

Joyce King
Benjamin E. Mays Endowed Chair for Urban Teaching, Learning and Leadership, Georgia State University; President, the Academy for Diaspora Literacy, Inc.

Shaun King
Columnist for the *Intercept*

Jonathan Kozol
Teacher; author, *Shame of the Nation, Savage Inequalities*; National Book Award–winner, *Death at an Early Age*

Jia Lee
Member, Movement of Rank and File Educators and Change the Stakes / NYC Opt Out

Barbara Madeloni
President, Massachusetts Teachers Association

Edwin Mayorga
Assistant Professor, Educational Studies, Swarthmore College, Latin American and Latino Studies

Deborah Menkart
Executive Director, Teaching for Change

Tom Morello
Musician, Rage against the Machine, Prophets of Rage

Pedro A. Noguera
Distinguished Professor of Education, UCLA Graduate School of Education and Information Studies

Nikkita Oliver
Community Organizer

Bob Peterson
Editor, *Rethinking Schools*; past President of the Milwaukee Teachers' Education Association

Bree Picower
Associate Professor, College of Education and Human Services, Montclair State University

Adam Sanchez
Organizer and Curriculum Writer, Zinn Education Project

David Stovall
Professor, Educational Policy Studies and African American Studies, University of Illinois at Chicago

José Luis Vilson
Math Teacher, New York City Department of Education; Executive Director, EduColor

Dyan Watson
Associate Professor of Education, Lewis and Clark Graduate School of Education and Counseling

Yohuru Williams
Dean of the College of Arts and Sciences, University of St. Thomas; Board of Directors, Network for Public Education

Securing Union Support: Successes and Struggles

CHAPTER 6

Black Lives Matter to the Chicago Teachers Union

*An Interview with Jennifer Johnson**

Jesse Hagopian: Start by explaining the conditions in the Chicago Public Schools, especially for Black students and Brown students. Also, what does the school-to-prison pipeline look like in Chicago?

Jen Johnson: Chicago Public Schools are made up of over five hundred individual school buildings, but close to 90 percent of our students come from low-income families, and 90 percent of our students are students of color. In terms of demographics, we're approaching a point where nearly half of our students are Latinx. Around 30 percent are Black students, but demographics are shifting. Thankfully, some of our school policy has shifted in recent years due to the advocacy work that students led and that the Chicago Teachers Union and other community organizations supported. The students were really at the center of calling for changes to the Uniform Discipline Code a few years ago, and the CTU made sure to support their efforts, and this advocacy helped lay the groundwork for

* This interview with Chicago Teachers Union Chief of Staff Jennifer Johnson was conducted on March 14, 2020, by Jesse Hagopian.

the passing of Senate Bill 100, which was aimed at shifting away from the school-to-prison pipeline.

But Chicago Public Schools (CPS) is definitely a kind of militarized school district in that we have the largest ROTC program in the country; we have armed police officers in our high schools; and metal detectors are very common. On the other hand, there were, like I said, efforts led by students to shift away from suspensions, police referrals, and so forth. The struggle's been going on for several years. That has led to a decrease in suspensions, which is a good thing.

And yet we have incidences where children have been arrested in schools. It's a pressing issue. There was a public incident at Marshall High School last year that was really horrific and traumatizing for students and staff. We in CTU did our best to intervene and were able to help ensure that the young woman was not put through the justice system, but this is still a work in progress.

Jesse: Was that the case where a girl was thrown down the stairs by a police officer?

Jen: Yeah, exactly.

Jesse: And it was caught on video?

Jen: Yeah, exactly.

Jesse: That was horrific.

Jen: It was horrific.

Jesse: That video was chilling. If I remember right, the officer lied about the incident, but the video clarified what had happened. Is that correct?

Jen: That's right. Again, because we've worked to have folks like Kim Foxx in positions like state's attorney of Cook County, Illinois, there are efforts like this where the CTU is able to intervene. We were in contact with Kim Foxx's office. We were able to make sure that this young woman was not prosecuted, but it was after the fact, after this horrific incident.

Another important issue is having teachers understand our role in building strong connections with students through culturally relevant pedagogy and seeing our young people as human actors with agency, power, and needs, rather than contributing to the criminalizing of youth.

Jesse: You all had one of the most heartbreaking instances of police killing a young person when officer Jason Van Dyke shot seventeen-year-old Chicago Public Schools student Laquan McDonald on the evening of October 20, 2014. Police reported at the time that McDonald had refused to put down a knife he was carrying and lunged at them. Internal police reports similarly described the incident, ruling the shooting justified, and Van Dyke was not charged in the shooting at that time.

Then, when a court ordered the police to release a dash cam video of the shooting over a year later, it showed McDonald had actually been walking away from the police when he was shot. Can you talk about the impact of the murder of Laquan McDonald on the city, on the students and teachers? How did this help shape demands around what it takes to make Black lives matter?

Jen: We were all devastated. We were all just shook to our core. When that video came out, it really exposed how then-mayor Rahm Emanuel was more concerned about his reelection than about this young man's needs and his family's needs—he suppressed the release of the video that showed what actually happened. We had already been supporting and working with local community organizations and religious leaders prior to Laquan's death, but this really just deepened our resolve. CTU's highest member leadership body, the House of Delegates, passed a resolution supporting more police accountability.

When the true nature of Laquan's death was exposed, we called for our members to participate in the marches downtown. That was hard for some of our members to understand, and certainly that kicked off a lot of dialogue and some pushback. But many of us in the CTU felt it was really important to call for justice and stand with the young man's family and let the world know that this young man's needs were not being met by our city or by our schools.

Jesse: Right on. It's astounding to me that you can have a mayor who is charged with running the public schools be somebody who's orchestrating a cover-up of a murder of one of the school students. Can you talk about the "Reparations Won" curriculum that the CTU supported as a way to teach students about the abuses of the Chicago Police Department?

Jen: For sure. For decades, Black men who were incarcerated in Illinois had been trying to be heard about the torture that they had experienced under police commander Jon Burge and other police underneath him in the '70s, '80s, and '90s. They struggled for decades to be believed. There were community organizations, legal groups, activists, and family members who fought for the survivors to be believed and to receive reviews of their cases. Multiple groups came together and made a huge push in 2015, and Rahm Emanuel, finally, for the first time, actually acknowledged that the torture had happened.

The organizers were very thoughtful about what they were fighting for. They didn't just say they wanted exonerations or pardons of those people who had been tortured in jail (that was and continues to be important work as there are still survivors who are incarcerated). They also wanted reparations for the survivors: monetary reparations, a counseling and community center where the survivors and their families and any other survivors of police torture could get counseling services, and a public memorial to be erected in the city to memorialize the survivors' fight so that no one would forget that this happened. They also included in their fight tuition assistance at city colleges for the survivors.

Jesse: Amazing.

Jen: But there's more. They also demanded that the history of the struggle against police torture be taught in the Chicago Public Schools in eighth and tenth grades. It was institutionalized with an ordinance that the school district had to now teach this history. It took a couple of years to get the curriculum developed, but along with community partners, the survivors and educators were able to be a part of that process of monitoring and supporting the development of the curriculum, which rolled out in the 2017–18 school year. It's now required curriculum.

It's mandated, but as things typically go, just because something's mandated doesn't mean it happens. We've done what we can to try to help teachers feel prepared to teach the history—we've done our own professional development. We had events with survivors; we had a survivor named Darrell Cannon come speak to CTU's House of Delegates in Deloitte, and we did a book event with Ronald Kitchen about his survivor story, *My Midnight Years*. There's plenty more work to do because we know in some communities this information is not being taught.

Jesse: The work you did around that curriculum could serve as a model because Chicago isn't the only city to have experienced abusive conditions in policing and jails. I hope people take that up around this country. That's really powerful.

Jen: I think it really does speak to the need for educators to listen to the community and think about how to involve community members in making decisions about what our students actually need to learn. The CTU didn't initiate the demand for the curriculum; the organizers and survivors did. And when we heard this demand, we made it a priority of our union.

Jesse: That's a great example. Talk specifically now about the Black Lives Matter at School movement and what value you see in this movement nationally. How has this movement impacted the Chicago Public Schools, and what are some of the successes and challenges for educators participating in the annual week of action?

Jen: Absolutely. First of all, I just want to say thank you to you all in Seattle and the folks in Philadelphia. You've done an amazing job of really focusing and prioritizing racial justice work in your union caucus spaces. We take a lot of inspiration from that in Chicago. Even though, obviously, racial justice fights are a part of our values and they're inherent to our work now that we're running the union, there is a focus coming out of Philadelphia and Seattle, and this has been inspiring. I think it's something we're still trying to achieve. We signed on to Black Lives Matters at school week the first year that it went national, and we have endorsed it every single year—we've made a point of actually passing the resolution every year so that people will have to confront it every single year.

Now is the time to double down on our support for social justice and think about how our collective bargaining rights are connected to our students and communities in Chicago. As educators and labor leaders, we have a responsibility to push the bounds of bargaining to include issues that matter to our communities, including fighting for affordable housing and supporting our homeless students.

We've had varying success making the Black Lives Matter at School Week of Action a widespread focus. I will say that our biggest critique of ourselves is that, while we're audacious and we're achieving a lot of great things, in some cases we're just not as focused as we could be. We take on twenty things rather than three. I wish I could say that we had done more school-by-school organizing around the Black Lives Matters at School Week of Action. But the week of action has really helped us to launch important events centrally. We've done film screenings and panels; we hosted a Black Lives Matter at School event for students that included dance, poetry, and other performances at the CTU building and was led by a teacher. We also make the BLM at School class activity resources widely available to the teachers, and we wear the BLM at School T-shirts, which have been wildly successful.

I think we've treated this as more of a part of our racial justice work in general, but it hasn't necessarily taken on the same focus as it in has other cities. We are still learning from other cities about how they're really making that week a powerful way to center the dialogue around racial justice.

Jesse: That's great that the week of action has contributed to your struggles for racial justice. The week, obviously, isn't meant to limit the work to a single week but to advance ongoing struggles. Let's move on to talking about this incredible contract battle that you all just went through—so much of it was about the struggle for racial justice and making Black lives matter at school. Can you talk about your demands and what you won?

Jen: We absolutely made the struggle for Black lives central to our contract demands. We have learned from other unions around the country and we are not alone in this work. I said before, 90 percent of our students are students of color in Chicago Public Schools.

We had a laser focus on four demands this time. First, we said that we were fighting for fair wages and benefits for our members—but in particular we highlighted our paraprofessional members, the school clerks, the teachers, the students, the folks who are mostly Black and Brown women who work in the school communities where they live. We said that it's not enough to provide raises that are across the board for all staff at a certain level; we need additional raises for those paraprofessional Black and Brown women.

Jesse: That's right!

Jen: We really won over the five years: on average, 40 percent raises for dozens of different paraprofessional job categories. We also won educational lanes for them that will phase in over the next couple of years. Paraprofessionals who have more than an associate's degree can move to a higher salary lane if they have a bachelor's or master's. These lanes will recognize their educational achievements and give them an incentive to keep going in their studies. It may also encourage more paraprofessionals, who already know their students well, to consider becoming classroom teachers. It's vital that we recognize their educational attainments, just as we do with teachers. We made a point of saying, "It's outrageous that there'd be Black and Brown women making poverty wages, working full time in CPS schools." That was a huge win.

Second, we said we must have enforceable class-size limits, particularly in our schools where students have high needs, special education needs, English-language learner needs, and in communities with high rates of violence. We won a $35 million annual class-size reduction fund and revamped the process so that now a council will actually have decision-making authority to spend money on recommendations to do things like split classes, add teacher assistance, or hire additional staff.

The priority will be on reducing class sizes in schools where students have the highest needs, which will obviously intersect, in particular, with schools that have mostly Black or Latinx students. Even in our class-size demands, we said we need funds that can address overcrowding overall, but the priority will be given to our students with the highest needs, which correlates to our students of color. The schools that are very, very white and affluent are still eligible for support, but they won't be prioritized.

Our third demand was around adequate staffing of our schools. We made the demand for a nurse in every school, every day.

Jesse: That demand for a nurse in every school has just been so prescient now with the outbreak of COVID-19. But really, a nurse in every school, every day, should be basic requirement for every school in the nation. It's not like kids only get sick on Tuesdays.

Jen: For sure. But we thought this through and we realized you can't just immediately, magically, hire enough nurses overnight. We won $2 million specifically allocated to support the nurse pipeline, money that can go toward tuition and other recruitment efforts. We're trying to create a pipeline of the folks who aren't fully registered and licensed to become fully registered and licensed, in order to build up the skill set of the nurses in the pipeline to grow the pool of folks who can care for our students. This will allow Black and Brown women who are currently nurses at the lower salary grades to get more qualifications and become fully certified school nurses with the maximum ability to do public health education and increase their salaries.

Jesse: That's really interesting. That's such an important model to show school districts around the country what it would really take to properly care for the students.

Jen: And there's more. We called for more school social workers and case managers in schools. We won a nurse and a social worker in every school, every day, by the end of this contract. Then on case management, we want to hire a specific allocation formula that's better than the current ratios so they will have to staff up additional case managers to manage special education services—and this is after we had a head of special ed in the district who just devastated our special ed services.

We were also fighting for additional counselors—every school gets a single counselor, but if you've got 1,500 kids in a school, one counselor is inadequate. Currently, it's up to the individual principal and their local school council to determine how their money is spent and if they want to have additional counselors. We also wanted more librarians. Right now we've only got a little over a hundred librarians at this point—maybe 120— and we have over five hundred schools. And adding more restorative justice coordinators was a priority to us because of the school-to-prison pipeline— something that you all have highlighted in the BLM at School movement.

We didn't win everything we wanted for all those positions, but we won a commitment to staff at least 120 more additional full-time positions if a school agrees to it. We're going to have to do organizing work to ensure that the school that are deemed eligible for a new position select someone who can help with instruction, like a librarian; somebody who can help with counseling; or someone who can help with social emotional support, such as restorative justice coordinator. This is about the needs of our students of color and trauma that they experienced in their communities that is not being addressed by other services. Finally, we wanted more staffing and supports for our English-language learners and special education students.

Jesse: Excellent. So tell me about your fourth demand.

Jen: The fourth demand was around different social justice issues. Even though really all of our demands were about social justice, this is where we focused on the fight for affordable housing and community schools. We didn't win a commitment from the school district or city to allot specific affordable housing policy, but we did end up winning additional full-time positions in our schools where students have the highest rates of homelessness.

In our last contract we won $10 million for twenty Sustainable Community Schools. These schools follow principles like self-determination and racial justice, and then they work with the community to enact these principles. There's more information about the principles of community schooling in the report by the Center for Popular Democracy and Alliance to Reclaim Our Schools.

These schools focus on culturally relevant pedagogy, effective teaching instead of high-stakes testing, restorative justice, wraparound services, cooperative decision making, and parent engagement. We fought really hard to win expansion of that program. The district was threatening to cut it off and so we won $10 million per year of the contract, so a total of $50 million to keep the twenty current Sustainable Community Schools funded and able to continue to work with community partners and build transformative schools.

Jesse: What an amazing example of how to fight to change the school system to make Black lives matter. I thought I would end by asking what you think the role of unions should be in the struggle to make Black lives matter at school. And what is your vision for education that would truly make our Black students lives valued?

Jen: Wow. Beautiful, big questions, Jesse. I think the role of teachers unions is critical. I am only a union leader because my rank-and-file colleagues in our caucus and our leadership believe that racial and social justice is inherently built into our work as educators. I would not be the leader that I am in our union if it were otherwise. The students that we serve are our partners. We need to be working with our students to design a future that we think is collectively best. We can only do that if we recognize the inherent value of our students' identities, their families, their communities, and their challenges.

I am a Black woman myself, and so this is not something that I had to learn, but it's something that teachers and union leaders have an opportunity to teach those who might not see it this way. I think the unions have a very particular role in reminding all educators that it's their responsibility to contribute to antiracist work. That includes unions that are in mostly white districts. We have to actively push people to see their role, regardless of their location or the students they teach, as contributing to a more just society. The week of action is just such a powerful call because it gives educators everywhere the ability to join in this racial justice work. BLM at School provides concrete activities to make that work real and tangible. It's more than just talking about it or saying you believe it; the week is about making space and sharing resources across the country. It's a clarion call to hold educators accountable. This action asks educators: What does it look like in your classroom? What does it look like in your school? and What does it look like in your district and your union?

Our goal must be to create a school district where students, parents, educators, administrators, and community members are in partnership with a mission of racial and social justice. That requires educators and administrators, in particular, to relinquish some control and power, to see themselves as a part of a collective effort to educate one another. It's not just about educating our students in a one-way direction, but learning from our students and finding areas where *we* need to grow.

Our Sustainable Community Schools program is not perfect, but it's a contribution in the struggle for the kind of education we want to see. We need to work at building more schools where decision making is shared, because once that happens, community voice and community wisdom can be respected. That's not easy—this is about breaking down power dynamics, and that's something that school districts, with their inherent hierarchies, tend to resist. Sometimes teachers unions also resist this change because they, too, can be hierarchical. We have to struggle against those instincts and push for the more democratic instincts that we have as educators, namely to listen, to debate, but to also be able to hear parents, students, and community wisdom. When we include everyone our decision making—especially the Black and Brown voices that have been marginalized for too long—the vision of Black students' lives mattering to the school becomes attainable.

CHAPTER 7

Pushing Our Union to Do Antiracist Work

Los Angeles Teachers Union Tackles Racial Justice

by Cecily Myart-Cruz and Erika Jones

Michael Brown was murdered on August 9, 2014, and almost immediately after his death, "experts" emerged, eager to condemn an eighteen-year-old child. We've heard it all before: "He was a thug, a thief, and maybe he deserved what he got."

What we weren't prepared for was having colleagues in our own union write and express those sentiments.

When this tragedy took place, we were in our first year as elected leaders within our union, Cecily as a vice president and Erika as a member of the board of directors. Collectively there was a feeling that we could not stay silent at this moment. United Teachers Los Angeles (UTLA) put out a press release after Michael was murdered to affirm that we, as educators, stand in the gap for our children. We do not condone police violence, and we aim to end the criminalization of our youth.

We received over one thousand comments about the press release, and very few were positive. The vast majority of the comments were from female union members who were married to police officers. The emails included statements like the aforementioned "He was a thug, a thief, and maybe he deserved what he got," but they also said things like, "We aren't a racial and social justice union." Many of these emails even closed with the slogans "Blue Lives Matter" or "All Lives Matter." It is notable that these emails almost always included the member's name, employee number, and school. It disheartened us to realize that most of the members who objected to our press release were teaching students that looked just like Michael Brown.

However, at the same time, we were seeing teachers becoming more and more vocal about racial justice and pursuing outlets for their advocacy. Nikki Schop was one of those teachers. She was teaching at Washington Preparatory High School in South Central Los Angeles and was fed up that even on her own campus, youth were criminalized and subject to police brutality. She called on UTLA to condemn criminalization and police brutality. After that motion was passed, we formed the UTLA Racial Justice Taskforce.

Formed in 2015, the UTLA Racial Justice Taskforce included educators, students, parents, and community members. Two of the key questions the committee had to address at the outset were "Why is making Black lives matter in schools important? and "How do we garner buy-in around a subject that no one seems to want to speak to?" Our committee dove in headfirst, creating a position paper entitled "Why Is Making Black Lives Matter at School Important?" This position paper came equipped with a teaching guide, frequently asked questions, and a few memes meant for small group discussions.

We had the paper produced for thirty-five thousand members in an effort to begin to educate our members and initiate conversation and reflection. Next, our committee wanted to go deep into the challenges around racial injustice at school and host a series of forums, complete with student panels. While we needed a mass education of our members, we wanted to make sure to center students—not teachers and other adults—in the fight for educational justice.

It was clear, though, we needed a broad coalition of support. Our committee began to take a critical look at who was at our table and decided that we wanted students, community organizations, and rank-and-file members to join our movement in changing outcomes for our babies.

Black Lives Matter Los Angeles, Los Angeles Community Action Network, Integrated Schools, Students Deserve, Students Not Suspects, and Stop LAPD Spying Coalition were community organizations that came to the table in the fight for justice.

Our first action was to mark the anniversary of the murder of Ezell Ford (a former student at Bethune Middle School). When we met at Bethune Middle School in deep South Central LA, we knew it would be a long fight to communicate the message that racial justice is educational justice. The scene that day was telling: the school police showed up in force that day; there were more school police and LAPD in the room than members.

After that meeting at Bethune, we continued to hold events, trainings, student-led conferences, and our first Conference on Racial and Social Justice for educators. One critical moment during this work was the forum we hosted at Susan Miller Dorsey Senior High School in Central LA in September of 2016.

September 29, 2016, Dorsey High School: Making Black lives matter in our schools—Erika remembers this important evening

From the stage, I could see people filling every space in the large auditorium; all eight hundred seats were taken, and people were flooding down the aisles. News reporters with cameras tried to get in, and the school police surrounded us outside, forcing students, educators, parents, and community members to weave between and around them just to get into the auditorium. Student-made posters celebrating Black lives adorned the walls, and in the middle of the stage sat five brilliant young Black scholars and one parent who was also a community organizer.

This was our third panel on making Black lives matter at school and our largest attended yet. As I moderated this panel, the young activists on the stage dropped so much knowledge on the audience, discussing how they wanted to attend schools with people who looked like them but quickly realized that those schools were underfunded and underserved; they spoke about how there are more military recruiters than college counselors on campus and more cops than psychologists. They stated that their classes did not even have enough desks for all the students in attendance and, on many days, they were pulled from their class for what were supposedly random searches that left them feeling humiliated and targeted.

The audience held onto every word as the students detailed what it was like to walk past cops who notoriously harassed students on their way home from school, making sure that if they were in a group they stayed quiet and kept their hands to their sides and their heads down. They called out educators of color who were not advocating for their success and were instead playing into destructive and stereotypical racial narratives. During a small-group discussion period, youth from across the city facilitated solutions-based dialogue between all stakeholders in a way that was authentic and, unfortunately, not the norm when we talk about education reforms and outcomes. I looked out into the audience, and the energy and love in the room were overwhelming. I was so proud of this moment and the fact that we'd managed to stop talking *at* students and instead let them lead while we listened. A movement was sparked in that room, on that day.

That event had been a long time coming. We had planned for it for months in advance by holding a series of events put on by the UTLA Racial Justice Committee. Saying "Black Lives Matter" was not comfortable for a lot of educators, so we took time before the committee to have deep discussions with our colleagues, making that our union's work. Community groups such as Black Lives Matter Los Angeles, Students Deserve, and Stop LAPD Spying all had a place on the committee, and we ensured that there were permanent committee seats for students, parents, educators, and other community members. We'd fulfilled our vision of creating a student-centered committee that would fight for revolutionary change. But that event sparked a fire and truly showed us that, as educators, students, parents, and communities, we have much work to do around racial justice within the Los Angeles Unified School District.

Working at the local level would be critical for us as union activists. However, Cecily and I both knew that we needed to have this conversation on a national level. After the Dorsey event, we created a training program for educators called Making Black Lives Matter at Schools. We began facilitating this training at union events both statewide and nationally. The training centered around three elements: gaining an understanding of the BLM movement, understanding how school policies and procedures affect Black students, and devising a plan for how to begin racial justice work within your own area to change policies that lead to the criminalization of our youth. The training also covered the need to fight for the creation of ethnic studies programs and community schools.

Ensuring national union support: Cecily takes on NEA

After the successful work within our union around racial justice and connecting with educators nationwide to uplift the Black Lives Matter at School Week of Action, we felt it was time to take this advocacy to the National Education Association.

In 2016, I brought a new business item (NBI) to the NEA Representative Assembly, asking the body to recognize and promote Black Lives Matter at School Week of Action in our schools. I hoped for the best and planned for the worst. The NBI needed to pass by a majority on the floor of ten thousand delegates. As I waited at the microphone for my name to be called, I reread what I had written. I knew that my words could help make or break the endorsement of the NEA supporting Black Lives Matter at School. Finally, my name was called, and I looked out at the crowd and stated: "The Black Lives Matter movement is a powerful nonviolent peace movement that systematically examines injustices that exist at the intersections of race, class, and gender. This week of action promotes a set of national demands that focus on improving the school experience for students of color."

I spoke calmly, stating that the national demands were guiding principles. We demanded that the NEA stand in solidarity with the national Black Lives Matter at School Week of Action in order for educators to access the curriculum and materials to be used in school. We sought, above all, to lift up and affirm students of color.

When the NBI passed overwhelmingly, shouts of joy, cheers, and crying erupted in the assembly hall. I came away from that victory with the words of Frederick Douglass echoing in my thoughts: "This struggle may be a moral one, or it may be a physical one...but it must be a struggle. Power concedes nothing without a demand."

Sample Union Endorsements

The efforts of rank-and-file union members in educators unions around the country to secure endorsements for the Black Lives Matter at School Week of Action have been crucial to its success. Gaining the union endorsement has infused confidence into schools organizing Black Lives Matter efforts and helped many more educators take the important step of joining the movement. The many educators union local resolutions have also helped to secure the endorsement of the National Education Association, the largest educators union in the country. As of this writing, the American Federation of Teachers has not yet endorsed the Black Lives Matter at School Week of Action, although many AFT locals have. Below are some of the union resolutions in support of the week of action that have passed around the country; these should serve as models for educators who want to bring the movement to a school district that has not yet joined.

National Education Association*

New Business Item 4 (2018) Action: Adopted NEA will promote the Black Lives Matter Week of Action in schools during Black History month in 2019, using existing communication resources, specifically calling for clear efforts to demonstrate support for the three demands of the BLM at School Week of Action in schools:

1. ending zero tolerance policies and replacing them with restorative justice practices
2. hiring and mentoring Black educators
3. mandating that ethnic studies be taught in pre-K–12th grade schools in age-appropriate ways

*NEA endorsed BLM at School Week of Action before the fourth demand was added.

Seattle Education Association

November 13, 2017, Seattle Education Association Representative Assembly; November 12, 2017, New Business Item from Bruce Jackson, "Black Lives Matter at School"

Whereas The Seattle Education Association has taken a national leadership role in the Black Lives Matter at School movement, now inspiring a dozen major cities to join us in our movement for change,

Whereas there are far too few Black educators and educators of color in proportion to the number of students of color in the schools,

Whereas zero tolerance discipline and over-policing of our youth have proven to be ineffective in the reduction of discipline, and Restorative Practices have proven to be a powerful tool in the reduction of disproportionate discipline,

Whereas according to the *Washington Post* this year there have been 898 police-involved killings, including 204 of Black people,

Whereas the creation and implementation of an Ethnic Studies curriculum is of critical importance to supporting the diversity of students, and currently in development in SPS, and The Seattle Education Association RA unanimously voted to support mandatory K–12 Ethnic Studies curriculum in SPS,

Be it resolved that the Seattle Education Association join the national call for Black Lives Matter at School Week to kick off Black History Month during February 5th to February 11th,

Be it further resolved that SEA encourage its members to wear Black Lives Matter shirts to school that week and teach lessons that week about the school-to-prison pipeline, Black immigrant youth, Black women empowerment, Black LGBTQ community, and Black history.

Chicago Teachers Union
Resolution for Black Lives Matter at School Week of February 3–7, 2020

The Chicago Teachers Union House of Delegates passed the following resolution at its January 8, 2020, meeting:

WHEREAS the closing of public schools in Chicago, turn-arounds, and other school actions have negatively and dispro-portionately impacted Black and Brown communities; and

WHEREAS according to the *Chicago Reporter* (December 2017), "In the past decade, Chicago's public schools lost more than 52,000 black students" and, according to the *Chicago Sun Times* (October 2019), Chicago has lost 256,000 Black residents, "more than any other city in the U.S." as housing becomes more unaffordable; and

WHEREAS as of December 2019, Chicago Teachers Union members served Chicago Public School students who are nearly 90% students of color (46.6% of students are Latinx, 35.9% Black, 10.8% White, 4.2% Asian, and 0.3% Native American); and

WHEREAS since 2001 (when Black teachers made up 40% of CPS teachers) the number of Black teachers in CPS has dropped by 5,500, and as of 2019, there were too few Black teachers and teachers of color (50.4% of teachers are White, 20.7% Black, 21.2% Latinx, 3.9% Asian, and 0.4% Native American) in proportion to the number of students of color they teach; and

WHEREAS Illinois House Bill 2859 was signed in 1991 and section 27-20.4 of the Illinois School Code mandated that "every public elementary school and high school shall include in its curriculum a unit of instruction studying the events of Black History;" and

WHEREAS Chicago Public Schools rolled out a K–10 Interdisciplinary African and African American Studies curriculum in 2013 and a K–10 Interdisciplinary Latino and Latin American Studies curriculum in 2015; and

WHEREAS in 2015 Chicago City Council passed a reparations resolution requiring that the history and fight for justice of the Jon Burge police torture survivors be taught to all eighth and tenth grade students in CPS; and

WHEREAS the CTU supported the development and implementation of this now named "Reparations Won" curriculum which was a part of the nationally historic and precedent setting reparations package; and

WHEREAS the implementation of ethnic studies and culturally sustaining curricula is of critical importance to supporting the learning needs of all students, but particularly Black and Brown students who make up the vast majority of CPS students; and

WHEREAS according to the *Washington Post*, in 2019, 885 people have been shot and killed by police, down only slightly from the nearly 1,000 people killed in each of the previous four full years, and of those killed Black men were still disproportionately represented; and

WHEREAS the CTU House of Delegates, "as a matter of our commitment to the fair treatment of all citizens in the city of Chicago" passed a resolution in December of 2015 supporting the creation in Chicago of a Civilian Police Accountability Council among with community members; and

WHEREAS according to the "Handcuffs in Hallways" report by the Shriver Center (February 2017), "In total, between 2012 and 2016, the police officers assigned to CPS schools accumulated $2,030,652 in misconduct settlements for activities on and off school grounds," and "of that total, nearly $1.5 million resulted from excessive use of force against a minor and $215,000 from incidents that occurred on CPS grounds;" and

WHEREAS according to the University of Chicago CCSR (September 2015), Black and Brown students face suspensions from school at disproportionate rates even when risk factors "such as poverty and low achievement" are controlled for; and

WHEREAS Illinois Senate Bill 100 was signed in 2015 and was intended to reduce exclusionary discipline which disproportionately kept Black and Brown students out of school and contributed to them entering the school-to-prison pipeline; and

WHEREAS discipline, criminalization, and over-policing of Black and Brown students has proven to be ineffective in the improvement of outcomes, damaging on their health and well-being, and restorative practices are proven to be a powerful tool in the reduction of disproportionate discipline and improved school climate; and

WHEREAS CPS often ineffectively implements restorative practices without adequate training, support, and understanding of their role in a developmentally appropriate system of accountability, consequences, and harm reparation; and

WHEREAS the CTU fought for and won in its most recent contract increased staffing of social workers and nurses and the protection of counselor time to do counseling work and will continue to fight until CPS hires, staffs, and retains clinicians and counselors in schools at levels recommended by their respective national professional organizations in order to support and address students' socioemotional and other needs; therefore, be it

RESOLVED that the Chicago Teachers Union (CTU) endorses participation in Black Lives Matter at School Week to begin Black History Month the week of February 3–7, 2020; and

RESOLVED that the CTU will host events during or around this week and engage in advocacy on an ongoing basis aligned to the national demands for hiring more Black teachers and ending the pushout of Black teachers in our schools, proper implementation of restorative practices in schools and ending zero tolerance discipline, teaching students Black history and other ethnic studies curricula, and funding more counselors in schools as opposed to police officers; and be it finally

RESOLVED that the CTU encourage its members to wear Black Lives Matter at School shirts to school that week and teach lessons about related topics.

Maryland State Education Association

At the 2018 Maryland State Education Association (MSEA) Convention in October, the MSEA Board of Directors unanimously voted to move an NBI on behalf of the Board, endorsing the Black Lives Matter at School Week of Action.

NB1 15: MSEA will endorse the 2019 Black Lives Matter (BLM) at School Week of Action, specifically calling for efforts to demonstrate support for the demands of the BLM Week of Action at School:

1. ending zero tolerance policies and replacing them with restorative justice practices
2. hiring and mentoring Black educators
3. mandating that ethnic studies be taught in pre-K–12th schools in age appropriate ways
4. fund counselors, not cops

MSEA will support efforts by individual members or local associations by providing financial support through 10 total grants in the amount of $500 each. Grant application process and the selection of awardees will be determined by the MSEA BOD. In addition, MSEA will promote events and curriculum/resources using existing communication resources.

Rationale: The 2018 NEA Representative Assembly overwhelming voted to adopt NBI 3 which calls for NEA to promote the 2019 Black Lives Matter Week of Action as a way to further begin to dismantle institutional racism. MSEA should demonstrate its commitment to the implementation of NBI 3 at the state level. Furthermore, acknowledging and promoting this week will demonstrate MSEA's commitment to supporting the Black Lives Matter movement in a tangible, student-centered, action-based way.

CHAPTER 8

The Struggle for Union Support in New York City

An Interview with Myrie*

Denisha Jones: Where do you teach?

Myrie: I teach at MS 391 in the Bronx, in District 10, one of the largest school districts in NYC.

Denisha: What do you teach?

Myrie: I teach eighth-grade social studies.

Denisha: Tell us a little bit about your union and your union involvement.

Myrie: The United Federation of Teachers has roughly 200,000 members with roughly 70,000 retirees. The union was formed in 1960 as Local 2 of the American Federation of Teachers. The UFT has three gov-

---

* Denisha Jones conducted this interview with United Federation of Teachers chapter leader and Bronx teacher Dermott Myrie, who prefers to go by Myrie, on February 8, 2020.

erning bodies: (1) the 3,400-member Delegate Assembly (DA), which is the union's legislature, with elected representatives from every school; (2) the 102-member elected Executive Board that sets policy on a variety of education, labor, and union issues; (3) the Administrative Committee, composed of the eleven officers, borough representatives, and selected department heads, which oversees day-to-day operations. I am an elected chapter leader for my school.

Before I was elected chapter leader, I was elected as the delegate, or number two person. My role as the chapter leader is multifold: representing all chapter members in informal resolutions of problems with the administration/principal and in grievances; involving the chapter with the union by advising members of meetings, programs, rallies, and other activities; attending Delegate Assembly, district, and citywide chapter leader meetings and divisional meetings where the concerns of the chapter can be transmitted.

The UFT has several caucuses. The Unity Caucus has been in power since the union's inception. I ran on the social justice slate of the Movement of Rank and File Educators (MORE) Caucus for president of the UFT in the 2019 election. MORE is also a part of a nationwide collective called the United Caucuses of Rank and File Educators (UCORE). We are fighting for social justice in many states: Arizona, California, Colorado, Illinois, Maryland, North Carolina, and Pennsylvania to name a few, and here at home in New York. I have been active with my caucus and within communities as we fight against school closings and displacement of BIPOC due to gentrification. I have been active with other MORE chapter leaders and delegates in the Black Lives Matter at School Week of Action organizing. We have brought resolutions to the DA about undoing-racism training and supporting the Black Lives Matter at School Week of Action, but our efforts have been hijacked by the UFT leadership. To be clear, the work I do is really what my caucus does—in other words, what we do collectively with allies. This work is not about me.

Denisha: Please describe the first time you attempted to get union support for the week of action? What worked? What roadblocks did you face?

Myrie: The first time our caucus attempted to get union support was in the 2017–18 school year. The resolution was written by Adam Sanchez and Jia Lee. Jia is an NYC Opt Out parent and teacher who testified before Congress on the negative impact of testing. She later ran as a New York State lieutenant gubernatorial candidate on a progressive Green Party platform. Our action in the UFT was effective since our caucus utilized the resolution process and distributed the resolution to all attending delegates to read, and it brought awareness to the legislative body. The roadblock was overt; African American Assistant Secretary Leroy Barr argued against the resolution, saying that it was "divisive" and more so in a year when the Janus case was looming, "it is crucial to remain united." He was called out immediately in an open letter entitled, "We Want a Union That Believes Black Lives Matter." Several op-ed pieces in the media were written by parents, advocates, and community allies who came to our defense after the attack from leadership.

Denisha: If you were unsuccessful, what do you think prohibited your success?

Myrie: The UFT leadership has prescriptively ensured that issues of race and discussions of undoing racism are unwelcome at the Delegate Assembly (DA). In 2019, the second year of organizing, we brought up the resolution in December 2018, to be placed on the agenda for the January DA. Leadership used two African American Executive Board members to argue the point that the resolution was redundant since the UFT was already involved in equity work for all and not just for one group (African Americans). I argued that the resolution was different, and eventually the body voted to place it on January's agenda by a narrow margin. At the January 2019 meeting, things went downhill. The UFT introduced a resolution calling on the body to support all ethnic groups, and it passed. Leadership used maneuvers to move up other resolutions on the agenda ahead of the BLM at School resolution and were successful. They introduced new resolutions to exhaust the meeting time.

Eventually, the UFT president called on the resolution with three minutes remaining before the meeting ended. A white woman from Staten Island stood up and spoke against the resolution, arguing that it was redundant since one was just passed supporting all racial and ethnic groups. I spoke to the resolution, explaining that it was a no-brainer since the NEA earlier in the summer had endorsed the week of action with the demands of BLM. I said that he, as president of the union, should proactively keep updated with info from the NEA, especially on social justice issues. The president ruled me out of order and ruled the resolution out of order. This is unheard of—to rule a resolution out of order.

Denisha: Why is securing union support/endorsements important to this movement?

Myrie: Securing union endorsement/support is very important to the movement. As educators and social justice warriors, we constantly remind ourselves that our working conditions are our students' learning conditions. Union support is crucial for the BLM at School movement. Look around the country at all the unions who support the struggles of BIPOC and the intersectionality of education, poverty, homelessness, school closings, criminalization of our youth, and lack of funding for schools, and remarkably, they are directing the political winds in the country with a progressive agenda. Where are the UFT, New York State United Teachers, and American Federation of Teachers as it relates to BLM at School? They are scared and scary as hell. Leadership is lacking in these named unions, even when they endorse Democrats; many of these politicians regularly refuse to talk about racism and how to address the oppression and poverty that families are facing.

You see the difference in LA and Chicago unions as leadership and the rank and file immerse social justice demands in their contracts. This is the way it is done. The leadership of the LA and Chicago unions is part of UCORE, and hence the urgency to engage its membership about the students they serve and meeting students' and their families' needs. This year we included in our BLM at School resolution a specific demand for the UFT to work with the New York City Council to allocate funds to build thirty units of housing in each borough for students and families in shelters.

As you know, the resolution did not reach the floor of the DA. Leadership ensured that the meeting went on and with only seven minutes for resolutions that were already on the agenda. Three days later, the president of the UFT was at a church service on MLK day urging parishioners to fight for housing. This is a first for the UFT in publicly talking about homelessness and engaging the African American community about homelessness.

Denisha: What advice would you give to other teachers who are trying to get their local union on board?

Myrie: It is worthwhile. There will be pushback in some unions. In other unions, it is a no-brainer. Talk to members in your schools. Use the BLM at School Starter Kit to bring the BLM at School Week of Action to your colleagues and into your schools. Most importantly, challenge the union to get on board. Write letters to the leadership, and voice your concerns. Network on social media and follow #BlackLivesMatterAt-School. Follow NEA EdJustice links on the internet and share it at your union meetings. Hand out flyers about the week of action. Hold rallies in front of union headquarters. We recently rallied in front of the UFT on January 12, 2020, and shared our four BLM demands and handed out resolutions to attending delegates. Never give in. Never give up.

This year, Senators Elizabeth Warren and Bernie Sanders, Democratic presidential candidates, tweeted about the week of action. This shows that unionism pays off. My hope is that neither candidate co-opts the movement for political advantage but for doing what's right for public education and meeting our four national demands.

CHAPTER 9

Successes and Challenges Garnering State and Local Union Support in Howard County, Maryland

An Interview with Erika Strauss Chavarria*

Denisha Jones: Where do you teach, and what do you teach?

Erika Strauss Chavarria: I am a tenth-year Spanish teacher at Wilde Lake High School in Howard County, Maryland.

Denisha: Tell us a little bit about your union and your union involvement.

Erika: I currently serve on the National Education Association Board of Directors, representing the state of Maryland. I also serve on the Maryland State Education Association Board of Directors. I have been involved in union work for around ten years now. Previously I was a building rep and

---

* Denisha Jones conducted this interview with high school teacher and social justice advocate Erika Strauss Chavarria on February 10, 2020.

served on my local union board of directors. I have represented Maryland as a delegate to the NEA Representative Assembly for over five years now.

Denisha: Please describe the first time you attempted to get union support for the Black Lives Matter at School Week of Action. What worked? What roadblocks did you face?

Erika: After the Free Minds, Free People conference in Baltimore in 2017, I brought the idea of participating in the Black Lives Matter at School Week of Action to what was at the time the Howard County Educators of Color Coalition, started through a grant that my colleague Matthew Vaughn-Smith had written and received. The Educators of Color Coalition voted to endorse the week of action and to bring a new business item (NBI) endorsing the week of action to our local union's representative assembly. After much debate back and forth, hesitation, fear, but also excitement, the NBI passed. The following year the National Education Association endorsed the week of action through an NBI written, moved, and supported by the NEA Black Caucus. There was much pushback to that NBI as well, but we ultimately gained enough support and power to have the NBI pass. It was after that representative assembly that I was able to write an NBI for the Maryland State Education Association's representative assembly and was successful in getting support from the entire board of directors to move the NBI. Much of the debate for that NBI revolved around the fourth demand, for schools to fund counselors, not cops. Many educators were uncomfortable with the terminology and the idea of not supporting cops in schools. There was a debate about removing the fourth demand on the NBI, but the supporters of the NBI were successful in explaining the importance of and justification for the fourth demand and clearly conveyed the message that the national Black Lives Matter at School movement wrote the demands and we did not have the power to alter them in any way.

The NBI did not pass unanimously; however, ultimately it did pass with all four demands intact, as well as a financial component of ten grants giving out $500 each for local union organizations or individuals who wanted to use the money for activities related to the Black Lives Matter at School Week of Action in their communities. Much of the pushback and debate have always been around the controversial nature of the Black

Lives Matter movement, as well as the underlying racism and bias that still exist in systemic and individual forms in our education system.

By far, the most debated and controversial part of the week of action in terms of the demands is the "fund counselors, not cops" demand. There are still many educators who do not understand that police do not represent safety for many Black and Brown communities or students. These educators do not see how the presence of police officers leads to the school-to-prison pipeline. Just in the past two days there were two incidents of police brutality against students of color in schools! These are not rare occurrences. Schools need to be a place of safety and learning. Period.

Denisha: What do you think most contributed to your success?

Erika: The success we have seen thus far has been through true grassroots organizing to build collective power toward fighting against racism and uplifting and affirming the lives of our Black students, parents, families, and communities. The data clearly demonstrates the disparities in the severity of discipline, suspensions, and expulsions of Black and Brown students versus their white peers for the same offenses. It is also impossible to deny the lack of Black and other educators of color in our schools.

One of the most important contributors to success has been the growing number of education justice organizations and alliances doing antiracist work; these groups have built a grassroots movement for racial justice and education justice. Many union members are also members of these important alliances and grassroots organizations and have been tirelessly pushing national, state, and local unions to make racial justice and equity a priority. In the NEA, for example, racial justice educators were able to pass very important NBIs related to racial justice and antiracist work, such as an NBI on institutional racism, NBIs on the Black Lives Matter at School Week of Action, and, most recently, an NBI that acknowledges white supremacy culture, an important step toward dismantling this same culture. None of this work would be possible without the Black and Brown leaders who have laid their lives on the line for equality, equity, and justice throughout history.

Denisha: Despite your success, what challenges do you continue to face working with unions to support the week of action?

Erika: Our challenges thus far have been pervasive racism throughout our communities and the racism that also exists within our unions. The majority of our educators are white women. Although many educators do believe in antiracist work, many do not. Explicit and implicit bias and racism are persistent within our schools and show up through disproportionate discipline of Black students, as well as biased and inauthentic curriculum.

Unions can be reluctant to support the week of action because of the fear of angering white educators and ultimately losing membership. Unions are also fearful of the controversial nature of Black Lives Matter and the stereotype of it being a radical organization that is "anti-cop." This country has a long way to go in the fight against racism and oppression, and our unions are not devoid of these attitudes. I am very proud of the many local and state unions, as well as the NEA, who have committed to affirming the lives of Black students. But we have long way to go.

I wanted to note (not specifically related to unions, but important) that in my particular county, racism is hidden under a veil of utopianism and "diversity." Also, because of politics and outside influences, Howard County school board members in the past were reluctant to vote yes on a board resolution for the Black Lives Matter at School Week of Action, citing lack of time to research and/or financial and fiduciary concerns as their basis for abstention. Due to the controversial nature of their lack of support for the Black Lives Matter at School resolution last year, we were successful in passing a resolution this year with a unanimous yes vote.

However, we are now seeing signs of a restrictive nature when it comes to the curriculum and the activities that are supported or unsupported by the district, despite the passage of the resolution. It is important to note that the curriculum offered by the Black Lives Matter at School Week of Action curriculum committee does not require implementation with 100 percent fidelity, particularly since 85 percent of the education profession consists of white educators who may end up causing more harm than good when trying to teach the lessons. There have been some stories that have come to light about educators using the Black Lives Matter at School Week of Action as a justification to teach incorrect and racist history in the name of teaching for the week of action.

Denisha: Why is securing union support/endorsements important to this movement?

Erika: Securing union endorsements and support is crucial in that it allows educators to feel like they have protection in participating in the week of action. It also enables information and resources about the week of action to be shared widely among the millions of union members across the country. Endorsements and support also put pressure on local school districts to demonstrate their commitment to Black students and families through supporting the week of action and by supporting the four demands. Maybe equally as important, endorsements demonstrate a collective power and voice in the affirmation of Black students by educators across the country.

Denisha: What advice would you give to other teachers who are trying to get their local union on board?

Erika: My advice for other teachers is to go to the Black Lives Matter at School website and use the tool kit for how to participate in the week of action. One of the most important things is to reach out to local community grassroots organizations who are already focused on racial justice work and to come as a unified voice to put pressure on local unions to support the week of action. Reaching out to parents of Black students is also essential in putting pressure on local unions to get on board.

One must have a lot of courage and tough skin to do this work. Do not let defeats discourage you from pushing harder and working toward the goal of support by local unions. Our Black students' lives are literally on the line. We must do right by them and their families and the communities that we support and that we represent. The marginalization, oppression, criminalization, and unequal and inequitable treatment of our Black students and other students of color cannot continue. We must fight back. Teachers doing this work must decide if they are willing to risk their jobs in the name of justice. That risk comes with the territory of doing this work, and it's up to the individual teacher or educator to decide how much or how little they can handle and how much or how little they are willing to risk.

Poster created by Matthew Vaughn-Smith to recognize the passing of the Black Lives Matter at School Resolution in Howard County, Maryland.

CHAPTER 10

Seattle Educators' Lesson Plan for City Officials

Defund the Police and Spend the Money on Social Programs and Education!*

By Jesse Hagopian

On June 8, 2020, my union, the Seattle Education Association (SEA), overwhelmingly passed seven resolutions in solidarity with the Movement for Black Lives. These included removing police from the Seattle Public Schools (SPS) (which was won) and from the King County Labor Council (achieved by a subsequent vote of the council); educating SEA members on alternatives to calling 911 on students; and, my own resolution, to defund the Seattle Police Department and reinvest the money in education, healthcare, and programs to support families.

These bold resolutions were surely spurred by the police killings of George Floyd, Breonna Taylor, and Ahmaud Arbery, and the ensuing uprising that swept the nation. But this vote wasn't only about injustices occurring elsewhere. Seattle's educators have been fighting institutional

---

* A version of this entry appeared in the June 19, 2020, issue of the *Seattle Times*.

racism and the school-to-prison pipeline here for some time.

The Black Lives Matter at School movement erupted in Seattle in September 2016. A white supremacist threatened to bomb John Muir Elementary School when the educators there—in conjunction with parents, community, and the group Black Men Uniting to Change the Narrative—declared that they would celebrate Black students with an assembly and by wearing "Black Lives Matter" shirts to school.

Black Lives Matter at School then went national, thanks to educators in Philadelphia who organized a full week of action and broke down the thirteen principles of the movement into teaching points for each day of the week. Last year, educators in more than forty cities participated in Black Lives Matter at School, reaching many thousands of students.

Each year since, Seattle's educators have voted to support the demands of the national Black Lives Matter at School week of action during the first week in February, including the fourth SEA demand, "fund counselors, not cops." And when SPS parent Charleena Lyles was killed in her own home in front of her children by Seattle Police Department officers on June 18, 2017, the SEA urged our members to wear their Black Lives Matter shirts to school and join a rally to stand with Charleena's family.

Building on that legacy, educators took a bold, new step to call for a 50 percent cut from the $409 million already budgeted for the Seattle Police Department this year. Seattle educators echo the words of Michelle Alexander, leading human rights advocate and author of *The New Jim Crow*, who recently wrote, "After decades of reform, countless commissions and task forces, and millions of dollars poured into 'smart on crime' approaches, the police behave with about as much brutality today as they did in 1966. . . . More than 95 percent of arrests every year are for nonviolent offenses like loitering, fare evasion, and theft."[1]

Yet the resolution passed by Seattle's educators wasn't simply about shrinking the size and malignancy of the police but about reimagining justice, education, public safety, and our society. The resolution also demands that

> Seattle's Mayor and City Council must protect and expand investments to make our communities safe, prioritizing community-led health and

safety strategies. Full access to affordable housing, community-based anti-violence programs, trauma services and treatment, universal childcare and free public transit are just a few of the non-police solutions to social problems.

As the saying goes, "Hurt people hurt people; whole people heal people." Massive wealth inequality and structural racism are hurting people in Seattle—and people in cities around the country—and constitute the biggest threat to public safety. Now is the time to invest in housing, education, and healthcare, to create whole and healthy communities and new paradigms for addressing the root causes of violence.

Several Seattle-based organizations are already providing a restorative justice and community-building approach to public safety, including Community Passageways, Safe Passage, and Creative Justice. These programs provide alternatives to youth incarceration and mentorship to youth who are involved with the legal system. Their staff are trained in de-escalation techniques to help mediate conflicts, providing an alternative model for public safety. These and other programs are limited by their budgets, however, which pale in comparison to the funding lavished on the punitive system of policing.

Minneapolis has already vowed to dismantle its police force and start over with a new vision for investing in social workers, public health workers, and conflict mediators who are trained to care for people's well-being.

Seattle's educators have a lesson for city officials. We hope they are sitting up straight and taking notes: We can create safe and thriving communities by joining the growing number of cities who are reappropriating funds from a punishment-based system and re-aiming them toward a new system that builds thriving communities.

Seattle Education Association new business items (NBIs) in solidarity with the Black Lives Matter movement and against police violence

The following documents are the seven resolutions for Black lives that passed overwhelmingly at the June 8, 2020, Representative Assembly of the SEA. Here's a brief summary of the main ideas behind each NBI that passed, with the language of the full resolutions included below:

1. endorse Black Lives Matter statewide march and general strike

2. affirm our union's support for the Black Lives Matter movement and the SEA's Center for Racial Equity

3. call for Seattle Public Schools to divest ties with the Seattle Police Department and use the funds to invest in counselors and other educators

4. call for the removal of the Seattle Police Officers Guild from the Martin Luther King Jr. County Labor Council

5. defund the police, use the funds to invest in the community, and don't prosecute arrested Black Lives Matter protesters

6. educate SEA members on alternatives to calling 911 against students

7. work with SEA members on discussing and implementing social and emotional learning (SEL) in our schools

1. NBI: Endorse Black Lives Matter statewide march and general strike

Background: In solidarity with the community which includes SEA members, SPS students, and SPS families,

In support of the victories and continuing the progress towards addressing anti-Blackness through collective action,

In recognition that the continued harm to the Black community harms all our communities,

And the risk to the Black community has been and will continue to be greater than the potential risk of the march,

And "anti-Blackness is a greater threat to our survival, and racism in itself is its own pandemic" (according to Black Lives Matter Chair Ebony Miranda),

Be it resolved that...

SEA Interests: End anti-Blackness and promote racial equity. Solidarity with our community.

Recommendation: SEA will endorse and advocate for SEA members to participate in the Black Lives Matter Statewide March and General Strike organized by Black Lives Matter Seattle–King County on Friday, June 12, 2020, at 2:00 p.m., at Judkins Park. If participating in the march is not possible, members engage in other ways that advocate for affirming that Black lives matter.

2. NBI: Affirm and sustain Black Lives Matter and SEA's Center for Racial Equity

Background: In response to the recent Seattle Police Department use of force, including pepper spray and flash bang grenades, against youth protestors on Saturday, May 30,

In grief and mourning for the lives lost to police brutality, white supremacy, and racist violence, including George Floyd, Breonna Taylor, Tony McDade, and uncountable more people of color killed by racism,

In understanding that Seattle Public Schools has committed to racial equity, through its current strategic plan and policy 0030,

In understanding that the current research of the effects of the COVID-19 pandemic shows that people of color, and people who are Black and Brown, are predominantly at risk and affected by the current healthcare crisis,

And, in solidarity with educators, students, and families of Seattle Public Schools who are people of color, and who are at great risk for violence by racism within the social institutions of policing, education, and healthcare,

And to affirm the work of educators within our community who lead racial equity work and education for our staff and community,

And with care for our community, students, and families at the forefront of our decisions,

Be it resolved that...

SEA Interests: Improve the quality of and access to public education for all students. Safety and solidarity with our community.

Recommendation:

1. SEA will make a monetary donation to Black Lives Seattle Bail Fund ($2,000); Black Lives Seattle ($1,000); Families of Color Seattle ($1,000); and Seattle Children's March ($1,500).

2. SEA's Budget and Finance Committee will increase funding towards SEA Center for Racial Equity, to continue its work to develop resources (e.g., an online Racial Equity Toolkit and curriculum resources), and SEA will make those resources widely available to students, staff, and families (e.g., through the CRE website).

3. NBI: Divest and redirect

Background: In response to the recent Seattle Police Department's use of force, including pepper spray and flash-bang grenades, against youth protestors on Saturday, May 30, 2020,

In grief and mourning for the lives lost to police brutality, white supremacy, and racist violence, including George Floyd, Breonna Taylor, Tony McDade, and uncountable more people of color killed by racism,

In understanding that Seattle Public Schools has committed to racial equity, through its current strategic plan and policy 0030,

In understanding that the current research of the effects of the COVID-19 pandemic shows that people of color, and people who are Black and Brown, are predominantly at risk and affected by the current healthcare crisis,

In solidarity with educators, students, and families of Seattle Public Schools who are people of color, and who are at great risk for violence by racism within the social institutions of policing, education, and healthcare,

And with care for our community, students, and families at the forefront of our decisions,

Be it resolved that…

1.   SEA will submit a request using the Freedom of Information Act to ascertain any contracts, funding, or relationship between Seattle Public Schools and Seattle Police Department, and if/when funding or contracts are found between Seattle Public Schools and Seattle Police Department,

2.   SEA will write a letter to the Seattle Public School Board and Superintendent Juneau, to call them to divest from of any funding toward, contracts, relationship, or outreach with Seattle Police Department, and furthermore,

3.   SEA will call for Seattle Public School Board and Superintendent Denise Juneau and Seattle City Council to use any divested funds to hire counselors, social workers, family support workers, student family advocates, restorative justice educators, gender and sexuality educators, ethnic studies educators and curriculum, or social support relief positions in partnership with SEA. This letter will be shared publicly through SEA communications, and will include language advocating for training around safe de-escalation strategies, transparency from SPS and the city, and centering student and family collaboration within Seattle Public Schools.[2]

4. NBI: Remove Seattle Police Officers Guild from the Martin Luther King Jr. County Labor Council

Background: In solidarity with the Black, Indigenous, people of color (BIPOC) union members' petition, we demand that the Seattle Police Officers Guild (SPOG) be removed from the Martin Luther King Jr. County Labor Council.[3]

SEA Interests: Increase respect for the profession and public education. Improve the quality of and access to public education for all students. Forge partnerships with families, businesses, other unions, and community groups. Ensure Black lives matter in our schools and communities.

Recommendation: The Seattle Education Association will publicly call for the removal of the Seattle Police Officers Guild from the Martin Luther King Jr. County Labor Council (MLKCLC), send out a press release announcing this demand, and communicate this demand to all SEA members through SEA emails, texts, social media, and website. In addition, the SEA delegate(s) to the MLKCLC will propose this demand be voted on at the earliest possible MLKCLC meeting, and work with other area unions to urge that they pass similar resolutions.

5. NBI: Defund the police

Background: To stop police violence, the police must be reduced in size, in budget, and in scope. Some cities are already beginning this process—Seattle should join! Police are rooted in violence against Black people. To protect Black lives, this moment calls for investing and expanding our safety and well-being beyond policing.

SEA Interests: Increase respect for the profession and public education. Improve the quality of and access to public education for all students. Forge partnerships with families, businesses, other unions, and community groups. Ensure Black lives matter in our schools and communities.

Recommendation: The SEA will endorse the following demands and sign onto the "Defund the Police" statement:[4]

1. Seattle's Mayor and City Council must immediately defund Seattle Police Department (SPD). The city faces a $300 million budget shortfall due to COVID-19. Seattle City Council should propose and vote for a 50 percent cut from the $363 million already budgeted for SPD.

2. Seattle's Mayor and City Council must protect and expand investments to make our communities safe, prioritizing community-led health and safety strategies. Full access to affordable housing, community-based anti-violence programs, trauma services and treatment, universal childcare, and free public transit are just a few of the non-police solutions to social problems.

3. The Seattle City Attorney must not prosecute protesters, including those arrested for violating curfew, and those living in encampments. Protesters took to the streets to call for the end of the murders of Black people by police, and SPD unnecessarily escalated tensions and violence.

   In addition, the SEA will send out a press release announcing these demands and communicate them to SEA members through SEA emails, texts, social media, and website.

   Finally, the SEA will donate $2,000 to COVID-19 Mutual Aid Seattle to support their efforts to further build the movement in Seattle for these demands.

6. NBI: What is a threat? Alternatives to calling 911
Background: Our students need to be distanced from the Seattle Police Department. Aside from the 4–5 school-based officers, police are allowed into our schools when called in by educators. At present, it is up to each educator to decide when they feel threatened enough to call the police. We must specifically define situations in which 911 is called, and which 911 department is requested.

SEA Interests: Increase respect for the profession and public education. Improve the quality of and access to public education for all students.

Recommendation: Whereas the Seattle Police Department continues to serve and protect in ways that harm BIPOC,

Whereas our union is dedicated to creating a safe and nurturing environment for those furthest from educational justice, including BIPOC students and teachers,

Whereas police are called into our schools by educators, who are given the right to call 911 whenever they feel threatened,

I propose that a committee be formed to study the relevant sections of our collective bargaining agreement (CBA) in order to propose a Memorandum of Agreement for our next meeting that defines much more specifically when educators will have the right to call 911 and in which cases the call should be made to request the police, as opposed to a medic or other first responder. If necessary, this committee might suggest the right of educators to call a different community crisis resource instead of the police. The CBA, as it stands now, has the potential to protect and encourage teachers who make their building unsafe for their colleagues and students.

Furthermore, while this committee convenes, SEA will educate its members on alternatives to calling the police when they feel threatened.

7. NBI: Social and emotional learning in our schools

Background: SPS has been looking to implement SEL in schools as a way to fulfill part of their Strategic Plan. In anticipation of this, SEA has an opportunity to seek member input on how SEL can be introduced in a way that is authentic, benefits students, and adheres to our contracts.

SEA Interests: Maintain member input and agency over the design and implementation of our professional practices; ensure district directives conform to the CBA.

Recommendation: SEA leadership works with membership to define and shape what meaningful SEL does/could look like in our schools. As part of the outreach to members regarding the reopening of schools in the fall, SEA will include in its survey to members questions to generate feedback around key areas for implementing SEL, such as curriculum, professional development, how/when content is delivered to students, who delivers that content, and effect on member workloads. This data will be made available to all members and will be aggregated by schools. This information will help SEA better represent member interests and concerns when working with SPS to bring quality SEL to our students.

Defending the Boston Teachers Union from the Boston Police

On February 3, 2020, Boston Police Patrolmen's Association President Michael Leary sent a scathing attack letter to the Boston Teachers Union president, Jessica Tang, demanding that educators cancel their participation in the national Black Lives Matter Week of Action.

The letter from Officer Leary was leaked to the media, and police and others critical of the Black Lives Matter movement organized pressure on the union to stop their demands for racial justice. President Tang conferred with her membership, reached out to national organizers of Black Lives Matter at School for support, and then refused to back down in the face of this intimidation.

Then, just two days after receiving the letter from Officer Leary, President Tang went to the Boston School Board meeting and delivered a stirring speech in which she refused to back away from the struggle to make Black students' lives matter in school. Below are President Tang's words to the Boston school board and the solidarity statement that Black Lives Matter at School wrote in support of President Tang and the Boston Teachers Union.

Pro-students, pro-love: A response to the Boston police union's opposition to BLM at School, delivered by Jessica Tang, president of the Boston Teachers Union, February 5, 2020, Boston school board meeting

Good evening, Chair Loconto, Superintendent Cassellius, members of the Steering Committee.

Although it's important to celebrate Black history every month, the month of February is an opportunity to elevate and highlight the work that we're doing in this district when it comes to affirming Black lives and nurturing Black futures in the Boston Public Schools. And of course, a baseline budget is a part of that.

At the BTU, we're proud to be part of a national movement that started in Seattle and is now taking place in around forty cities. Four years ago, a group of teachers stood with their elementary-age students that were feeling the effects of anti-Black racism. The events impacting Black youth, including the tragic death of Trayvon Martin who would be twenty-five years old today, fueled these educators' desire to affirm and show support for their Black students. Unfortunately, the action of solidarity resulted in a bomb threat and the cancellation of a unity event. In response, thousands of Seattle teachers wore Black Lives Matter shirts. This action became the catalyst for the Black Lives Matter at School movement, which started in February of 2017 and has taken place every February since.

Each day of this week of action corresponds with a lesson and inclusive values that educators are encouraged to teach. This started on Monday with Restorative Justice, Empathy, and Loving Engagement; yesterday's lesson was Diversity and Globalism; today, Trans-affirming, Queer Affirming, and Collective Value; tomorrow, Intergenerational, Black Families, and Black Villages; and Friday, Black Women and being Unapologetically Black.

There are also four national demands:

- First, ending zero tolerance. We were proud in 2017 to be the first union to negotiate restorative practices into our contract and more recently to support Congress-woman Ayanna Pressley's PUSHOUT Bill that offers comprehensive solutions to this issue.
- Second, mandating Black history and ethnic studies because we know that the identities of our students are often not reflected in a standardized curriculum.
- Third, hiring more Black teachers. We have a court mandate from 1974 to hire 25 percent Black teachers, and that goal has not always been met. While we have the highest rates of teachers of color in the state and we have partnerships with the district to recruit and work on retention, we can still do better.
- Fourth, funding more counselors in our schools. And we believe counselors need to be a higher funding priority over theoretically increasing the number of police in schools. With limited budgets and cuts we believe adequate access to social-emotional well-being, restorative practices, and other efforts are more effective than increasing police presence in our schools.

It's about being pro-students, pro-love, and being guided by the lessons grounded in the values of inclusion and equity as well as the thirteen Black Lives Matter principles, which we hope people will take the time to read, know, and understand better.

We want, again, to thank the district for their support and collaboration in ensuring that we continue to push our district, and ourselves, to make our schools a welcoming, safe place for all, and that includes our Black students, families, and educators. That is what this week is about, and these are the stories and experiences our members and allies are here to share tonight.

Boston Teachers Union President Jessica Tang gives testimony during a Boston School Committee meeting February 5, 2020. Image credit: *Bay State Banner*.

"This is a movement for equity, inclusion, and the uplifting of Black students": A solidarity statement in response to the Boston police union's attack on Black Lives Matter at School

The following statement was posted to the Black Lives Matter at School website on February 13, 2020.

We, the organizers of the Black Lives Matter at School movement, strongly condemn the shameful attack on Boston educators launched by Boston Police Patrolmen's Union President Michael Leary.[5] During the first week of February 2020, thousands of educators in over forty cities and towns around the country organized the third annual Black Lives Matter at School Week of Action. On February 3, Leary wrote a letter on behalf of the 1,400 members of his association attacking the Black Lives Matter at School movement and strongly urged that Boston Teachers Union President Jessica Tang withdraw her union's participation from the national Black Lives Matter at School Week of Action.

In his letter, Leary wrote that Black Lives Matter has made policing more dangerous—without citing any examples or statistics—and claimed, "Vilifying those who serve the public as police officers only increases distrust and puts police and citizens at risk of increased violence from an emboldened group of angry anti-police individuals."

This attack on educators who seek to support the lives of Black students is shameful, misguided, and harmful to Black students and educators. The suggestion that uplifting and affirming Black students in school—the true purpose of the Black Lives Matter at School movement—is putting police and citizens at risk of increased violence is shocking and reprehensible.

In a statement, Tang responded to the Boston police union by saying, "Through our participation, we're demonstrating support, love, and affirmation to our Black students, families, and educators."

The national Black Lives Matter at School Week of Action has four demands for supporting Black youth's education: ending zero tolerance discipline policies in schools; mandating Black history and ethnic studies in curriculum; hiring more Black educators; and funding counselors, not cops. In response to the last demand, Leary wrote in his letter, "Even the 'Week of Action National Demands' you posted on the BTU website includes the goal, 'Fund counselors, not cops.' While more counselors may be a good idea, the idea that spending less on public safety will make our communities better or safer is ridiculous."

As in any social movement, the people who make up the Black Lives Matter at School movement have many different opinions about the role of police in society. However, what we can agree on is that when school districts have precious scarce resources, they should invest their money in upstream interventions that support the social and emotional well-being of children—such as counselors, school psychologists, social workers, and educational programs like Dignity at Schools' "Counselors Not Cops" campaign—to build relationships with students in order to get at the root of problems that could potentially cause conflicts, and thereby prevent safety concerns. As data from recent reports reveal, school-based mental health providers not only improve student outcomes, but can also improve overall school safety. As the ACLU wrote in a report on the topic, "There is no evidence that increased police presence in schools improves school safety. Indeed, in many cases, it causes harm. When in schools, police officers do what they are trained to do, which is detain, handcuff, and arrest. This leads to greater student alienation and a more threatening school climate."[6]

The United States is one of the very few countries in the world that polices children in school, and it is especially inappropriate when so many schools fail to provide services to support whole child development and positive discipline, and promote conflict resolution. According to the ACLU report, 1.7 million children go to a school in the United States where there is a police officer and no counselor—and some fourteen million students attend a school without a counselor, nurse, psychologist or social worker, yet do have a cop.[7] This is why the Advancement Project, Dignity in Schools, youth organizations such as Students Deserve, and others across the country call for #PoliceFreeSchools as they continue to catalog the numerous police assaults on youth of color across the United States and push forward a vision of school safety that is not reliant on policing.

What is truly upsetting about officer Leary's letter, is that nowhere in it does he acknowledge the inequities in education that have left Black students in the most underfunded schools[8] in the nation, that have led to Black students being suspended at dramatically disproportionate rates,[9] or that have left students with a curriculum that obscures the many great contributions to the world by people of African descent.

We call on the Boston Police Patrolmen's Association to withdraw its letter against the Black Lives Matter at School Week of Action. Black Lives Matter at School is a national movement for equity, inclusion, and the uplifting of Black students, not an attack on police, and deserves to be supported by everyone who believes in justice and an empowering education.

Sincerely,
Black Lives Matter at School Coalition, February 13, 2020

Educators Doing the Work

CHAPTER 11

Our Schools Need Abolitionists, Not Reformers

*By Bettina L. Love**

This essay is not to enumerate the recent murders of Black people by police, justify why protest and uprising are important for social change, or remind us why NFL player Colin Kaepernick took a knee. If you have missed those points, blamed victims, or proclaimed "All Lives Matter," this article is not for you, and you may want to ask yourself whether you should be teaching any children, especially Black children.

This article is for teachers who understand that racism is real, anti-Blackness is real, and state-sanctioned violence, which allows police to kill Black people with impunity, is real. It is for teachers who know change is necessary and want to understand exactly what kind of change we need as a country.

Politicians who know the words "justice" and "equity" only when they want peace in the streets are going to try to persuade us that they

---

* This article was originally published in *Education Week* on June 12, 2020.

are capable of reforming centuries of oppression by changing policies, adding more accountability measures, and removing the "bad apples" from among police.

These actions will sound comprehensive and, with time, like a solution to injustice. These reforms may even reduce police killings or school suspensions of Black students, but as civil rights activist Ella Baker said, a "reduction of injustice is not the same as freedom." Reformists want incremental change, but Black lives are being lost with every day we wait. And to be Black is to live in a constant state of exhaustion.

Centuries of Black resistance and protest have had a profound impact on the nation. As Nikole Hannah-Jones, the creator of "The 1619 Project," points out: "We have helped the country to live up to its founding ideals.... Without the idealistic, strenuous, and patriotic efforts of Black Americans, our democracy today would most likely look very different—it might not be a democracy at all." Those civil rights achievements were critical, including the reformist ones.

But reform is no longer enough. Too often, reform is rooted in whiteness because it appeases white liberals who need to see change but want to maintain their status, power, and supremacy.

Abolition of oppression is needed because reform still did not stop a police officer from putting his knee on George Floyd's neck in broad daylight for eight minutes and forty-six seconds; it did not stop police from killing Breonna Taylor in her own home. Also that: largely nonwhite school districts get $23 billion less in state and local funding than predominantly white ones; Black people make up 13 percent of the US population but account for 26 percent of the deaths from COVID-19; and with only 5 percent of the world's population, the United States has nearly 25 percent of the world's prison population. We need to be honest: we cannot reform something this monstrous; we have to abolish it.

Abolitionists want to eliminate what is oppressive, not reform it, not reimagine it, but remove oppression by its roots. Abolitionists want to understand the conditions that normalize oppression and uproot those conditions, too. Abolitionists, in the words of scholar and activist Bill Ayers, "demand the impossible" and work to build a world rooted in the possibilities of justice. Abolitionists are not anarchists; as we eliminate these systems, we want to build conditions that create institutions that are just, loving, equitable, and that center Black lives.

Abolitionism is not a social justice trend. It is a way of life defined by commitment to working toward a humanity where no one is disposable, prisons no longer exist, being Black is not a crime, teachers have high expectations for Black and Brown children, and joy is seen as a foundation of learning.

Abolitionists strive for that reality by fighting for a divestment of law enforcement to redistribute funds to education, housing, jobs, and healthcare; elimination of high-stakes testing; replacement of watered-down and Eurocentric materials from educational publishers like Pearson, McGraw-Hill, and Houghton Mifflin Harcourt with community-created standards and curriculum; the end of police presence in schools; employment of Black teachers en masse; hiring of therapists and counselors who believe Black lives matter in schools; destruction of inner-city schools that resemble prisons; and elimination of suspension in favor of restorative justice.

Abolitionist work is hard and demands an indomitable spirit of resistance. As a nation, we saw this spirit in Harriet Tubman and Frederick Douglass. We also see it in twenty-first century abolitionists like Angela Davis, Charlene Carruthers, Erica Meiners, Derecka Purnell, David Stovall, and Farima Pour-Khorshid.

For non-Black people, abolitionism requires giving up the idea of being an "ally" to become a "co-conspirator." Many social justice groups have shifted the language to "co-conspirator" because allies work toward something that is mutually beneficial and supportive to all parties. Co-conspirators, in contrast, understand how whiteness and privilege work in our society and leverage their power, privilege, and resources in solidarity with justice movements to dismantle white supremacy. Co-conspirators function as verbs, not as nouns.

The journey for abolitionists and our co-conspirators is arduous, but we fight for a future that will never need to be reformed again because it was built as just from the beginning.

CHAPTER 12

NYC Teachers Bring the Black Lives Matter at School Week of Action to the Early Years

By Laleña Garcia and Rosy Clark

Laleña on adapting the thirteen principles into child-friendly language

When I heard that New York City was going to join the Black Lives Matter at School Week of Action after a call from educators in Philly, I was thrilled. Then I thought, "Oh, geez. The first thing people will say is, 'We can't talk about this with young children.'" I knew from experience that some folks will say things like that out of misguided desire to protect young children from conversations about race (and other differences). However, I also knew that many more early childhood educators would want to be involved. Many of these educators are committed to social justice and regularly have conversations with their students about topics such race, class, and gender, but they perhaps felt hesitant to bring up Black Lives Matter because of the horrific police violence that the movement was responding to. Remember, this was after the summer when a four-year-old child watched as Philando Castile was murdered. We urgently needed to help our young ones, but we had to do it in a way that best met their needs.

Luckily, I learned that the week of action centers Black Lives Matter's thirteen guiding principles, and these principles support values consistent with quality early childhood education; many of us teach in classrooms where we already explicitly discuss empathy and diversity, as well as a variety of family structures and the importance of community. I attended a meeting with other New York City educators who were hoping to bring the week of action to their schools, and I became familiar with the thirteen guiding principles and listened as folks volunteered for tasks. I decided that my first job would be to translate the principles into kid-friendly language, which could then be disseminated, along with a short essay providing language to introduce the Black Lives Matter movement. I hoped that the kid-friendly language would provide a jumping-off point for educators who wanted to bring the principles into their classrooms, while remaining age appropriate for their young students.

This was both easier and more challenging than I had anticipated. I started with the principles that are present in every early childhood classroom: empathy and diversity. Many early childhood educators already spend time teaching children about empathy, asking them to look closely at each other's faces to determine "what our friends are feeling." We talk about our responsibility to think about and be gentle with each other. The principle of restorative justice is an extension on this way of thinking. If you knock down someone's block building, you cannot just say sorry, you must rebuild.

But what about some of the harder principles? How do you discuss globalism with children who barely know the name of their city? Or the meaning of "transgender" and "queer affirming" with families who struggle with accepting their gender nonconforming children and diverse family structures? Or the importance of affirming Black women, in schools that are majority white, or schools that have been actively involved in the pushout of Black girls?

In the end, it took time, intense collaboration, and self-scrutiny to adapt the material for young children. I wanted to remain true to the essence of each principle, while keeping the language simple and accessible. I reached out to early childhood educators and talked with my co-kindergarten teacher, Anna Sobel, who was an invaluable person to bounce ideas off. I made sure to talk to trans* educators, too. Finally, I was lucky to have a colleague, Alaina Daniels, who helped me formulate the language.

I finally had kid-friendly language ready for each principle. I then wrote a brief statement to adults to reassure them that we would *not* have to talk about police brutality to address Black Lives Matter in our classrooms or with our children. In 2018, Anna and I workshopped the language in our classrooms, and our five- and six-year-olds were not only receptive but excited. I was thrilled to see them absorbing the ideas and trying out the language themselves.

The summer afterward, I collaborated with Caryn Davidson, a BLM educator who is a high school art teacher and highly gifted artist. She made posters of each principle featuring the wording I had developed. Early in the fall of 2018, I had an insight: what if we had a coloring book that would allow children to actively engage with the principles? I called Caryn, and through our discussion, we decided that it should be an activity book with prompts for each principle, which would make it a more authentic and meaningful learning experience for children. We met at a crowded midtown coffee shop before one of our organizing meetings to flesh out this idea and to think of a prompt for each principle. Again, I enlisted the help of my colleagues Anna Sobel and Alaina Daniels to think of questions to ask children.

As 2019 began, I decided to use the posters in my classroom with my students. I was unprepared for how enthusiastically they greeted the material. My kids loved the posters and were thrilled to have them up on the walls of our classroom, where they remained for the rest of the year. They would refer to the posters often. "That reminds me of one of the posters," became a common refrain. "They just needed some transgender affirming," a child remarked, shaking her head, after we read the picture book *From the Stars in the Sky to the Fish in the Sea* by Kai Cheng Thom. And after we'd finished *Little Melba and Her Big Trombone*, by Katheryn Russell-Brown, one child had this to say: "Melba was like 'loving engagement' because she loved her fans and didn't care about the people who were mean. And 'Black women,' because some people thought she couldn't play because she was a girl, but they were wrong."

And the coloring book? That was a huge hit.

I teach at an independent school with a commitment to social justice. With no racial majority, our school is the most racially and economically diverse school in New York City. My administration was unswervingly supportive, and I received very little pushback from parents. The process of adapting and integrating the thirteen principles of BLM went well for me. But what would happen at another school? I turned to other educators to find out if these same materials would be useful in other settings.

Rosy on reaching children who may not be personally affected by racial oppression

As a pre-K teacher in a public school in Brooklyn, I was both excited and apprehensive when I heard about the Black Lives Matter at School Week of Action. I knew that this was exactly the kind of social justice education work that I wanted to be practicing in my classroom, but I also knew that it would be a delicate subject to broach, and I was not sure what the response would be.

I teach pre-K at a public elementary school in a primarily white, upper-middle-class neighborhood, so I was concerned that the subject matter would not be as applicable to my students who have, for the most part, never experienced discrimination or racial oppression. However, I knew that it was important to help them understand the world outside of their own experiences.

As I dove into the organizing work of planning the week of action around the city, I looked for other teachers who were making curriculum for this week and what they were doing. Finding Laleña's child-friendly language for the thirteen guiding principles of Black Lives Matter quickly changed my thinking about how to do this work in an early childhood classroom. I realized that these principles were the foundation of everything I was already teaching in my classroom. Working within this framework would give my teaching new depth and clarity.

The coloring book was an especially helpful tool in my pre-K classroom. I had the children color the lovely illustrations designed by Caryn Davidson and talked about each of the principles as we colored them in. We read books that connected to each principle to help think more about how these ideas operate in our daily lives. One of my favorite moments was when I read the book *Willow Finds a Way*, by Lana Button, in which a child stands up to a bully in her classroom. At the end of the story, one of my students exclaimed, "Ms. Clark, Willow is doing 'loving engagement'! She helped Kristabelle practice being kind!" Talking about the principles and reading stories that connected to them seemed to reach my students and help them understand.

Laleña on the value of accessible language for all learners

After the 2018 week of action, I got feedback from teachers from pre-K to high school that the "kid-friendly" language had been helpful in their classrooms. My hope has been that the language will be useful to young children and to people of all ages. It turns out, many of us are still about five years old when it comes to talking about race and gender. We have not had much practice discussing these subjects, and having simple, straightforward language to use as a jumping-off point has been useful to teachers of older students, as well. After 2019, we got similar positive feedback about the coloring book. Several New York City educators are working on a middle school version to use during the 2020 week of action.

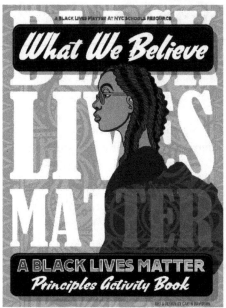

Covers of Black Lives Matter Principles coloring book and activity book, created by Caryn Davidson.

How to Talk to Young Children about the Black Lives Matter Guiding Principles

By Laleña Garcia

As we think about discussing big ideas with little people, we consider age-appropriate language so that our young students can grasp the concepts we're introducing and incorporate these ideas and language into their own thinking and conversation.

While adults can certainly talk about any of the principles (and many of us already do) without mentioning the Black Lives Matter movement, we can also describe the movement as a group of people who want to make sure that everyone is treated fairly, regardless of the color of their skin. We can say something along these lines:

> The civil rights movement, with people we know about—like Martin Luther King Jr. and Rosa Parks—worked to change laws that were unfair. The Black Lives Matter movement is a group of people working together who want to make sure

that everyone is treated fairly, because, even though many of those old, unfair laws were changed many years ago, some people are still not being treated fairly.

The idea of police violence is frightening to young children, and just as we wouldn't discuss the violence inflicted on civil rights activists, we avoid discussing contemporary racist violence with our youngest children.

After each principle, I have suggested some language that you can use when talking to young children. Whenever possible, try to make connections to children's lived experience, in the classroom, the home, or out in the world.

Restorative justice

Restorative justice is the commitment to build a beloved and loving community that is sustainable and growing.

"We know that if you knock down someone's block building, you have to help them rebuild it. You can't just say, 'sorry' and walk away. But when you help someone rebuild, that is called *restorative justice*. It's the idea that we have to help people when something hurtful happens to them, even if it happened by accident."

Empathy

Empathy is the ability to connect with others by building relationships based on mutual trust and understanding.

"It's so important to think about how other people feel, because different people have different feelings. Sometimes it helps to think about how you would feel if the same thing that happened to your friend happened to you. Another way to say that is *empathy*."

Loving engagement

Loving engagement is the commitment to practice justice, liberation, and peace.

"It's so important to make sure that we always try to be fair and peaceful. We have to keep practicing this so that we can get better and better at it. Another way to say that is *loving engagement*."

Diversity
Diversity is the celebration and acknowledgment of differences and commonalities across cultures.

"Different people do different things and have different feelings. It's so important that we have lots of different kinds of people in our community and that everyone feels safe. Another way to say that is *diversity*."

Globalism
Globalism is our ability to see how we are impacted or privileged within the Black global family that exists across the world in different regions.

"Globalism means that we are thinking about all the different people all over the world and thinking about the ways to keep things fair everywhere."

Transgender affirming
Transgender affirming is the commitment to continue to make space for our trans siblings by encouraging leadership and recognizing trans-antagonistic violence, while doing the work required to dismantle cisgender privilege and uplift Black trans folk.

"Everybody has the right to choose their own gender by listening to their own heart and mind. Everyone gets to choose if they are a girl or a boy or both or neither or something else, and no one else gets to choose for them."

Queer affirming
Queer affirming is working toward a queer-affirming network where heteronormative thinking no longer exists.

"Everybody has the right to choose who they love and the kind of family they want by listening to their own heart and mind."

Collective value

Collective value means that all Black lives, regardless of actual or perceived sexual identity, gender identity, gender expression, economic status, ability, disability, religious beliefs or disbeliefs, immigration status, or location, matter.

"Everybody is important and has the right to be safe and happy. Another way to say that is *collective value*."

Intergenerational

Intergenerational is a space free from ageism where we can learn from each other.

"It's important that we have spaces where people of different ages can come together and learn from each other. Another way to say that is *intergenerational*."

Black families

Black families creates a space that is family friendly and free from patriarchal practices.

"There are lots of different kinds of families; what makes a family is that it's people who take care of each other. It's important to make sure that all families feel welcome."

Black villages

Black villages is the disruption of Western nuclear family dynamics and a return to the "collective village" where individuals take care of each other.

"There are lots of different kinds of families; what makes a family is that it's people who take care of each other; those people might be related, or maybe they choose to be a family together and take care of each other. Sometimes, when it's lots of families together, it can be called a *village*."

Black women

Black women is the building of women-centered spaces free from sexism, misogyny, and male-centeredness.

"There are some people who think that women are less important than men. We know that all people are important and have the right to be safe and talk about their own feelings."

Unapologetically Black

Unapologetically Black is the affirmation that Black lives matter and that our love and desire for justice and freedom are prerequisites for wanting that for others. These principles are the blueprint for healing and do not include, nor do they support, ignoring or sanitizing the ugliness and discomfort that comes with dealing with race and anti-race issues.

"There are lots of different kinds of people, and one way that we're different is the color of our skin. It's important to make sure that all people are treated fairly, and that's why we and lots of other people all over the country and the world are part of the Black Lives Matter movement."

CHAPTER 13

Bringing the Team Along

When Solidarity Leads to Progress

By Makai Kellogg

N early every US institution, from healthcare to banking to education, demonstrates through policy and practice that Black lives don't matter. In response to racist and harmful systems, teachers around the country organized the Black Lives Matter at School coalition. The Black Lives Matter at School Week of Action focuses on centering Black lives and bringing racial justice to the forefront by integrating the thirteen guiding principles into the curriculum and planning school activities and events. Teachers and schools involved in the movement call for implementing restorative justice practices, eliminating zero tolerance discipline, hiring more Black teachers, mandating Black and ethnic studies, and replacing police with counselors.

So, where do young children fit into this movement for Black lives?

As an early educator in Washington, DC, I learned about the Black Lives Matter at School Week of Action through the nonprofit Teaching for Change and teacher activist groups on social media. In January 2018, I introduced the week of action to my preschool. After receiving approval from my administrator, I ran around the building asking individual teachers if they were interested in participating. I bombarded them with resources and pulled books from our library that could be used for planning. I began crafting a letter to families informing them of the ways that the guiding principles align with our Quaker values and antibias mission; I also had the same discussions on a more informal basis with my colleagues. The Friday before the week of action, the teachers met during a staff meeting and reviewed the letter to families that would go out that day. I was excited and ready for the week ahead, but when I looked around the room, I realized there was a problem.

Introducing something new to a teaching staff, such as a new break policy or use of curricular materials, is one thing. Introducing something new that addresses racism and white supremacy is another. Some teachers expressed discomfort about informing parents with short notice, fear of how white parents would react to the material, and concern that they were unprepared to adequately teach the lessons. The decision reached in the meeting was to use the materials and instruction but not the name "Black Lives Matter Week of Action"; it wouldn't work if all the teachers were not on board. Teachers still led their activities, read books, and even wore the shirts, but they made no mention of the purpose of these actions.

I felt deflated and disappointed. My biggest pitfall, I realized, was overestimating others' interest and understanding of the social justice concerns of the BLM movement. I needed to recognize that everyone was coming from different places of comfort and safety when it came to discussing race and naming racism. In retrospect, I could have taken the time to gauge how the staff felt about and understood the movement before suggesting the new curriculum. I also could have created opportunities for the relationship building that's needed for these conversations. As Dr. Bettina Love writes, "The push for justice by students, parents, and community members cannot be done without solidarity and a reflectiveness of self."[1]

This led to a question: How can we teach young children that Black lives matter without fully understanding what that means ourselves? As they learned about the week of action, some teachers expressed their concerns and objections. One teacher brought up media coverage that stigmatized the movement as violent. Another asked, "Why now?" and, "If we do this week, what about other groups? Shouldn't we focus on

Latinx, Asians, and others?" Some of the staff simply felt uncomfortable at the idea of having conversations about race, especially with parents.

All this gave me an action plan to make the following year a success. The next year, in order to make sure that all teachers had their questions addressed, I asked Dr. Denisha Jones to lead an info session. Bringing in an outside expert is very useful when engaging in equity work at a school, especially when you are usually the one pushing the agenda. Dr. Jones explained the week of action from a national standpoint as an educational movement and talked about how to adapt the ideas with an early childhood lens.

The DC Area Educators for Social Justice also held events specifically for early educators on discussing race, representation, and history in children's literature and about the purpose of the week of action. I also provided more books that specifically addressed the guiding principles and practical guidance on how they could be used. In January, I wrote a letter to parents about the week. My administrator and I both signed it, and she sent it out to the school community of families and teachers.

The info session and guidance on curriculum helped teachers feel more confident, and I noticed the hesitancy from the first year had dissipated. With the added preparation and support, one teacher said that she "was more into [the topic] because we had more options to meet the kids' needs in the classroom and express it in a more age-appropriate way." In developing the curriculum, we decided that the material for the younger children, ages 18 months to 2.5 years, should be focused on the guiding principle of empathy, while the older children, ages 3 to 5, would explore all of the guiding BLM principles. Psychologist and educator Dr. Beverly Daniel Tatum believes that "when we talk to children about racial issues, or anything else, we have to keep in mind each child's developmental stage and cognitive ability to make sense of what we are saying."[2] The teachers of younger children felt comfortable using empathy as a focal point and incorporating other guiding principles such as diversity and intergenerationality when choosing children's books. With the older children, who have more language, inquiry skills, and problem-solving capabilities, teachers tackled issues such as bullying, being an ally, and questioning gender norms.

With support and encouragement, teachers were seeing that the beauty of the guiding principles is that they are flexible; often several principles are discernable in a single activity. Children's literature was an especially effective vehicle because multiple guiding principles can be entwined in a single story. Many of the teachers began sharing their own ideas, and some collaborated on the curriculum. Along with reading books, teachers were using puppets and baby dolls to model empathy. The older classes were exploring the color black, working collectively to build a structure, creating language to describe their skin color, and using puppets to solve problems.

While all was well in the classrooms, the real work had to be done internally. As a routine part of the staff meeting schedule, we began holding antibias meetings where ongoing, self-reflective practice takes place. I provide equity and diversity resources to teachers, and all interested educators are welcome to attend DC Area Educators for Social Justice events. These opportunities underscore what we already do in our classrooms: model kindness and coach children on daily interactions to build empathy. Also, as antibias educators, we help children recognize and act against unfairness, learn how to be allies, and affirm and celebrate the diversity of students and their families. Reflecting on how we are already doing this work makes celebrating Black Lives Matter business as usual.

As I reflect on my experience bringing Black Lives Matter at School Week of Action to my school, there were missteps, roadblocks, surprises, and finally, a meaningful outcome. Introducing an important curricular change starts with teacher buy-in and willingness to do the work.

The movement's guiding principles, especially the excellent early childhood version developed by Laleña Garcia, promote compassion, self-love, and respect for others—all things that parents and teachers want children to understand. The guiding principles provide this language. Using these principles throughout the year in the early childhood years actively challenges white supremacy. It also helps ground and focus our purpose as educators as we introduce and explore social justice topics and social and emotional learning. As a teacher, I've been gratified to see just how well children remember and reiterate the guiding principles, comparing, for example, themes of acceptance from the book *I Walk with Vanessa* to similar ideas in *Julian Is a Mermaid*, or to real-world examples of injustice or exclusion. The week of action is now on our school calendar, demonstrating our collective commitment to equity norms by proudly stating that is what we do and who we are as a program.

Black lives matter in early childhood and beyond. I and other educators have seen firsthand that even quite young children are eager to discuss justice, fairness, and empathy. By initiating these conversations in age-appropriate ways, we are building the foundation necessary to critically examine the atrocities and legacy of this country's past and present. With more children actively working against oppressive and inequitable systems, we may actually have a chance.

Image credit: Wear Out the Silence.

CHAPTER 14

Centering the Youngest Black Children

An Interview with Takiema Bunche-Smith*

Denisha Jones: Let's start with a little bit about you. Tell me what you do at Bank Street College of Education.

Takiema Bunche-Smith: I'm the executive director of the Center on Culture, Race and Equity at Bank Street College of Education. At CCRE, we provide research-based professional development to education professionals and institutions to help them create antiracist and culturally responsive, sustaining environments for children, families, and staff. In the work that we do, we center race in these conversations. We work in settings that include birth to twelfth grade and beyond. We even recently started working with a school that serves individuals up to age twenty-one, so we really cover the whole spectrum of childhood. We adapt our development frameworks based on the ages of the children, but our consistent focus is helping adults become aware of their own mindsets and behaviors around race, culture, and equity, which means our model is applicable across all settings.

---

* This interview was conducted on Wednesday, May 20, 2020, by Denisha Jones.

A while back, as we were doing our work with schools, I started to identify places of potential growth in our curriculum and approach. We would often get questions like, well, why is this just about Black and white people? Where is everyone else? I had actually raised that question myself when I first came to CCRE. Trying to answer it pushed me to really ask, why *are* we talking just about Black and white people? The answer is that we have to. We need to talk about Black people specifically, and people who are racialized in other ways. And we need to talk about Black and white people because there are specific issues we need to understand related to Black oppression in the US context and around the world. We need to understand our racialization and how it has been woven into every single system in the United States.

And so I asked myself, do people genuinely understand that? No. Do we talk about it? No. Do we talk about the impact of anti-Black racism in the field of education? No. We need to be talking about it at the personal, professional, and institutional levels. The heart of CCRE's approach is to discuss concepts, research, and practice on those three levels. But there was a gap in our curriculum on the topic of how racism impacts people of all races, and anti-Black racism in particular.

Denisha: You are so right. We are not talking about it enough—and not in early childhood.

Takiema: Early childhood education has this hidden side. It is presented as a "raceless" field. This has been my experience for the longest time, even in my early training at Bank Street. I remember having lots of questions about race and culture. It was always the question that came up for me after I was presented with the canon, or standard wisdom, on an issue. A substantial part of the socializing piece of early childhood education is to speak objectively to what *all* children need, such as, "All children need care and relationships." But nobody would say what it means to be understood culturally and what impact race and racism have on the field of early education. I have been doing this work for a long time, as I've tried to find my way, and only over the past four years have those discussions begun to take place more broadly within the field. I know that Bank Street's graduate programs have also grown tremendously in this area and have incorporated culturally responsive and antiracist curriculum, approaches, and frameworks into their courses.

When I saw the Black Lives Matter at School Week of Action, I was immediately drawn to it as a way to shine a spotlight on the experiences of Black students. I quickly realized that the focus for most was on K–12, and I began to question that approach. Children are Black before kindergarten, and families are Black before kindergarten, and all these disparate, disproportionate outcomes are happening before kindergarten. Kids don't just wake up at age five and start getting suspended or excluded or not seeing themselves represented. I wanted to bring the focus of early childhood to the week of action. That was the starting point. At CCRE, we began to adjust our curriculum to explicitly address anti-Black racism on the personal, professional, and institutional levels. And then, when the Black Lives Matter as School Week of Action came about, it was an opportunity to take that perspective and push it in terms of early childhood.

Denisha: As an early childhood teacher and teacher educator, everything you said profoundly resonates with me. What made you decide to plan an early childhood symposium for the 2019 Black Lives Matter at School Week of Action?

Takiema: In 2018, I was invited to speak on a panel organized by a parent working with the Institute for Collaborative Education (a progressive public school in New York City). She's someone who has done parent activism work primarily around opting out and pushing back against standardized tests in education. She said, "We're planning this panel that's focused on the fact that standardized tests are racist." Up until that point, although I was one of the leaders in the NYC opt-out movement, I hadn't explored much of the research and theory that supported that assertion, so it led me to do additional research that confirmed what I intuitively knew to be correct.

The event was great because there were people from different perspectives and positions within the educational field on the panel. And all but one identified as Black. My opening remarks on that panel were about young Black children, and I wanted to situate our understanding within a historical context. As Michael Dumas and Joseph Nelson point out in "(Re)Imagining Black Boyhood," when we look at Black people's history, we see how their humanity has always been denied in a white supremacist society.[1] And that doesn't start when they are an adult; it starts at birth. When we think of a three-year-old, we may picture a child playing, but for Black children, their bodies have been seen as commodities, and they've been denied that opportunity. During enslavement, Black children as young as three were made to work in the fields.

I felt it was important to interject the space with those kinds of necessary discussions. I wondered why we didn't have an event that specifically focused on early childhood education and anti-Black racism. I didn't see anyone else doing it, and I thought it would provide a way for people to learn and consider the youngest Black children.

Later that year, in October of 2018, I approached College leadership, and we received enthusiastic support and resources across all divisions of Bank Street College of Education to host the 2019 symposium.

Denisha: Tell me more about that first symposium.

Takiema: The theme was "From Theory to Practice in Early Education: Black Children Learning and Thriving." (A video recording of the symposium is available on the CCRE webpage.) We wanted to take the CCRE philosophy of having a strength-based approach. That is, we wanted to focus the conversation on our magic, joy, resiliency, strength, and all the things that are wonderful about Black children. I didn't want people to leave the symposium depressed by stats and numbers but instead to come away feeling like what they were seeing and hearing was amazing—that *we* are amazing. I wanted them to see strengths they had never seen before and discover how they could build on them. And that is precisely what people took away from the event.

I'm someone who wants to highlight the problems and then ask, what is our agency to change? I would be super discouraged if I just kept looking at the stats. I want to know what we are *doing*. For the learning portion of the symposium, we had two panels, and the focus was on examining early childhood education to find out what is happening around Black children learning. What are the opportunities, the challenges? What are some things we can start to rethink? And then, when it came to thriving, we were like, what are people doing that's working? Some people and institutions are serving Black children and doing it well. So how do we highlight their work and learn from them, and shift to a place where our work nurtures Black children?

We realized that we don't have to create something that doesn't exist. If we think historically, during segregation—when Black people, by and large, were left to their own devices—we were doing a great job educating Black children within the context of violent white supremacy, prior to school integration. So we have historical models for how best to educate Black children that we can look to.

The push for integration was predicated upon assimilating Black children into white dominant social and cultural norms, instead of fully funding and providing resources that Black children need to be successful. And it created this notion that what Black children need most is not play and open-ended activities but worksheets and academic preschool—essentially to sit down and practice the letter A. But that's not what white people are giving their kids when they can offer them the best opportunities. They encourage their children to play in the dirt and sand, and to experiment. Black children need those same opportunities to thrive.

Denisha: Absolutely, this is such an important point. Black children need more play, more engagement, and more hands-on activities!

Takiema: Yes, they do! So overall, the event was very successful. We got tremendously positive feedback and an enormous amount of interest for both years. I was blown away by the number of people who reserved a spot in advance and reached out about coming, which showed me that there was a vast need and considerable interest.

However, there were still very few opportunities for people to approach thinking about Black children and early childhood from a strengths-based perspective. During the first symposium, we did a poll asking how many people had had specific professional development (PD) on how to support Black children to thrive in early childhood. We asked if the PD was specific for children birth to age eight and if it was longer than a one-day or half-day training. Around 84 percent said they had never had that kind of training. That was fascinating to me because we have all these disparities for Black children, but only about 15 percent of people receive any specific training on how to support them. No wonder we still have disparities in education! Not enough people within education are thinking about what to do to truly ensure that Black children are able to thrive in a way that is race specific and strength based.

Denisha: Wow, that is a powerful connection and essential for teacher educators to understand. Can you tell me a little bit about the event this year? I had my students watch the 2019 event through the livestream, and this year I was fortunate to be able to attend the 2020 symposium in person. Can you talk a little bit about how you organized the event for this year and how you made it different from the first one?

Takiema: It was definitely very different this year. We wanted to model what high-quality professional development looks like through our symposium. Our goal is always to model individualized and robust learning experiences. We spent a lot of time after last year's event looking over the feedback, both the anecdotal responses and the surveys. We'd asked people what they wanted to learn more about, and we'd collected feedback about the format. Reviewing all of the responses allowed us to shift our focus this year.

In terms of topic, the symposium focused this year on the intersection of gender and race for children birth to eight years old. Two things stood out for me as leader of the development of the symposium. First, in 2019, we had a panelist, Akiea Gross, who is nonbinary. When they were on the panel and during all of our planning meetings and conversations, I learned a lot from hearing about their experiences. And afterward, I got to thinking about my own learning curve around gender expansiveness. Listening to Akiea Gross talk about their experiences as a child, a teenager, and then a kindergarten teacher, I realized I had more to learn and that I wanted to explore this more.

And the second thing that came up was the feedback and the responses we received when we asked participants in the 2019 symposium to identify questions they had. Many participants said the focus had been mostly on Black boys, but what about Black girls? During the first symposium, we had a panelist who specifically works with Black boys. We also had Akiea talking about limitations of the gender binary. We realized others were excluded if we only focused on that binary. Again, I turned to the research, and the data demonstrated the danger of being silent with respect to Black queer, trans, and gender nonconforming children.

My approach is usually to look at problems or challenges that adults experience, and then trace them back to their origin. Most problems do not start when a person is an adult, and they do not start when someone is five. Gender oppression begins even earlier. The imposition of a gender construct begins during pregnancy and birth, which can be oppressive if a child, when born, does not align with their assigned gender. And that simply wasn't a conversation we were having in education. In the Black Lives Matter at School Week of Action, I see lots of nuanced curriculum and activities around gender that concern children older than kindergarten, but when you look at the stats, the need to address these topics in younger children is clear.

I wanted to use the space of the symposium as a way to resist trying to fit everything into a neat box. When we look at suspensions and preschool, there is one dynamic for Black girls. There's a dynamic for Black boys that is different and equally harmful. Both Black girls and boys are adultified, but the intersection of gender plays out differently for each of them. Black girls are labeled mouthy, too fast, loud, and aggressive. Black boys are also adultified, but they are considered threatening, aggressive, and less compliant, leading to higher rates of special education.

And then when you look at Black children who identify as transgender or gender nonconforming, there is invisibility, in part because most adults don't have a framing for how to speak about gender identity and development in early childhood. While we're not sure what's happening with trans and gender nonconforming children in childcare and preschool in real time, we have evidence that they don't have positive school experiences shortly after early childhood. We know that they experience extremely disproportionate numbers of suspension, expulsion, and violence in K–12 schools, as well as mental health issues, and referrals to juvenile justice systems by the time they're sixteen. If you trace that back, you recognize that the educational system has not supported them in all of their identities from the very beginning. We know that the school system did not support them as Black preschoolers and in early childhood. When we add in gender, and we look at the intersection with race, the outcomes are even worse. So that left me asking, what can we do?

Denisha: Thank you for sharing your insight and your process. The 2020 symposium did a fantastic job exploring those issues and educating everyone on the need to learn more about the intersection of race and gender. What is your long-term goal for organizing the week of action? What are your thoughts for next year's symposium?

Takiema: My long-term goal is to make sure people realize that these are conversations that need to happen well beyond the week of action. I want people thinking about very young Black children and education, and their role in supporting Black children fifty-two weeks a year, not just one week or one month. And that requires keeping the conversation open and evolving. When we discuss or research any educational issue starting from early childhood, I want us to ask how the issue relates to Black children and Black families. And I want that approach to be happening in every setting, from higher education to elementary classrooms, to family engagement to mental health. As it stands, we're failing Black children educationally.

Our generation is not as successful as it theoretically should be based on the desegregation interventions from the '70s or '80s, like magnet schools and busing. The group of people who received those interventions were somewhat successful by mainstream standards, but it came at a cost. Having to leave one's largely Black community to find "good schools" and academic success should never be a choice that someone has to make. I want to ensure that every educator, regardless of their race and the age of the children they serve, speaks about Black children and how we can support them and build upon all the strengths they bring to schools. I want to move from a deficit-based attitude that locates Black children's challenges within themselves, their families, and their cultures, and shift to understanding and disrupting the impact of anti-Black racism at the personal, professional, and institutional levels in education. Those are my long-term goals.

Denisha: Thank you so much for your amazing labor and your commitment to the Black Lives Matter at School Week of Action. I look forward to the 2021 symposium!

CHAPTER 15

Organizing the Black Lives Matter at School Week of Action in New Jersey

An Interview with Raquel James-Goodman

> *They tried to bury us. They didn't know we were seeds.*
> —Dinos Christianopoulos

Planting the seeds:
A preface by Awo Okaikor Aryee-Price

My conversation with Raquel James-Goodman is rooted in our shared gratitude for the collective past, present, and future work of those who came before us and those who will come after us. Our own stories, springing from Hackensack, New Jersey, are part of a larger narrative of Black and African diasporic peoples resisting oppression, as well as the interlocking struggle for liberation and decolonization on the Indigenous lands of the Lenni Lenape, the Ramapough Lenape Nation, and others who occupied this land prior to colonization, and the continued and perpetual attempt at genocide. We understand the genealogical linkage between the struggles of the Indigenous people of this land (which we now refer to as the United States of America) and the African diasporic peoples of this land. Our own stories are extensions of this past.

About three years ago, I was targeted by administrators and others in my school district as I fought for racial justice, and the attacks were supported and perpetuated by the union leadership within the district and county. After being called racist and "anti-police"[1] and having to endure the anti-Black racism that comes with being a Black womxn committed to liberation, I was eventually dismissed and even prohibited from certain future work opportunities. I am certain I was dismissed because of the racial justice organizing work I was engaged in, although the district would never admit to that. It didn't matter that I had an excellent teaching record and strong support from students and the community. None of that mattered when anti-Black racism and white supremacy were the order of the day.

My own story, however, is about the seeds we plant and continue to plant. It is about how we do not always get to bear witness to the fruits of our labor, and how other times we do get to see those fruits taking form in ways that surpass our imagination. The seeds that I planted by organizing within the district required us to take an honest look at the ways in which systemic oppression and racism impact the experiences of Black, Indigenous, and Latinx students, educators, and their families. These were conversations that the district leadership—the superintendents, the principals, and the union leadership—resisted to such a degree that they needed to force me out of the district. It is a story of the ways that white supremacy will go to great lengths to silence dissenting voices and make an example of one individual in order to maintain power, dominance, and existing structures. But this is also a story of triumph and the power of organizing as a tool to interrupt power and dominance.

In July of 2019, as I was returning home from the Free Minds, Free People conference in Minnesota, I received an unexpected phone call from Raquel James-Goodman. It had been almost exactly three years since I had been dismissed from Hackensack and last seen Raquel's name flash across my phone's screen. A hesitancy sat in my belly. The plane was still taxiing toward the gate. I was surrounded by the chaos of anxious, inattentive passengers rushing to retrieve their carry-on luggage before hurriedly disembarking the plane. I wasn't sure if I should answer the phone. When I was dismissed from Hackensack, Raquel and I were not speaking. Raquel, along with many others, had abandoned me during a time when I was being ostracized from my profession. It had been three isolating years.

But I did pick up the phone. Curiosity answered the call.

Radical love and reconciliation brought us together.

And here we are today, collectively writing about the power of reconciliation, radical love, and organizing for our collective liberation. Here is our story.*

Awo Okaikor Aryee-Price (left) and Raquel James-Goodman. Photo credit: Awo Okaikor Aryee-Price.

Awo Okaikor Aryee-Price: Where do you teach? Why do you teach? Feel free to include information on your background.

Raquel James-Goodman: I'm a sixth-grade English language arts teacher in Hackensack, New Jersey. I've always been attracted to learning, and right before I started kindergarten, my mom explained that schooling is a means of survival. My mother, an Afro-Panamanian immigrant, emphasized that for me and my siblings, we would have to work twice as hard at anything we do to get the same opportunities white Americans get. She rationalized this by explaining that it was just the way things were in this country. When it was finally time for me to go to school, my mother rented an apartment in a four-family classic colonial on a busy

---

* Awo Okaikor Aryee-Price conducted this interview with Raquel James-Goodman in the spring of 2020.

road in a working-class white suburban town. My mother felt we would have a better educational opportunity because it was a white school. We were the only Black family in town.

Decades later, I think about my mother's rationale. A school is a place full of possibilities, and for my mother, a white school had more opportunities and possibilities for her Black children. I think about this great compromise my mother had to make and I cringe. Black and Latinx kids still have the burden of feeling they must work twice as hard to counter white supremacist ideas and oppression. For Black children, our society never allows them to just be kids. So teaching is my way of preparing kids to challenge structures of oppression and explore all the possibilities. I teach because I believe it is important for students to see teachers that look like them and share linguistic and cultural similarities. I wish I had this opportunity as a child.

Okaikor: Tell me about how you first learned about the Black Lives Matter at School Week of Action.

Raquel: The first time I learned about the week of action was from you, Okaikor, a dedicated soldier in the fight for equitable schools. You shared the work of the coalition and advised me on grant opportunities within the New Jersey Education Association and hosting events during the week of action.

Okaikor: What made you decide to organize the week of action in your school district?

Raquel: I proposed an intergenerational panel discussion with students, educators, and community members on the topic of racial bias and education. There has been increasing racial tension in my district. Most of the students are Latinx and Black; however, the teaching staff and administration are overwhelmingly white. Teachers and administrators routinely claim to be "color-blind" and blame systems and practices of inequity on uninvolved parents and unmotivated kids. The district is culturally destructive. Educators in denial of the role they play in creating and sustaining systems of oppression need to hear from the students that are sitting in their classrooms right now. Adults cannot simply silence the experiences of the youth. I organized this event to elevate student voices and force stakeholders to listen.

Okaikor: Describe the events you organized for the week of action at your school/district. Were they successful?

Raquel: Students, educators, parents, and community members engaged in a powerful evening of courageous conversations that focused on the impact of racial bias on education. A seventh-grade student spotlighted recent headlines from New Jersey news that highlighted some of the challenges Black and Latinx students face today. The headlines included "NJ schools among 'Most Segregated' in the Nation, Suit Says," "Black Kids in NJ Schools Are Suspended at a Higher Rate Than White Kids, Data Shows," and "NJ Wrestler Forced to Cut Dreadlocks Still Targeted over Hair, Lawyer Says." She expressed personal connections to the headlines and said that in her four years at Hackensack Middle School, she has only had four Black teachers, none of whom have been male.

Next, an eighth-grade student read his poem, "I'm Hispanic," which listed the many stereotypes he has combated in school. The first stanza of the poem reads, "I'm Hispanic so I'm not legal / Disrespected by Americans / looked down on by the bald eagle / Discrimination is prohibited/ but we're still not treated equal."

A senior at Hackensack High School currently taking an elective called Race and Representation spoke about the intersection of race and culture as a Dominican American woman. She recalled straightening her hair because she thought her curly hair did not meet the standard of beauty she had internalized. Today, she rocks her curls with pride, countering the ideal Western beauty standards. She also expressed the need for educators to see the whole child. She described herself as a talented artist who "never took an art class in school" and advised that educators need to help students explore their talents and areas of interest instead of focusing on testing.

Another senior described the impact of implicit bias on her teacher's expectations for her. She said, "Stereotypes have affected me in a way that people assume I'm not meant to achieve. When they see me, they don't see the typical high GPA honors student." She further explained the importance of the event:

In order to create equality for our students at school, we must encourage those who feel neglected. Students who aren't typically given the opportunities to excel or are not taught in a way that affects their identity may not feel included at school. Conversations are necessary because if we don't talk about these situations, they won't change. I guess my goal is to see more people who look like me represented in spaces that aren't typically made for us.

Throughout the panel discussion, attendees were able to participate by posting comments through an app using real-time feedback. Audience members remarked that their own educations had done little to nothing to teach them about racial diversity. One wrote, "I was educated in the '50s and '60s in New Jersey and did not learn about the broadness of Black and Brown history," while another attendee noted, "The curriculum did not represent me or hold my culture in high esteem."

Some attendees recalled how stereotypes and other racist narratives impacted their schooling. One observed, "Bias impacted my schooling tremendously. I was never pushed, because my teachers thought average was 'good enough' for me. Looking back, I believe I could have done more if my teachers had believed I could do more."

The majority of attendees agreed on the need for staff training. When asked the question "What must we do first to create equity for all students?" over 50 percent of the audience chose "train staff in culturally responsive teaching."

The evening ended with attendees gathering for a post-discussion reception sponsored by Hackensack Education Association's PRIDE that included refreshments, book giveaways, and a book signing by author Nathaniel Sojourner Truth. More than 120 people from across Bergen County attended the panel discussion. The event was a success for several reasons. Attendees shared their experiences, made new connections, reflected, and are now in the process of mobilizing to demand staff training in culturally responsive pedagogy. This event created the groundwork for change.

Okaikor: A few years ago, this would not have been easily embraced in the district. What do you think has changed since then?

Raquel: The demand for justice is growing. We can no longer be patient. As I said before, education is survival. We have a responsibility to arm our kids with the necessary tools to survive. If we do not actively disrupt the systems of oppression, then we are taking part in maintaining them. I've made it a personal mission to move forward in the direction of equity, even when the district does not support me, because we, as a people, are suffering. We are failing kids, and I feel an urgency to push forward and demand change. This steadfast determination has mobilized me to build relationships with community leaders and make my mission public.

Through this process you coached me, Okaikor. I was humbled and grateful for your guidance. I also felt great personal guilt for turning my back on you years earlier when you called out the oppressive culture in Hackensack, which was allowing racist structures and practices to continue. You actively tried to seek allies in the fight for justice and equity for our most vulnerable kids, and I turned a blind eye to you and the cause. I now know how it feels to reach out to a school community and get very little support in return. I am still embarrassed by my betrayal. By dismissing you, the district thought they could sweep their racism under the rug, hide it, and pretend it does not exist, but it is spilling over in so many ways that it's unavoidable.

People are becoming aware of the ways that racism manifests in how Black and Latinx students are treated, suspended, and tracked, and in the kinds of college counseling they receive. It cannot be ignored. The numbers are atrocious. Black educators are suffering and continue to suffer. We are not supported, promoted, or celebrated without compromise. Black and Latinx students are suffering here, and they continue to suffer, yet no one is held accountable. Stakeholders are saying enough is enough, and with the growing voice of concern, the district can no longer silence us as they have done in the past. The district is in a crisis and the work is urgent.

Okaikor: Ahhh! I definitely don't think you should feel guilt, embarrassment, or shame. Those can be paralyzing emotions if left without resolution. I can certainly name a time—probably several times—when I didn't completely show up for folx who needed me. I think about it all the time. At an early age, many of us learn to go under the radar, to "go along to get along"—don't rock the boat. That's part of our social conditioning under what bell hooks refers to as a white supremacist capitalist patriarchy. What makes this commendable is the reconciliation that happened. Each time we hurt or harm each other, we are pushed further away from our own humanity, but when we reconcile, we gain back a piece of that humanity we've lost.

So, tell me more about some of the barriers that you faced in trying to get the week of action recognized.

Raquel: Thank you for that. There's myriad ways you could have responded to my rejection years ago. Our reconciliation and solidarity is most commendable, but so is your ability to forgive. I am moving to a place where I forgive too, especially the administrators that look like me and are paid very well to masquerade as advocates for equity.

So the barriers: there are parallels to the hurdles that you faced while organizing in Hackensack. I mean, the entire process of getting Black Lives Matter at School up and rolling in my district was systematically delayed. It became obvious that the work of social justice was not a priority for the district. This realization made me angry at first. Why is this only important to me? I soon realized that people don't feel obligated to demand educational equity if they are comfortable.

Also, just the mention of BLM was apparently offensive and "anti-white." So when I first began organizing, very few people in my district were interested in participating. I sent out literature about the mission of Black Lives Matter at School Week of Action and included resources to plan for activities in classes for different age and subjects. Overall, my efforts were met with silence, though there were a few teachers that right away offered assistance and applauded my efforts. The closer we got to the event, the more the support began to build. But overall, I felt like the staff were closed-minded. I personally invited all the administrators in my school to attend. My principal was out sick with the flu but extended his support. Out of four vice principals, two attended; the two that did not attend are both white. I wonder if they did not feel the need to understand the shared experiences of Black and Latinx students in their schools. One teacher confirmed my hunch with an email suggesting that I provide more information on the BLM movement to help white staff members better understand that BLM has nothing to do with rejecting white educators. I replied that if an educator is so closed-minded and unable to listen, question, or research the goal of BLM at school, and jumps to unfounded conclusions, then I question why are they educators in the first place. How can they possibly facilitate critical thinking with our students? And why in the world would you teach in Hackensack?

Okaikor: How did the community receive the week of action? Was there any opposition?

Raquel: One parent publicly expressed anger that this event was happening. She wrote an email to district administration and school staff expressing her rage at the fact that the district didn't recognize that "all lives matter." She demanded to know how a Black Lives Matter at School event could be approved and wondered if it had to do with Black History Month. I found that in the end, my district and some of my school administration were supportive. Whether their support was the result of a heavy conscience or a calculated move to win the Black community's approval, I don't know. But they showed up and did not fold when confronted with opposition.

Okaikor: What are your long-term goals for organizing the week of action in your district?

Raquel: Moving forward, I am hungry to learn more about the root causes of social, economic, and educational inequality instead of only addressing the symptoms and manifestations of these inequalities. I want to learn with others. So, the next step is educating myself and others so that we have a common language and platform to build from. I am actively seeking funds to pay for this experience.

I will also be working with the NAACP of Bergen County to host conversations with educators of color in Bergen County. They have agreed to provide the event space for a series of conversations. We need a space in New Jersey where we can come together to process our experiences, develop our pedagogy, and organize for better school environments that center our full and collective humanity. That is not something that we currently have, especially in Bergen County, New Jersey.

Additionally, I am going to present local demands based on the data collected at the event to our district's Affirmative Action Committee. Students recognize the harm they have endured within the district, and they also recognize what they need. I will be leaning on their collective wisdom to push toward a more just and equitable school system for my students.

CHAPTER 16

This Is My Education

Bringing the Black Lives Matter at School Week of Action to an African American Immersion School in Milwaukee

By Angela Harris

"This is my education, it is my right, my passport, my weapon to change the world." These are the words we start our day with at Dr. Martin Luther King Jr. African American Immersion School in Milwaukee. Ours is the only public African American immersion school in the country. We formed as a result of a task force organized in 1989 in Milwaukee to make recommendations about the crisis facing Black boys in education and in the community. One of the resulting recommendations was to establish two schools for African American boys: an elementary and a middle school. But because Black girls in our area were also struggling, the decision was reached to make the two new schools coeducational. In 1990, the Milwaukee Board of School Directors decided to give the two schools the designation "African American immersion schools." In 1991, the elementary school opened, and the middle school followed in the fall of 1992.

This was a unique educational opportunity and a departure from the traditional public school setting for Black children. In a study of the first five years of African American immersion schools, *African-Centered Schooling in Theory and Practice*, the editors stated that the African American immersion schools in Milwaukee "represent a contemporary example of a historical ongoing effort by African Americans to realize their educational aspirations for their children."[1] African American immersion centers the lives, current and historical experiences, culture, and experiences of our students in every aspect of their school day. Immersion schools move the work of the week of action beyond just a week and embed it into our teaching practice and pedagogy.

Our school has not always existed as an African American immersion school. After the 1990s, priorities changed, the administration changed, and the vision of the school changed. My journey at Dr. King Jr. School started as the school staff and administration were in the second year of reviving the tenets and practices of being an African American immersion school. It was my interview with the principal that convinced me, as a new educator, to take a position as the kindergarten teacher in what some might consider a "high-needs school." Prior to that interview, I had researched the school and read these words on the school's website: "Dr. Martin Luther King Jr. School is a learning center that cultivates self-determined learners through an African American Immersion learning experience that equips them with the academic, socio-emotional, and life skills necessary to excel in a global economy and improve the conditions of their communities."

After reading that statement, I immediately felt at home. I knew that this was the type of school environment where I wanted to begin my career as an educator. I wanted to build a pedagogy that centered the lives of students who had been marginalized for far too long. During the interview, the principal spoke about the values that our school instills in our scholars: scholarship, peace, justice, equality, courage, community, and service. Walking through the school, I saw myself on every wall and in every poster. I heard scholars addressed with dignity and encouraged to "be the boss of their brains" and "make strong choices." It was a feeling that was unfamiliar and unexpected. During the '90s, staff were required to have a certain number of college credits in African American studies, and even after that requirement was lifted, the staff at Dr. King remained predominantly Black and is today 95 percent Black.

Dr. King Jr. School offered me the remarkable experience of being an educator and being educated at the same time. As a Black student, I can say I rarely had teachers who looked like me or the chance to be surrounded by my own cultural history; my first Black teacher was when I was in high school. I never felt seen or reflected in the school culture or curriculum of any school I attended during my education. The feelings of hope, aspiration, self-determination, and joy I felt when I accepted the position at Dr. King Jr. marked an extraordinary turning point in my life.

I felt that same hope and optimism when I was first introduced to Black Lives Matter at School Week of Action. The movement is another, more recent example of helping Black students reach the educational heights they deserve. Like the immersion school where I work, the week of action provides Black students with an alternative to the traditional public school experience and curriculum.

A key breakthrough for teachers and students in Milwaukee occurred in 2015 when the school district passed a resolution in support of Black Lives Matter that called for a number of outcomes, including

> creating safe spaces, quality restorative justice practices, community and parent involvement, and involvement of student leaders of all types; discussions of biases, racial micro-aggressions, fears, cultural ignorance, and stereotypes of Black youth; discussions that lead to training of school staffs in methods of de-escalation, mindfulness, creating a culture of trust, and cultural relevance and reviewing and strengthening curriculum, and creating critical ethnic studies. [...] [B]ringing community into our schools and strengthening schools as centers of support for communities; and that the district review its programs that may be contributing to unfair, unequal power relationships with community and school policing.

Those of us in the Black Educators Caucus (a group of Black educators from Milwaukee Public Schools) leveraged that resolution to secure continued support from the district.

My first introduction to the week of action was as a member of the Milwaukee Teachers Union when our union voted to support a resolution to endorse Black Lives Matter at School Week of Action in 2017. The goal of the week—to center Black lives and experiences—resonated with the work that was happening at Dr. King Jr. School. As a rank-and-file member and organizer of the teachers union, I was provided an opportunity to attend the 2018 Labor Notes Conference. At the conference, I attended a session with the Philadelphia Black Lives Matter at School organizers and gained essential knowledge about grassroots organizing, curriculum sharing, and community events.

When I returned home from the Labor Notes Conference, I hit the ground running. As chair of the Black Educators Caucus, my group worked with the vice president of the Milwaukee school board and determined that the first week in February would be Black Lives Matter at School week across the district. The week became a resolution in Milwaukee Public Schools in November of 2018. A commitment by the board and district made this a reality in practice and policy.

The resolution called for an "advisory committee," which would provide access to educational materials and curriculum for students, staff, and district personnel, as well as plan and promote community events relevant to the week of action and the national demands. Our first year as a district BLM at School advisory committee, we engaged the community in a week's worth of events, including a panel discussion about our hopes for students in Milwaukee as well as the Black Lives Matter movement's national demands. We hosted a screening of the film *Talking Black in America* and engaged in rich discussions of Black language and vernacular. We hosted an intergenerational night, a social night, and a poetry and open mic night. We utilized our district-wide communication to provide access to the BLM at School week curriculum and created a pledge to participate that was made available to staff, students, family, and community members. It was a tremendous undertaking for our first year as a district; I recall the feeling of urgency and hope among the advisory committee while we planned and the pride we felt when the week was complete.

District buy-in was the key to making the week of action a rule across the district rather than just an event held in a few area schools. For me, getting involved at the national level was a critical part of our success in Milwaukee; it allowed me to see what was happening across the nation with the movement and develop strategies for implementation locally.

My new opportunity to learn

As a teacher, I know from experience that even very young children are interested in discussing race, identity, and colorism (discrimination based on skin tone). These issues aren't just abstract topics but real-life, daily concerns.

"Mrs. Harris, they being mean again," one of my scholars (let's call her Shamiah) yelled out in the classroom one day.

"Who is 'they' Shamiah, and what are they doing?" I asked.

"They saying I can't play cause I'm too Black." The scholars Shamiah was talking about were what some might describe as light-skinned; that is, they represent lighter shades of brown, and Shamiah is a darker shade of brown.

Another day, one of our scholars, Noel, confided that students in the class were calling her "white." Noel is Latinx.

"Mrs. Harris," she said, "tell them I'm not a white girl."

Black Lives Matter at School Week of Action gives all educators the time and space to tackle these and other conversations. As early childhood educators, we have a responsibility to lay a foundation for our students for what it means to be valued and to value others, and the period from K3 to second grade is when conversations about inclusion, diversity, expression, and justice should begin.

Even as young children, many of our students have burdens, trauma, and stories to tell. During my first full year educating at an African American immersion school and participating in Black Lives Matter at School Week of Action, I remember being pulled aside by students who, in a whisper, confided that a parent was, or had been, in jail. That week we took a walking field trip to Martin Luther King Jr. Library, which is right next door to the district police station, and the scholars were visibly frightened. There's a question we ask a lot in my classroom: "Is this hurting or helping?" As we walked back to school that day, I was bombarded with stories about how students felt the police hurt them instead of helping them. As a Black educator and early in my career, I knew I needed to create an environment where students felt that their lives and stories mattered. During that first week of action, we read books like *Mama Did You Hear the News?*, by Sanya Whittaker Gragg, in which parents talk to their young son about the police shooting of an unarmed

Black man, and *The Night Dad Went to Jail,* by Melissa Higgins, a story about the pain of having an incarcerated parent.

Some people feel that the early childhood years are too soon to talk about race, but these conversations are happening anyway, whether or not we like it. The idea that topics like race, racial justice, and Black Lives Matter at School are too complex to teach in early childhood years is often simply an excuse for educators to stray away from content and curriculum that moves beyond simplistic diversity in the early elementary years. But injustice is a lived experience for my scholars and for so many students of color around the nation. What kind of educators would we be if we didn't address issues that are central to the lives of our students?

The week of action became policy and practice in Milwaukee in 2018. However, well before this, the principles that shape the movement had been part of my practice. Creating a space where the lives, experiences, beliefs, attitudes, feelings, and opinions of Black students are centered is challenging even in the most progressive of environments. It creates a discomfort that many would rather avoid. My first full year in the classroom and planning for the week of action underscored for me why we have to persist—even with the discomfort. We have to be determined and hopeful when working with our schools and our districts. We have to meet people where they are, knowing that beloved community is not built overnight. Folks, especially educators in elementary grades, need to feel supported and know that they have the capacity and resources to teach on behalf of Black lives inside and outside of the classroom.

I matter. I'm worth it. My future has a purpose.

When we hosted the kick-off event for the BLM at School Week of Action at our school, every scholar, from kindergarten to eighth grade, participated in a school-wide chant, "I matter, I'm worth it, my future has a purpose." We spent that first day of the week of action talking about a topic that had come up many times in the classroom: the color of our skin.

As a class, we sat in a circle, and I asked the scholars if someone ever said something about how they look that made them feel bad, sad, or even angry. We recalled the times that Shamiah and Noel were singled out on the basis of their skin color, and we talked about how that made them feel. We read the story *Shades of Black,* by Sandra Pickney, and we drew self-portraits and wrote on the outside of the picture what others might see or assume about us, and on the inside we wrote the things that others may not see or know about us. We discussed as a class how colorism and prejudice affect us and how who we are on the outside may be different than who we are on the inside.

The book adaptation of Useni Eugene Perkins's poem "Hey Black Child" is a classroom staple. Perkins invites children to think about the strength, knowledge, and bravery that defines and empowers them. My scholars performed this poem at the Black Lives Matter at School kickoff event, and we recite it just about every day. Participating in the week of action is about reaffirming our Black students' identities and experiences. It's not just about telling them they matter but showing it. Our students need to believe in the excellence that we know exists inside all of us.

In my building, there is a beautiful mural filled with deep colors and an even deeper history of the African diaspora. The second day of the week of action is connected to the guiding principles of diversity and globalism. For both novice teachers and advanced educators alike, this day can and should be used to talk about a history that began prior to slavery. "I am Menes and Mansa Musa, Hannibal, Nefertiti, Queen Nzingha, Tubman, and Turner, and King," goes one of the lines of our school's scholar declaration. The goal of discussing diversity and globalism is to get scholars to realize that the excellence that exists inside them came from the ancestors who came before them. That day, we read *Young, Gifted, and Black* by Jamia Wilson and picked a different person to read about and add to our word wall. We ended the lesson talking about our greatness, our excellence. We used "Hey Black child, do you know who you are?" as a sentence starter for a journal prompt. Some of their responses included "I am Black girl magic," "I am brave, strong, and proud," and "I am a king and a ruler."

I am because we are

"I am because we are and because we are, therefore, I am," goes another line from our scholar declaration. At Dr. King Jr. School, we teach collective value—we are all connected. Along with Kingian values, we have a Kwanzaa principle of the month, Ujima. This Kwanzaa principle means collective work and responsibility. Our problems are connected, and the solutions to those problems are connected as well. There is an African proverb that states, "Sticks in a bundle are unbreakable." Our students are the sticks, and, as educators, we create the bundle.

On day three of the week of action, we read *Seven Spools of Thread*, by Angela Shelf Medearis. The story is about seven Ashanti brothers who fight all the time. Their father dies and leaves them seven spools of thread, which they must turn into gold to receive their inheritance. "What lesson did the father want the Ashanti bothers to learn?" I asked. "They should work together instead of fight," one scholar answered. "To not just help themselves, to help others," answered another. We made unity chains and each link was a unique design and a valued contribution to our chain.

Unapologetically Black is what Black students become when their lives are at the center of their educational experience. It is what they become when they see themselves in the pictures on the school walls, in the school culture, and most importantly in the curriculum. The book adaptation of the poem "My People," by Langston Hughes, is another staple in our classroom library, and it's the work I used to close the week of action last year. We listened to the poem and discussed Hughes's theme of the beauty of the Black people. Then I posed the question to my scholars: What other things are beautiful about our people?

The answers flowed freely that day on the carpet.

Photo collage created by Angela Harris for district professional development on Black Lives Matter at School Week of Action. Photos credit: Joe Brusky.

Frequently Asked Questions about the Week of Action

These responses to common questions about the purpose, value, and implementation of the Black Lives Matter Week of Action were created by teachers in New York City in 2018 and adapted by the Black Lives Matter National Steering Committee.

Justifications

Why is a week of action important right now?

Black Lives Matter is currently in the news. Most students are aware, to some degree, of this movement. Addressing this in the classroom is acknowledging an important current events topic. Bringing issues of racial justice into the classroom not only affirms the identities of our students but is crucial to fostering critical engagement with the world—regardless of where you, your students, and their families stand on the issues.

As an educator, I have way too much to do already. Why do I need to add something else to that list?

Informational reading and argumentative and informational writing are a part of the national standards. These materials and content will add a topical and inclusive element to the lessons you already need to teach. In addition to teaching students these required skills, it is important for us to work with students to understand and analyze the world around them. Also, many of the resources we offer can be used as short activities, if that better fits the needs of your classroom.

How does this curriculum relate to Common Core?

Close reading of informational texts and critical writing of argumentative and informational texts are important parts of the Common Core standards. The texts we provide lend themselves to analytical reading and critical writing.

I'm not sure if my grade group / teachers in my department would be on board with this. How do I explain to them why I am participating / wearing this shirt?

Start by sharing this FAQ and curriculum ideas. (Lesson plan idea are available on the Black Lives Matter at School website). Explain to them, from your heart and mind, why making room for learning about Black Lives Matter this week is important to you and your students. Create a space where you can listen and talk, as a group or in pairs.

What if my principal tells me to take off the shirt or button and not teach this to my students?

The goal of BLM week is awareness and discussion, not political agitation. You are the best judge of your school environment and what, if anything, needs to be put in front of your administration ahead of time. As you plan your week with fellow educators, use your collective knowledge of the climate in your building to figure out what actions will encourage engagement without pushing people away. You will have the support of educators everywhere who are working to organize.

Purpose

What place does Black Lives Matter have in my daily curriculum?

Integrating culturally diverse opinions into your daily curriculum allows students to gain a deeper understanding of pertinent issues affecting our students and their classmates. The principles associated with Black Lives Matter highlight the historical exclusion of BIPOC and the recognition of the value of human life regardless of racial and gender identity. Also, the thirteen guiding principles of Black Lives Matter define a multifaceted approach to justice that can create the conditions for improving relations between people of different races. The lessons and activities that we are offering for teachers to use fit directly into Common Core State Standards (CCSS). CCSS encourages the use of rigorous and complex texts, with the practice of certain standards to use with such texts. We encourage teachers to look through the folders of recommended resources (available under "Lesson Plans" on the Black Lives Matter at School website) and see which ones would fit this criteria as well as the focus standards that they are currently on based upon the "Standards Map" for the second quarter.

Is this material age appropriate for my students?

Issues of equity and fairness are important in all aspects of all our lives, and in each of our classrooms. Having students of all ages discuss and process these deep issues at their own level, using grade-appropriate materials, strengthens their critical thinking abilities and provides them with the opportunity to be fully engaged learners.

Implementation

I'm an elementary teacher, and I'm not used to openly raising issues of race in my classroom. What are some

actions I can take and what kinds of materials can be helpful?

Does your classroom have students of more than one race? Do your instructional materials include people of different races? Are you a different race than some (or all) of your students? If any of these are true—and likely all are—then issues of race are already present in your classroom. You can raise awareness about this omnipresent aspect of our society without triggering conflict or anxiety in your students. Take a look at some of our elementary-specific resources to find a lesson that suits your environment.

I don't know how to do this in a big way. What is one small thing I can do?

There are many small, manageable ways to get involved—from wearing a button or T-shirt to journal prompts and discussions to class period–length lessons, to planning a school-wide event that invites in students, educators, and families.

Can I integrate this into my teaching beyond the week?

Absolutely! One of the goals is to provide deeper connections between educators, parents, students, and community organizations. We encourage you to use these materials, resources, and ideas throughout the school year.

How can I get my colleagues on board with this at my school? How can I reach out to parents and get them on board?

The best way to get anyone on board is through conversation—encourage all parties to ask and answer questions. When talking with colleagues, encourage them to consider that these are issues that affect the majority of our students on a daily basis. Teachers and parents share the common goal of helping our children navigate the difficult conversations that they will inevitably confront in this world. Reach out to parent networks in your school and let them know what your building is planning. Consider holding an informational picket, sharing information with parents in the morning before school starts.

What are my rights when teaching materials that some parents might find inappropriate?

Many items that teachers include in their curriculum are considered controversial. That is one of our jobs as educators: to raise our students' awareness of issues that affect the world around them and to help them consider potential solutions. If you are concerned that parents will object to a topic you will be teaching, then write a letter home and explain your goals in teaching the material. Use responses from this FAQ to help jump-start your letter.

How can I prepare young students and their families for discussion of sensitive topics?

Think of writing a letter that you will send home to parents. Inform them of the topics you will be discussing and the reasons why they will be included in the curriculum.

I teach math and science. How can I integrate racial justice into my teaching?

There are a lot of ways to integrate justice-driven curriculum into science and math lessons. Science and math are based on problem-solving, research, and use of numbers to understand the world. Ways to incorporate this content into math pedagogy can be found in the text *Rethinking Mathematics: Teaching Social Justice by the Numbers*. You can use numbers and maps to look at the impacts of housing discrimination, low minimum wage, and the school-to-prison pipeline. You can ask your students to think about ways to solve deep social problems. How can we reduce the number of losses of life to police violence? What are ways to end deep poverty? In science class, we learn about the world by asking questions that can be solved with research questions and materials. What questions do students have about healthcare? What are the innovations and inventions that we can design?

It's also possible to take time out of math and science class to talk about how students are doing and feeling about the world around them. If we view students as humans first and learners second, it's possible to see value in carving out necessary time to engage with our kids around the work of social change, organizing, and building power in the world that we live in.

In my classroom, students are from different communities and racial backgrounds. How should I approach this?

Every time we plan a lesson, we make choices about which perspectives, cultures, histories, and experiences we want to present. No lesson we teach will ever fully encompass the personal experiences of all of our students. Instead, our goal as educators should be to choose content that is relevant, meaningful, important, and thought provoking for our students. The Black Lives Matter movement meets these criteria. It is a major current events issue with roots throughout American history, a topic many students have been exposed to (often without context), and a defining social movement of our time. It is also an opportunity to introduce vital conversations about topics such as empathy, discrimination, activism, privilege, and public policy.

Isn't it my job is to expose students to different viewpoints, not take sides in the classroom?

Indeed! This is a great opportunity to design lessons that encourage thoughtful discussion and formation of informed opinions. We also want to point out that not addressing these issues in the classroom is a political statement, one that students can pick up on.

I do not feel like my principal would be okay with me participating, but I'm totally down with this cause. What are other ways I can get involved?

If you do not feel safe to participate fully in this campaign, there is an incredible amount of important work to do. Finding time to have conversations about racial justice, the Black Lives Matter movement, and other issues with your co-workers is invaluable. Building strong relationships and organizing in your building can be very helpful in dealing with a tough principal.

I'm afraid of retribution from parents and students. How can I explain what we're doing in a way that they won't feel threatened and will be supportive?
Let your students and parents know that you are doing this to encourage critical thinking and awareness of current event issues that are directly impacting all of us. Also, allow them to voice their concerns and ask them plenty of questions. Read through this page—many of the FAQs can be helpful.

Pushback

Isn't this too emotionally stressful for students? Can we really open up a sensitive conversation when we can't devote legitimate time to covering this issue?
Students are confronting these issues on a daily basis in the world at large. It's our obligation and role as teachers to create safe environments for our students to process tough issues. Helping students begin the conversation by framing their feelings and questions is the first step toward them identifying their own values and worldview regarding these tough issues.

As a teacher who is married to a police officer, I am not down with Black Lives Matter. Isn't this just about Black rage at the police?
The police are also victims of our society's push toward mass incarceration and underfunded schools and social services. What we're all dealing with is a systemic breakdown that leads to increased violence across the system. Policing is just a tiny part of what we're talking about—so let's start the discussion. Check out all thirteen guiding principles of Black Lives Matter as a starting point.

Isn't Black Lives Matter racist against white people?
Black Lives Matter helps us to analyze the quality of life for marginalized groups in our society—groups who happen to make up the majority of students in many of our urban schools.

Though these conversations can sometimes be provocative, bringing up these conversations strengthens our community. Relationships deepen in the process, and hidden truths become sites of understanding.

As a white teacher, I feel like it's not my place to have conversations about Black Lives Matter, police shootings, and related topics in my classroom with students of color.

This is a conversation for everyone. Everyone has a right to understand the historical context that has led to this moment. If this is something you would want your own child to know, then your students, too, will understand that this comes from an authentic place. And remember—choosing not to have these conversations is also making a stance. If you're not ready to wear a shirt or teach a lesson at this point, that's Okay. However, we are asking you to be willing to engage in this important conversation about racial justice.

The Black Lives Matter message is already embedded in the way I teach—everyone is valued. So why set aside time for one group of people and not others?

That's so important! But this is not about respect and kindness. This is about unpacking your backpack of privilege with your students, which will help them understand their own identities and how that shapes our society. Relying on "colorblind" rhetoric around kindness and tolerance only perpetuates the issues at hand and does nothing to challenge structural racism and white supremacy.

CHAPTER 17

Higher Education Organizing for the Week of Action

An Interview with Anthony Dandridge and Kiersten Greene*

Screenshot of the SUNY New Paltz Library website page containing a research guide for Black Lives Matter at School.

Denisha Jones: What is your name? Where do you teach? What do you teach? Feel free to include information on your degree.

Anthony Dandridge: My name is Anthony Dandridge, and I teach

---

* Denisha Jones conducted this interview with State University of New York at New Paltz professors Anthony Dandridge and Kiersten Greene on Monday, February 10, 2020.

undergraduate students in the Department of Black Studies at State University of New York at New Paltz. Established in 1969, Black Studies at New Paltz is one of the oldest such departments in history. The discipline itself was the first to be established in accordance with the grassroots protest struggles of the masses. That unique designation continues to frame its objectives and legitimacy in a variety of ways that in part complement those same challenges that people of African descent continue to endure globally. Generally, the teaching we participate in is centered within the very human and intellectual contributions of people of African descent. The primary focuses of my courses are the overlapping fields of culture, politics, history, art, religion, and philosophy. Some courses I have taught are Introduction to Black Studies, Black History, Race and Racism in US History, and History of Black Political Thought. I hold a bachelor's degree in philosophy, a master's degree in African American studies, and am currently ABD in my PhD in Africology and African American studies.

Kiersten Greene: My name is Kiersten Greene, and I also teach at SUNY New Paltz. I educate aspiring teachers in the Department of Teaching and Learning, and I primarily teach literacy education teaching methods to undergraduate and graduate students seeking teacher certification in early childhood and childhood education. I most often teach classes in how to teach reading and writing, as well as education technology. I hold a master's degree in early childhood and elementary school and a PhD in urban education, and prior to seeking a career in higher education, I taught photography at a residential treatment center in Yonkers, New York, and then taught third and fifth grade and was a literacy coach at an elementary school in New York City.

Denisha: How did you each first learn about the Black Lives Matter at School Week of Action?

Anthony: I have participated in these struggles on many levels, as I have been aware of those issues that have impacted people of African descent almost my entire life, primarily because I am Black. I first learned of the Black Lives Matter at School Week of Action in November of 2017 when I attended a conference in Philadelphia at MLK High School on

Philly students and Black Lives Matter. After I accepted an appointment in Black Studies at New Paltz in the fall of 2018, I was made aware of the growth of the movement on campus by Kiersten, a newly found friend and member of the Critical Pedagogy Study Group I had recently joined.

Kiersten: I have been an antiracist union activist and community organizer for the last twenty or so years and have been following the work of Jesse Hagopian and Wayne Au for a while now; therefore, I heard about Black Lives Matter at School at its inception. In summer 2018, I had the opportunity to hear Jesse and Wayne speak about their experiences at a gathering of socialist activists in Chicago, and during that discussion, we talked briefly about bringing the K–12 effort into higher education, and especially into schools and colleges of education. That fall, I connected with other scholars and practitioners bringing BLM at School to their campuses and worked with my colleague Michael Smith (now at The College of New Jersey), and Anthony to plan several events during the 2019 national BLM at School Week of Action.

Denisha: What made you decide to organize the week of action at an institution for higher education?

Anthony: Given that a significant objective of Black studies is social change, I have consistently sought out spaces to engage in the long tradition in which this work has expressed itself. Whether it is the classroom, conference, faculty meeting, or lunch line, we need situations and opportunities where we can challenge unjustifiably incomplete narratives of human inquiry. In deciding to extend this movement to SUNY New Paltz, I knew there would be resistance, but I understood the benefits to the lives of all our students, faculty, administration, and global community.

Kiersten: As a white teacher educator and antiracist activist who teaches future and current teachers about literacy education, I am constantly looking for ways to connect the socio-political, historical, and economic underpinnings of education to the teaching of reading and writing. Literacy educators, generally, are often perceived as acritical and disconnected from the theoretical foundations of education, and I actively work to push back at this dominant narrative. I see dismantling racism as inextricably linked to the labor of teaching and firmly believe it is incumbent upon all educators, and especially white educators, to examine how racism is either resisted or reproduced in the classroom through pedagogy and curriculum. Establishing Black Lives Matter at School at SUNY New Paltz was a logical extension of this work. Initially, I hoped that the School of Education would embrace BLM at School programming, but in the fall of 2019, BLM at School planning quickly evolved into a wide and deep cross-campus effort that stretched far beyond the School of Education—largely due to our collective efforts, and especially those of Anthony and my colleague Laura Arias. At present, our planning committee is comprised of forty-five students, staff, faculty, and community members of the SUNY New Paltz campus community.

Denisha: Describe the events you organized for the week of action at your school. Were they successful? Why or why not?

Anthony: We have had multiple events in 2019 and 2020 at SUNY New Paltz. In 2019, we had three events during the week, and in 2020 that has expanded to fourteen or more events throughout the month.[1] There's an extensive history of attempts to reduce the impact of racism in our educational institutions, as well as a parallel history of resistance to these efforts. Hosting events like the week of action is key. SUNY New Paltz, while not a bastion for Black lives, has definitely maintained an evolving, progressive disposition toward dismantling racism.

Kiersten: To build on what Anthony shared, in February 2019, we held a roundtable discussion of James Baldwin's "A Talk to Teachers," a screening of the documentary *Teach Us All*, and the fifth installment of Continuing the Conversation: Talking About Race and Racism in the Classroom, a series of conversations on our campus led by Carolyn Corrado in the Department of Sociology. The Baldwin roundtable was attended by a small group of students, staff, and faculty members. The documentary screening was a mistake in retrospect, and thus an opportunity to learn. I had watched parts of the film but hadn't watched to the end, where you quickly realize it ends by reinforcing the white savior narrative. We had a disappointing turnout—only about three people showed up to the screening, but it led to a critical discussion of what the film had exposed about the inequity that charter schools reinforce, and what solutions educators and community activists might offer in contrast. The 2019 Continuing the Conversation roundtable attendance was the largest our campus had seen for that event, exceeding one hundred attendees. So far, we have hosted two events in 2020, and both were extremely well attended. On February 4, we held a panel discussion called Black Struggle for Justice: Past, Present, and Future and heard the stories and lived experiences of BIPOC who have been fighting for justice on our campus since the 1960s. On February 6, we hosted the sixth installment of Continuing the Conversation, this time with a focus on antiracism in the classroom. We have a series of events—roundtables, art exhibits, cross-campus forums, and more planned for February 24–28.

Denisha: What are your long-term goals for organizing the week of action at your school?

Anthony: At minimum, because we would like to maintain the social, political, and cultural capital that has been gained by the current intellectual engagements of Black Lives Matter at SUNY New Paltz, we would like to expand these efforts into the future. Not unlike the establishment of Negro History Week by Carter G. Woodson as a week during the year where one highlights the work that has been learned and done throughout the year, our goals include the year-round institutional acceptance of these efforts.

Kiersten: Our campus community has engaged in multiple public discussions over the last several years about diversity, equity, and inclusion, and Black Lives Matter at School has united many participants in those discussions in an active way. As Anthony mentioned, our collective hope is to continue the conversation and planning long after February 2020. We will continue to bring events, discussions, and solutions to our campus in a way that explicitly marries theory with practice. We have talked about establishing ourselves as a cross-campus community organization that meets year-round and plan to strategize for how to do so in our upcoming meetings.

CHAPTER 18

White Educators for Black Lives

By Rosie Frascella, B. Kaiser, Brian Ford, and Jeff Stone

"If you put a chain around the neck of a slave," wrote Ralph Waldo Emerson, "the other end fastens itself around your own." Emerson was the author of a number of anti-slavery essays, but he also expressed racist ideas elsewhere in his writing, most notably in *English Traits*. Emerson is an example of the tension we hold as white people: espousing abolitionist, antiracist views (and acting on them), while at the same time retaining internalized racist ideas absorbed from a racist society. Emerson's words additionally capture how white folks in a racist society are themselves not free. Just as patriarchy harms men, racism and anti-Blackness constrain the minds of white people, leading them to invest in the idea of their supposed whiteness, which is really just a relationship to power. To live in a world that upholds whiteness and white supremacy is to be unfree.

Similar to the Marxist belief that universalizing the interests of the working class liberates all people, those of us who identify as white antiracists believe that our own liberation is tied up in that of Black, Indigenous, and people of color (BIPOC). This liberation is of the mind, yes, but it also has material benefits. In "A Herstory of the #BlackLivesMatter

Movement," Black Lives Matter co-founder Alicia Garza reminds us:

> When we are able to end hyper-criminalization and sexualization of Black people and end the poverty, control, and surveillance of Black people, every single person in this world has a better shot at getting and staying free. When Black people get free, everybody gets free. This is why we call on Black people and our allies to take up the call that Black lives matter.

The idea that the liberation of Black people liberates us all is a core tenet of Black Lives Matter and is at the center of our involvement in the Black Lives Matter at School Week of Action. This is not white savior charity work but a commitment to our collective freedom. For the four of us, this work takes place primarily in school—in teaching, in organizing, in curriculum development, and through participating in the week of action.

> *I am not in a classroom. Instead, I worked from my district's central office as a curriculum lead. Together with Black educators and Brown and Indigenous co-conspirators, we ran planning meetings with teachers, para-educators, families, and students to discuss and plan the week of action. Together we worked to try to center Black lives for this one week in the hopes that Black lives, Black history, and Black realities would be taught in our classes and found in our schools every day. —Jeff*

What does it mean to be a white organizer for Black Lives Matter at School Week of Action?

For us, the thirteen guiding principles of the movement have been invaluable, allowing us to honor the ways that Black and Indigenous people have been fighting for the ideals of this country from its inception. They also highlight the ways in which white supremacy, patriarchy, and capitalism have marginalized, oppressed, and terrorized all those who live under their grasp. None of us will be free until these systems are destroyed. We must be co-conspirators in this work, which means being will to be uncomfortable, take risks, and lose our privilege in order to truly dismantle white supremacy. To fail to do so is to cause harm to our students and ourselves.

In addition, as white people, we cannot shy away from discussing the role of white people in the construction of this brutal, violent, and oppressive nation. When words or actions are racist, sexist, classist, heteronormative, or ableist, we must call them out. As Ibram X. Kendi explains, the term "racist" is not pejorative; rather, it is an adjective that describes a behavior. If we can name and identify racist behaviors when they occur, we will learn and grow in the process. As educators, we challenge the idea of "neutrality" in the classroom. There is nothing neutral about a white person teaching a class almost entirely comprised of BIPOC. Our educational system has a *real* impact on students of color—from its curriculum, policies, and teaching force—and this impact is nowhere near neutral. If we truly care about understanding and honoring our students, we have to bring those realities into our teaching.

When we first started organizing the Black Lives Matter at School national movement, I was participating in the national steering committee. While brainstorming the national demands with others, I took up a lot of space in the conversation, sure that I knew what to do. This is part of white supremacy culture—the assumption that I, a white person, know what Black people need. My comrade called me in about it, and we had a real conversation. In that meeting, my behavior had been racist. I owned it and reach out to the person I had harmed, letting me rectify the situation and grow as a white ally. Then the national steering committee created a core of Black leaders to center Black voices and maintain the fidelity of the movement. My role as a white person was not to speak on behalf of Black people but rather to listen, learn, and support the leadership of Black educators, parents, and students. —Rosie

Co-conspiracy and our unions

Another important way that white co-conspirators can work alongside Black educators to promote the week of action is through our unions. Like the United States itself, our teachers unions were founded upon and continue to sustain white supremacy and anti-Black systems of power. To disrupt these oppressive systems, we recognize the need for unions to listen to Black voices of leadership and guidance, and to organize around their demands and visions for educational justice.

As critical white co-conspirators, we have sought to follow the leadership of the Black educators in our unions. Collectively, this has included serving in support roles on Black-led week of action planning committees, asking permission from Black union leaders to promote the week of action, proposing union endorsements, and working to encourage and support hesitant white teachers. Most importantly, we've learned that there are times when doing and saying nothing is the most appropriate action to take.

Yet, there are times when we do need to speak up. Across our unions, one of the common barriers to supporting the week of action has been the desire to avoid "divisiveness." There is a fear that by affirming Black lives, the union's ability to cast a wide net will be diminished. This is a misguided attempt to be palatable to white teachers at the expense of owning any real commitment to justice. We need to recognize when this is happening and speak out! Failure to do so is to perpetuate the very anti-Blackness we are seeking to disrupt.

At my school, student government begins brainstorming ideas for the week of action, and then teachers and staff plan backwards from the students' goals. Last year, some students decided to march across the Williamsburg Bridge from our school in Brooklyn to the citywide protest on the steps of the school chancellor's office. I don't believe that this march could have possibly been a success if it had been my idea: imagine a typical middle schooler's response if they were told to walk almost three miles in February for the sake of activism! But my students, like most young people, have an ingrained sense of justice and injustice, and they don't need me or any white teacher to give them a voice. All they needed was a chaperone. —Kaiser

What does this work look like in your classroom/school/workspace?

To do justice to the Black Lives Matter at School Week of Action, it cannot just last a week. The foundation and wisdom must live in our curriculum, our professional development, and our student groups. Simply put, to be antiracist at school means to actively and continually interrogate our curriculum, pedagogical practices, and our social engagement. We must create sustained spaces where educators, staff, and administrators can have conversations about the ways anti-Black racism shows up in our school community and policies. Listening is key. We recognize that BIPOC—whether students, educators, or parents and community members—are the experts on the experience of white supremacy in contemporary society. This means that their voices should be at the center of the conversation.

Solidarity with Migrant Families at the Border

The Black Lives Matter at School movement is organized around combating anti-Blackness in education. But we also know that Black liberation is bound together with the liberation of all other oppressed people. For that reason, when we learned of the Trump administration's policies separating families at the border and keeping little children away from their parents, we had to speak out. We were moved to support the Teach-In for Freedom on Sunday, February 17, 2019, at San Jacinto Plaza in El Paso, Texas. Teachers against Child Detention, a coalition launched by 2018 National Teacher of the Year Mandy Manning and other educators, organized the effort.

The teach-in featured lessons by more than thirty teachers from the United States and Mexico on US immigration policy and its impact on children. Members of Black Lives Matter at School traveled to El Paso in solidarity and to concretize the connection between Black and Brown people. BLM at School organizer Erika Strauss Chavarria delivered the following statement at the Teach-In for Freedom.

The Trump administration's "zero tolerance" policy of separating migrant children from their families at the border is cruel and inhuman. The US government has admitted to separating 2,700 children from their families and a recent Health and Human Services report indicates that there could even be thousands more.[1]

This gross injustice has prompted the national Black Lives Matter at School coalition to stand in solidarity with the Teach-In for Freedom, hosted by Teachers against Child Detention, and their demands of the US government for the immediate release of all immigrant children in US government custody and to shut down all immigrant detention centers housing immigrant children. On February 17, 2019, hundreds of educators from all over the country will raise their voices against the racist detention of refugee and immigrant children at the US border and the separation of children from their parents. We encourage all educators to join them on the border or teach lessons about the rights of immigrants and refugees in their own classrooms.

Educators will gather in the historic San Jacinto Plaza in El Paso, Texas, to teach lessons about the current impact and trauma of child detention as well as the history of immigration and child detention. We applaud the efforts of educators, their unions, faith-based organizations, and immigrant rights organizations in forming the alliance Teachers against Child Detention.

In addition, we believe their work in many ways overlaps with the struggles of the Black Lives Matter at School movement. Trump's rhetoric of "zero tolerance" on the border mirrors the "zero tolerance discipline" policies in schools that have led to a spike in suspension and expulsion rates—disproportionately impacting Black and Brown students. Zero tolerance discipline, then, contributes to the school-to-prison pipeline, which fuels the racist system of mass incarceration. The explosion in the prison population, or what Michelle Alexander calls "the New Jim Crow," rips apart African American families and separates Black children from their parents. In a June 2018 article, "Family Separation: It's a Problem for US Citizens Too," the *New York Times* estimated that 250,000 American children have a single mother in jail with another 150,000 having a mother in prison.[2] One in four Black children will have their father incarcerated before they turn fourteen. And it's not just Black parents who are incarcerated and then separated from their children—Black children are also over-policed and jailed. Some 30,000 youth are imprisoned in juvenile jails across the country, and Black children are imprisoned at a rate five times higher than white children.[3]

The movement for immigrant rights and the Black Lives Matter at School movement are both strengthened when we work together in common cause to stop the unjust detention and incarceration of all Black and Brown youth. We urge all educators around the country to support these movements and stand in solidarity with Teachers against Child Detention when they say:

WE BELIEVE

All children deserve to be in school.

All children deserve to be free.

We demand the release of our children.[4]

CHAPTER 19

The Week of Action Goes from Philadelphia Schools to Higher Education

*An Interview with Dana Morrison**

Denisha Jones: What is your name? What do you teach? Feel free to include information about your degree.

Dana Morrison: My name is Dana Morrison, and I am an assistant professor at West Chester University of Pennsylvania. I teach in the Department of Educational Foundations; more specifically, I teach philosophy and history of education, as well as education policy. I received a PhD in education from the University of Delaware where I specialized in socio-cultural and community-based approaches to education.

Denisha: How did you first learn about the Black Lives Matter at School Week of Action?

---

* Denisha Jones held this interview with West Chester University of Pennsylvania education professor Dana Morrison on February 16, 2020.

Dana: I learned about the Black Lives Matter at School Week of Action through friends and colleagues who were involved in Philadelphia's Caucus of Working Educators. In the first year, I shared articles highlighting the week with my students, who are mostly preservice teachers. We talked about the week of action as an example of critical pedagogy's commitment to making the pedagogical more political and what it might mean for teachers, students, parents, and communities—particularly teachers, students, parents and communities of color. A few months later I began working with teacher organizers in Philadelphia for my dissertation research. Many of these teachers were founders of the week of action and shared their experiences and commitments to racial justice in my fieldwork.

Denisha: What made you decide to organize the week of action at an institution for higher education?

Dana: Toward the end of my dissertation data collection I became actively involved with these teachers in coordinating outreach to local Philadelphia colleges and universities. At a citywide organizing meeting for the 2018 week of action, I facilitated a discussion with higher education faculty and graduate students about how we could get involved. This initial group of ten to twelve people grew to about thirty and spanned numerous institutions in the Philadelphia area, including the University of Pennsylvania, LaSalle, Swarthmore, West Chester University, and the Community College of Philadelphia. This initial work brought together educators of all levels around a common concern, racial justice. It re-centered my commitments as a critical educator and built relationships with other teachers in ways I never thought possible.

I often think back to a statement from one of my professors at the University of Delaware, Dr. Yasser Payne. He said that his primary goal in doing justice-oriented participatory action research was to bring the resources of the university to the community. I'm continually motivated by this analysis and see organizing for the week of action in higher education as a way to realign the university with its utopian purpose— serving the community. Particularly as a white educator, I organize each year to use whatever power I have to wield the university's resources for racial justice.

Denisha: Describe the events you organized for the week of action at your school. Were they successful?

Dana: This year we organized an antiracist training facilitated by educators from BAR-WE, a nationwide learning community seeking to Build Antiracist White Educators. This event was attended by over fifty preservice teachers and faculty at West Chester University, our most well-attended event to date. We succeeded by reaching out to colleagues and classes that would benefit from participating in such an event. When our university-wide organizing committee began planning back in September, one of the first things students recognized was the "work" that needed to be done regarding racism in our teacher education programs. Students of color recounted problematic conversations they'd had with white peers who planned on becoming teachers. This event was an important step, but just the first of many steps we need to take. That's why the Black Lives Matter at School Week of Action is such a critical movement. It provides a blueprint for racial justice work and a growing network of educators to support that work long term.

Denisha: What are your long-term goals for organizing the week of action at your school?

Dana: I want to bring more students and faculty into the planning of the week of action. At West Chester University we've been lucky enough to have some amazing Black students envision and direct our work, but those students are graduating! Looking to what folks in Philly and New York and other locales have accomplished, we need to grow a real community coalition of students, staff, and faculty to make sure this work has a lasting impact on our campus.

Flyer for West Chester University open mic, February 6, 2019. Image credit: Organizing committee, BLM Week of Action, West Chester University.

CHAPTER 20

The Black Lives Matter at School Pedagogy

Affirming Black Lives, Resisting Neoliberal Reform, and Reimagining Education for Liberation

By Denisha Jones

> *Let's begin by saying that we are living through a very dangerous time. Everyone in this room is in one way or another aware of that. We are in a revolutionary situation, no matter how unpopular that word has become in this country.... To any citizen of this country who figures himself responsible—and particularly those of you who deal with the minds and hearts of young people—must be prepared to "go for broke." Or to put it another way, you must understand that in the attempt to correct so many generations of bad faith and cruelty, when it is operating not only in the classroom but in society, you will meet the most fantastic, the most brutal, and the most determined resistance. There is no point in pretending that this won't happen.*
>
> —James Baldwin, "A Talk to Teachers,"
> reprinted in *Teaching for Black Lives*

Black Lives Matter Week of Action calendar of events for Philadelphia schools, 2017. Screenshot of a Facebook post by Denisha Jones.

I first heard of the Black Lives Matter at School Week of Action from a social media post in January 2017 from the Caucus of Working Educators in Philadelphia. The group shared a calendar of events for the week of action with principles for each day of the week; links to elementary, middle, and high school curriculum materials; and a list of activities and events. As I clicked on the links and reviewed the many resources, I immediately noticed how the lessons differed from traditional approaches to teaching Black history and the struggle for racial justice. Using the Black Lives Matter guiding principles as a foundation, the lessons shifted the usual focus from slavery and Civil Rights to affirming all Black Lives and uplifting those who engaged in past struggles and continue to fight for freedom.

Inspired by their labor, I reached out to members of WE through their Facebook page and asked them to submit a proposal to the Free Minds, Free People Conference in Baltimore, Maryland, in July 2017. At that gathering, we learned more about efforts to create the first week of action from presenters Kendra Brooks, Shira Cohen, Kelley Collings, Ismael Jimenez, and Shaw MacQueen. It was there that the national Black Lives Matter at School movement began.

As discussed througout this book, the week of action combines teaching the thirteen guiding principles and promoting the movement's national demands with a series of lessons and events throughout the week and beyond. As the movement grows and we hear about the challenges, struggles, and joys that those in participating cities are encountering, I am reminded that we who do this work are engaged in something truly new. Ours is a transformative, culturally relevant pedagogy that goes beyond the simple call to support "diversity" or promote "color-blind" ideologies but instead asks students to affirm Blackness in all its forms and to work collectively against anti-Blackness. Our pedagogy demands that this country finally recognize that Black lives do and should matter.

As an early childhood teacher educator and education justice advocate, I've long recognized the dangers of teaching Black children about their history through the lens of a single story. When I taught kindergarten in Washington, DC, I was committed to not teaching the history of the enslavement of African people as the genesis of Black history. Though #BlackLivesMatter had not yet formed in 2003, I was aware that the way public education presented Black history worked to reinforce Black inferiority and denied Black people's agency. I chose instead to focus on Black inventors and the idea that we can create new things that people across the world can use to improve their lives. This was a valuable corrective to the standard pedagogy, but it was not enough to ensure that all children learned a version of Black history that humanized the Black experience and invited them to engage in collective social action.

There has been a push to develop culturally relevant pedagogy and culturally responsive curriculums, which are increasingly regarded in the field of teacher education as requirements for preparing effective teachers. The earlier work of theorists Gloria Ladson-Billings and Geneva Gay called for a shift from blaming Black students for not succeeding in a Eurocentric system to creating an environment that allowed them to successfully navigate the educational demands of schooling and maintain their cultural competence.[1] Today, we see the continuation of that work in the contributions of contemporary scholars. Christopher Emdin, for example, seeks to dispel the perception of Black youth as unteachable and asks educators to engage in "reality pedagogy," which positions students as experts in their own realities and learning.[2] Bettina L. Love urges educators to identify teaching practices that manifest white privilege and lead to the spirit-murdering of Black children; she envisions abolitionist teaching as a tool to heal, protect, and liberate Black minds.[3] Jamila Lyiscott urges educators to adopt learning strategies that take action against inequities and racial injustice.[4] Those who teach the curriculum during the week of action enact a Black Lives Matter at School pedagogy connected to the historical push for culturally relevant teaching and representative of the current social movements and challenges to public education. The Black Lives Matter at School pedagogy affirms Black lives, resists neoliberal reforms, and presents a vision of education for liberation.

Affirming Black lives

In a review of the book *Teaching for Black Lives*, I suggested that teachers must recognize how traditional approaches to teaching Black history maintain anti-Blackness and white supremacy. The narratives of the happy and obedient slave, the respectable heroes of the civil rights movement, and the magical Negroes of today are offered up as examples of "good" Black people (i.e., Oprah Winfrey, Michael Jordan, and Barack Obama) and present a monolithic stereotype of Black people. The editors of the handbook resist such stereotypes by, in their words, "not only providing educators with critical perspectives on the role of schools in perpetuating anti-Blackness, but also by offering educators concrete examples of what it looks like to humanize Black people in curriculum, teaching, and policy."[5] In my review of the book, I praised *Teaching for Black Lives* as a vital tool for aiding in critical race pedagogy.[6] My only concern was that we need a version of the book geared toward educating young children. Most of the lessons portrayed in the book were from middle and high school teachers. We need resources that affirm Black lives in the early years so children can grow up prepared to respond to the historical assault on Black lives in the United States and around the world.

Before children learn about the enslavement of Africans, they must learn about Black villages, Black families, and the work of sustaining intergenerational networks. Before children are taught about emancipation and the Civil War, they must learn how restorative justice, empathy, and loving engagement are grounded in the work of those who have fought and continue to fight for Black people to be free. Before children celebrate Dr.

King and Rosa Parks, they must learn to respect all Black lives through the principles of trans affirming, queer affirming, and collective value. Before children come to know about the African transatlantic slave trade, they must learn how the continent of Africa birthed the rich diversity that is the global Black family. Before children can recite Dr. King's "I Have a Dream" speech, they must learn the joys of being unapologetically Black and honoring Black women.

The Black Lives Matter at School pedagogy is grounded in affirmations of Black lives that allow all children, but especially Black children, to develop a love and appreciation for Blackness. The creation of language for discussing the guiding principles for young children and the lists of age-appropriate books and activities are examples of how the movement's pedagogy lays the groundwork needed to enact a culturally relevant curriculum in the early years.

Resisting neoliberal reform

As Jesse Hagopian notes in Chapter 1, liberatory education often grows from the struggles for freedom that Black people have carried out in the United States and globally. Oppressive societies have used education to hinder the growth and development of oppressed peoples, thus making education a necessary tool for liberation. The growth of neoliberal ideologies and policies fueled the push for marketization and privatization within public education. Marketization is the practice of making the educational arena a more competitive environment where educational consumers (students and parents) have greater choice and control.[7] Privatization allows for businesses to provide those "consumers" new educational options under the mantra of school choice. The demand for choice offers a fertile opportunity for the growth of charter schools and vouchers to displace local governments as the only source of public education.

Although the impact of neoliberal reforms in education goes beyond Black children and families, the policies crafted to spread these ideas begin in Black communities. Cities with predominantly Black populations are the first to have public schools closed and turned into charter schools. Legislation that gives vouchers to low-income families to use in private schools is mandated in majority-Black cities like Washington, DC, by lawmakers who could not get similar bills passed in their own mostly white communities. Test-based accountability increases the use of high-stakes standardized testing to punish students and teachers, which disproportionately affects Black students, who remain on the losing end of the manufactured achievement gap. Thus, neoliberal reforms entrenched in white supremacy and anti-Black oppression pose specific challenges to the education of Black children.

Educators committed to racial justice utilize their pedagogy and the curriculum to resist neoliberal reforms that exacerbate the multiple adverse outcomes awaiting Black children in public education. The Black Lives Matter at School pedagogy expands the traditional narrow curriculum and fosters critical thinking and engagement in children often assumed to be "unteachable." At the heart of the movement's pedagogy is a curriculum that asks students to view the world through a critical racial and economic lens. By focusing on contemporary examples of Black community organizing and Black-led challenges to white supremacy, and by analyzing the role of schools in providing transformative justice, this pedagogy resists the hegemonic neoliberal curriculum.

Presenting a vision of education for liberation

During the first national Black Lives Matter at School Week of Action in February 2018, we asked students to creatively respond to the prompt "In a school where Black lives matter, we…" From the beginning of our collective endeavors, we sought to give students an opportunity to visualize an education steeped in the belief that Black lives do, in fact, matter. In 2019, we asked them to consider another prompt: "Schools show Black lives matter when…" In 2020, we introduced scholar Rudine Sims Bishop's notion of windows, mirrors, and sliding glass doors and asked, "What do the mirrors, windows, and sliding glass doors look like when we create a world where Black lives matter at school?"[8] Known as the Student Creative Challenge, the prompts invited students to construct a future where their schools would serve as stewards for promoting Black liberation, Black mattering, and Black joy.

One of the purposes of promoting critical thinking is to develop a critical consciousness to support individual efforts to respond to and change systems of oppression. Teaching students about structural oppression and deep-rooted inequities without giving them a space to enact social change is unlikely to yield positive results. The Black Lives Matter at School pedagogy asks students not only to think about how oppression impacts their life, but to work together to envision a better future.

In 2018, we asked cities to plan a rally during their week of action focusing on the national demands. Educators in New York City worked with youth to create a youth-led rally outside the city's department of education headquarters. Before the rally, youth made signs and signed up to speak about the demands. During the rally, the youth took the floor, and adults supported them. This year, the youth organizing event included youth-led workshops and performances. Students from high schools in multiple boroughs came together to learn from each other and work together to organize the rally. This is one example of how the Black Lives Matter pedagogy works with students to reimagine their education and demand that those with power turn their visions into reality.

Acknowledging the joys

James Baldwin's words to teachers, spoken in 1963, remain as relevant as ever today. Our attempts to correct the cruelty of a Eurocentric curriculum have been met with brutal resistance. From bomb threats in Seattle to conservative news outlets disparaging the week of action, each year our work is criticized and our participants are denigrated. Nonetheless, educators who use the Black Lives Matter at School pedagogy insist on "going for broke." They are seeing victories for students whose lives are made better by finally seeing themselves, their history, and their people uplifted in the school curriculum. They are acknowledging the joys inherent in the struggle and affirming that working to ensure that Black lives matter is a profound privilege and a worthy endeavor.

Flyer for a teen event in New York City for the 2020 week of action, created by B. Kaiser.

CHAPTER 21

The Black Lives Matter at School Year of Purpose Statement

This document was created by the steering committee of Black Lives Matter at School.

In addition to the BLM at School Week of Action (that is organized during the first week of February), educators, students, and parents are encouraged to participate in ongoing activations and reflection throughout the school year.

In the wake of the murders of George Floyd, Ahmaud Arbery, Breonna Taylor, Tony McDade, and others named and unnamed, a great Uprising for Black Lives has swept the nation and the world, inciting new urgency and radical possibilities for advancing abolitionist practice and uprooting institutional racism. The uprising has helped create a national discussion about what public safety could be. For too long public safety has been defined as spending more money on the legal punishment system and funding for more police in schools and communities. We believe it is vital to redefine public safety in terms of the holistic social and emotional wellbeing of students and educators. During this time of the coronavirus pandemic, public safety has to also mean not opening schools until the science supports it can be done safely, COVID-19 testing at schools and in communities is widely available, personal protective equipment is funded and supplied for educators and students, schools are provided functioning ventilation systems, and so much more.

The Uprising for Black lives has prompted the Black Lives Matter at School movement to expand its proposed activities to a "Year of Purpose," in addition to the annual Week of Action held during the first week of February. The centerpiece of the Year of Purpose is asking educators to reflect on their own work in relationship to antiracist pedagogy and abolitionist practice, persistently challenging themselves to center Black lives in their classrooms. In addition, educators will be asked to participate in intentional days of action throughout the school year uplifting different intersectional themes vital to making Black lives matter in schools, communities, and beyond (see the days of action below).

The learning environments we aspire to create reflect a deep understanding of the experiences of Black children, families, and communities, as well as our own ongoing work of critical self-reflection and personal transformation. Are we creating humanizing communities that respond to the concerns of our students? Are we committed to leveling up our expectations for Black students? As educators, we turn inward in order to reach outward, linking our efforts to broad, integrated movements for social justice. As our ancestor, the Black lesbian warrior poet Audre Lorde, stated, "There is no such thing as a single-issue struggle because we do not live single issue lives." This means we must commit to living our principles everyday, in and out of our classrooms, within our homes, and with our communities. It is a commitment to the village.

The excerpted questions we choose to focus upon are meant to support educators—and parents who are educating their kids at home during the pandemic—throughout the year. These questions, as well as pieces from our paragraphs above, first appeared in the book Planning to Change the World: A Plan Book for Social Justice Teachers (2019–2020). We invite educators and educators-in-training to meditate on the questions that follow, and—given that no such list can be comprehensive—to pose questions of their own. Only through deliberate reflection can we realign our teaching practices to meet our current challenges and invent new practices where there are none. Additional information about the Year of Purpose and opportunities to participate are available at BlackLivesMatterAtSchool.com.

SELF REFLECTION QUESTIONS

1. What is our school's relationship to Black community organizing? Do we have relationships with local movement organizers? Do they see our school as a place that believes in their mission? Do they see our school as a place to connect with local families?
2. How are school-wide policies and practices – especially disciplinary practices – applied across categories of race? Do problematic patterns emerge when we look at how policies are applied to Black students and when we also consider the intersections of gender, sexual orientation, and (dis)ability with Blackness?
3. How are the voices, accomplishments, and successes of Black folx uplifted in my lessons, units, and curriculum? Rather than focus on singular events or individuals, does my approach highlight the everyday actions and community organizing that will lead to change?
4. In what ways do our practices erase the histories of our students and prevent them from bringing their whole selves into the learning environment?
5. How do I understand the role that local/state laws and policies have on the educational experiences of my students? What is my role in working to change policies, regulations, and practices that harm Black students and families?*

ACTIONS AND ACTIVITIES

In addition to the self-reflection, we will encourage educators to participate in the following days of action throughout the year. Each action is grounded in the Movement for Black Lives Principles that we adopted as well:

1) FIRST DAY: Black to School (Whatever date that is for you)

- Wear the shirt
- Review the BLM at School reflection questions and write up your anti-racist action plan for the year

---

* These five questions appear in the "Not Just In February," feature section on page 214 of this book, along with other questions to help deepen antiracist practices in schools.

- Graffiti wall: "What are we going to do differently this year to further the movement for Black lives in our school."
- Post a video to social media
- Twitter chat

2) October 14th: Justice for George Day

Principle: Restorative Justice

October 14th is George Floyd's Birthday. Justice for George is a day to remember him and call for the defunding of the police and the redirecting of those funds towards social programs and education.

3) November 20: Transgender Day of Remembrance

Principle: Trans Affirming

Friday, November 20, Transgender Day of Remembrance 2020 William Dorsey Swann.

4) December 3: International People's with Disabilities Day

Principle: Globalism and Collective Value

December 3 is International People's with Disabilities Day. Harriet Tubman, Fannie Lou Hamer are two disabled freedom fighters we revere, even as the disabilities they carried with them into struggle aren't consistently lifted up as assets in their fight. To fight against societal ableism, we must celebrate our differences and understand how the lessons from Black disabled organizers teach us how to build inclusive, accessible movements.

5) Queer Organizing Behind the Scenes

Principle: Queer Affirming

January-During January, we find it critical to lift up Bayard Rustin, one of the principal organizers behind the March on Washington which is crowned as one of MLK's lasting achievements. To be queer-affirming means lifting up our queer ancestors who were at the foundation of our movements throughout time. This deepens the purpose of MLK day to understand that no one person makes a movement, highlighting how MLK's legacy encompasses the contributions of many.

6) Unapologetically Black Day

Principle: Unapologetically Black

Audre Lorde/Toni Morrison Birthday February 18th

7. Student Activist Day

Principles: Loving engagement and Empathy

March 6: Barbara Johns Black student activist day--Day to celebrate Black student activists.

8. Revolutionary Black Arts

Principle: Intergenerational

April- During National Library Week, we seek to center the classic contributions of Black Writers and artists across the generations: Zora Neale Huston, Faith Ringgold, Alma Thomas, Augusta Savage, Jasmine Mans. How are the themes and radical vision that they brought to their art reflected in your classrooms and communities? How can young people extend on these legacies?

9. Black Radical Educator Day

Principle: Black Villages
May 3rd: On Septima Clark's birthday we celebrate Black Radical educator day.

10. #SayHerName Day

Principle: Black Women
June 5, Breonna Taylor's Birthday—Day to call for justice for Breonna and uplift the #SayHerName movement

11. Education for Liberation Day

Principles: Black Families and Diversity
Juneteenth: Education for Liberation day—A day to celebrate the struggle that brought down slavery and reflects on what must be done to win Black liberation

12. A Day for Self Reflection

Review all 13 Principles
Last day of School, Reflection Day: reflect on your year of antiracist teaching. Possibly in groups.

Not Just in February!

Reflection Questions to Make Black Lives Matter Every Day at School*

By Awo Okaikor Aryee-Price, Maria C. Fernandez, and Christopher Rogers

Editor's Note

During the uprising for Black lives in 2020, the Black Lives Matter at School steering committee decided it was time to call for a "Year of Purpose" for Black lives, in addition to the week of action. As they participate in the year of purpose, educators are asked to continually reflect on their relationship to antiracist practices and join nationally coordinated actions throughout the year. The questions that follow include the five primary questions included in the Year of Purpose statement along with supplemental questions that are meant to deepen the reflection of educators throughout the year. A version of this feature first appeared in the book Planning to Change the World: A Plan Book for Social Justice Teachers (2019–2020).

---

* Originally published by Education for Liberation Network.

In a country that has always define norms and rules through a White, cis- hetero, Judeo-Christian, ableist lens, we have no option but to imagine and then build a radically different world in which Black lives matter. As educators, much of what is involved in how we create and design learning environments for our students must be situated in understanding the experiences of Black children, Black families, and Black communities. By creating more humanizing learning environments – by leveling up our expectations for how we treat Black students in school – we inevitably and consequently create a foundation for the treatment and support for all students.

We could not possibly set out an easy list of edicts that determine an isolated safe-zone for Black students within what we know to be a world still deeply invested in furthering Black suffering. Instead, we ask that educators meditate and reflect on some critical questions about how to make Black lives matter in the classroom, at school, and in the community. We also offer some fundamental guiding principles that drive any effort to center the mattering of Black lives.

Please use these questions as a starting point for conversations with your colleagues about how to transform pedagogy, practice, and organizing (within and outside the school environment). Like all transformative inquiry, this incomplete set of questions should lead to further questions and inquiry.

1. Is my school a force for social change?

- What is my school's relationship to Black community organizing? Do we have a relationship with local movement organizers? Do these organizers view our school as a place that believes in their mission? Do they view our school as a place where they can connect with local families?
- How do we see our school's mission of providing a quality education in connection with movements for healthcare? Housing rights? Fair wages? The environment? The abo-

lition of what Mariame Kaba calls the "criminal punishment system"?[1]

- What is the school's role in understanding the impact of
gentrification on the lives of Black students and their communities? How do we, as educators, work with community
members and parents to reimagine ways to create space for
self-determination?
- How do we uplift the ordinary/lay Black folx in our
community and include them in the co-creation of the
learning environment for students, parents, and community members?
- How do we, as educators, understand the role that local
and state laws and policies have on the educational experiences of our students? What can we do to change policies, regulations, and practices that harm Black students
and families?

2. Are my school's policies and practices helping or harming students?

- In what ways do my school's practices erase the histories of
our students and prevent them from bringing their whole
selves into the learning environment?
- What are some of our practices and policies that dehu-
manize Black students? How can we counter those policies
and practices?
- How are school-wide policies and practices applied across
race? And what does that look like when we intersect
across gender, sexual orientation, and (dis)ability?
- What is the impact of school discipline policies on Black
students? And what does that look like when we intersect
across gender, sexual orientation, and (dis)ability?
- How is my school communicating the promise of education and learning to our Black students? Does it repro-
duce the myth of meritocracy in its communication with
families? Is my school invested in collective uplift strategies

for Black families, regardless of their achievement in our school? How is my school disrupting narratives of individual exceptionalism that further notions of disposability for the overwhelming majority of Black students?

- What opportunities do educators have to engage in dialogue and unlearn biases and deficit ideologies about Black students, parents, and communities?
- How can we begin the process of internalizing restorative and transformative principles and practices at every level of daily operations of the school day?

3. How can I reenvision my own pedagogy as a force for change?

- Are the voices and accomplishments of Black folx uplifted in my lessons/units? Rather than focusing on singular events and figures, do I highlight the everyday actions, community organizing, and systems that led to tremendous change?
- How can I uplift the voices, accomplishments, and successes of Black folx in my lessons in ways that organically tie into larger content themes?
- Does my classroom celebrate Black forms of creative expression, in language, style, imagery, fashion, and beyond? Do my Black students feel that they can be their whole selves without fear of penalty or punishment?
- What are some of the ways that I can create space for Black students to bring their full selves into my learning environment?
- How might my classroom practices, principles, and overall learning environment design be limiting to Black students? What are some ways that I can change these practices, principles, and the design of the learning environment that will affirm students' humanity at all levels?

4. What values shape my teaching?

We offer these principles as starting points for reflection:

Self-determination: My learning environment and pedagogical practices affirm that Black folx and other oppressed groups have the right to determine what is right for their own individual and collective well-being.

A pedagogy of love: In *All About Love*, bell hooks frames love as a commitment to the spiritual growth and development of oneself and others. I am committed to my own spiritual growth and development, as well as those of my students, their families, and the community.

Healing-centered organizing: I recognize that social organizing and personal healing are not separate processes but deeply integrated ones. I embrace the concept of healing-centered organizing as an approach that creates a strong foundation for learning, political engagement, and advocacy.[2]

Ubuntuism: The traditional African/Pan-African cultural principle of ubuntu affirms the "oneness" and "togetherness" of all living beings. This philosophy shapes how I structure community, as well as how I envision learning, growing, organizing, and healing.

Creativity and imagination: As I imagine new worlds and design new learning environments, I believe in tearing down artificial borders and biases that have policed my imagination and those of students. I know that to solve the deepest conflicts of our time, I must embrace multiple modes of creativity and imagination, particularly for those we have marginalized, devalued, and delegitimized.

CHAPTER 22

Hire More
Black Teachers Now

A Research Statement from Black Lives Matter at School and Journey for Justice. Written by Denisha Jones with graphics by Beth Glenn.

*I*n 2018, members of the Black Lives Matter at School Movement col-*laborated with the grassroots alliance Journey for Justice to examine the problem of insufficient Black teachers in US public schools. Journey for Justice created a graphic report (below) using data drawn from the Albert Shanker Institute's* The State of Teacher Diversity in American Education, *Minneapolis teacher surveys, and the US Department of Education Civil Rights Data Collection.[1] The following statement, written by Jesse Hagopian, and the graphic report, created by Beth Glenn, first appeared on the Black Lives Matter at School website on February 7, 2019.*

What does public education have against Black Teachers?

You may think this is an exaggeration, but an analysis of the data from Journey for Justice (J4J) Alliance and the #WeChoose Coalition shows that in at least six major cities, Black teachers are becoming extinct. The same data shows us that each of these cities has a growing population of students of color, but many of them will not see a teacher who looks likes them in the course of their education. Instead, they will face discriminatory discipline and gaps in opportunities and attainment that negatively impact their future. From a 3 percent gap between the population of Black students and the number of Black teachers in Oakland to a 30 percent gap in Pittsburgh, Black students are attending schools increasingly taught by white educators. [Data on the growing extinction of Black teachers in major US cities is drawn from the graphic "The Purge of Black Teachers," below.]

This gap is even larger in charter schools, which tend to serve more Black students and hire fewer Black teachers. Both New York City and Chicago have seen gaps of 38 percent and 39 percent respectively between populations of Black students and the number of Black teachers within the charter school system.

To understand how the decline in Black teachers began, we must first look at New Orleans. After Hurricane Katrina, privatizers were able to push out Black teachers and turn the school district over to charter operators. In 2004, 71 percent of teachers in New Orleans were Black. In 2005, all New Orleans teachers were summarily fired, a mass dismissal of 8 percent of Louisiana's teachers and 24 percent of the state's Black teachers. By 2013, only 35 percent of new-hire teachers were Black, and only 22 percent of dismissed teachers were rehired, down from 33 percent in 2007. Nationally, we have seen a decline of Black teachers to 6 percent, while Black students make up 15 percent of the student population, and students of color account for more than half of the student population.

Often the removal of Black teachers is part of a broad effort to privatize public education by turning the public schools into charter schools. With an influx of charter schools comes an increase in mostly white teachers who have less experience and are likely trained in alternative teacher certification programs. New Orleans went from having teachers with an average of fifteen years of experience before Hurricane Katrina to teachers with just five years of experience post-Katrina. In 2007, Black teachers accounted for only 32 percent of new hires in New Orleans, and in 2013 that number increased to 35 percent. By contrast, 74 percent of the fired teachers rehired to teach in New Orleans in 2007 were Black. The majority of new hires in New Orleans since Hurricane

Katrina are white, even though the student population was 89 percent Black in 2013. [For New Orleans data, see the graphic "De-skilled and Disconnected," below.]

The lack of Black teachers in schools often leads to a cultural mismatch between Black students and white teachers and administrators. As a result, Black students in New Orleans are underrepresented in gifted and talented courses and AP courses, and a majority attend schools that do not offer calculus or physics. Additionally, Black students in New Orleans are disproportionately retained, suspended, and expelled. We know from the research that Black teachers are more likely to identify Black students as gifted and less likely to refer them for punitive disciplinary actions than are non-Black teachers. Black teachers often have higher expectations for Black students than do non-Black teachers, and we know that teacher expectations matter for student outcomes [see "De-skilled and Disconnected"].

Given these and other statistics, it is clear that we need more Black teachers in public education. As educators and activists across the country engage in the national Black Lives Matter at School Week of Action, February 4–8, 2019, it is imperative that we address the demand for more Black teachers. Black students deserve an education steeped in a culturally rich environment that honors and uplifts their socio-cultural identities, and this begins with having high-quality Black educators and administrators. We, the national steering committee of the Black Lives Matter in School Week of Action, join J4J and the #WeChoose Coalition to call on all districts to make explicit their plans to increase the hiring and retention of Black teachers.

The Purge of Black Teachers

The loss of Black teachers in New Orleans is an accelerated version of the national story. After a huge push-out right after school desegregation, the share of Black teachers has continued declining while the proportion of students of color has grown.

National Crisis

Since the mid-20th century, the share of Black teachers has declined to around **6%**. Today, about **15%** of students are Black, more than half of all students are students of color, & more than **80%** of teachers are white.

Share of Black and Hispanic Teachers

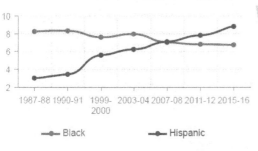

1987-88 1990-91 1999-2000 2003-04 2007-08 2011-12 2015-16

—●— Black   —●— Hispanic

A Leaky Pipeline

- Postsecondary education programs attract largely white students
- Across the United States, teachers of color experience challenging work environments
- Limited resources lower teacher retention rates
- Novice teachers of color lack support
- Teachers of color often leave their positions due these challenging environments

In the past two decades Black teacher turnover has outpaced that of non-Black teachers & undermined recent recruitment efforts. In 2012, the share of Black teachers leaving teaching or changing schools was 50% greater than that of non-Black teachers and far more likely to be involuntary.

New Orleans: *Privatization & Push-out*

2004
- Av teacher experience is 15.4 yrs
- 78% female
- 71% Black
- 60% attended NOLA college
- Overall, more experienced, more local and fewer white females than other storm impacted parishes

2006
- Mass firing wipes out 8% of LA teachers and 24% of states Black teachers

2005: Hurricane Katrina

2007
- 50% dismissed teachers rehired: 33% in NOLA and 18% in other parishes
- 50% not teaching in LA, a substantial increase from the 7-8% who left teaching annually before the storm
- privatization accelerates

2013
- 50% of initially rehired NOLA teachers dwindles to 37%: 22% in NOLA and 15% elsewhere in LA
- NOLA sees a dramatic drop post-privatization while vast majority hired into other parishes still employed
- NOLA teachers have substantially less teaching experience, are more likely female and are more likely to have only a bachelors degree compared to pre-Katrina cohort

"The Purge of Black Teachers," created in 2019 by Beth Glenn for Journey for Justice Alliance.

The Purge of Black Teachers In Cities

During Black Lives Matter at School Week, We Choose to Stop the Attack on Black Educators.

Organizers in the #WeChoose Campaign are striving to reverse the purge of Black educators that paves the way for the privatization of public schools & the decimation of Black communities. As cities nationwide hemorrhage Black talent, would-be educators are kept out & experienced leaders are pushed out, in favor of cheaper, less educated and culturally mismatched novices.

#WECHOOSE

EDUCATION EQUITY, NOT THE ILLUSION OF "SCHOOL CHOICE"

42% **20%**

2017 Black student v/s Black teacher percentage at district schools, a 22% gap

Until recently, the gap in Black students and teachers held relatively steady at around 13% in district schools, but in charter schools it varied between 37% and 39%.

The 2011 representation gap was nearly 3x larger at charter schools than district ones.:

39%

From 2002-11, the proportion of new district hires who were Black was consistently and meaningfully lower (by about 11 percentage points, on average) than Black representation among the city's teachers in the previous year.

Between between 2002 and 2011, the percentage of Black teachers decreased 11 points in district schools (from 38% to 27%) and 2 points in charters (from 25% to 23%).

Black females shrank from 31% to 22% of all teachers. Black males declined from 7 to 4%.

Over the past 5 years, Minneapolis has had an average retention rate of 86% for Black teachers. Around 3/4 of the teachers hired by school sites have been retained each year since 2013.Given the district's project $33 million budget deficit for the upcoming school year, schools will likely be forced to cut positions, rather than add new ones.Any teacher cuts will disproportionately impact teachers of color because a large portion of the district's teachers of color have not yet achieved tenure.

The MPS teacher force is only 5 percent Black (and one percent Black male), while Black students make up 38 percent of students

38%

5%

In 2017, 26.9 percent of new teacher hires were of color, compared to 19 percent in 2013.

Statewide, the average ratio of same-race teachers to students is the worst for Black students, compared to any other groups: on average 1 black teacher to 150 black students

In 2013, only 27 percent of new principal hires were of color. By 2017, that rate had risen to 57 percent.

More than 20 percent of all DPS teachers left their positions between 2012 and 2013, according to state data. And according to district information, half of all teachers leave the district within three years.

In 2015 65 percent of DPS paraprofessionals were educators of color, and they comprised 60% of the first class of a new new initiative in 2016 to help teacher's aides earn a bachelor's degree and a teaching license while keeping their jobs for most of the time they're in school.

About 5% of new teacher hires in 2017-18 were Black, along with about 14% of principal hires.

13%   4%   13%

This school year, Blacks made up 13 percent of the student body, but only 4 percent of teachers. 13% of Denver principals and assistants are Black

Denver

19%   30%

The 38% gap between the 2009 percentage of Black students and Black teachers was much more pronounced in New York City's charter schools.

38%

In 2012 19% of teachers were Black compared to 30% of students, an 11 point gap

The proportion of Black new hires in district schools was consistently below (by 5-8 percentage points every year) the proportion of Black teachers in the district workforce the previous year.

Between 2002 and 2012, the share of non-Black teachers in district schools remained stable, while the proportion of Black teachers declined modestly (about 3%). The 3-point decrease in the share of all teachers who were Black represented a 15 % decline in the total number of Black teachers.

The share of Black female teachers went from 17% to 15% while the proportion of teachers who were Black males hovered around 5% over the decade

New York

Schools in OUSD with a majority African American student body had the highest teacher turnover, averaging 38.3% of teachers leaving between the 2016-17 and 2017-18 school years.

Students at majority Black schools experienced 3.76 times more teacher turnover last year than those at majority white schools.

3.76x

Since 2016 Black teacher attrition has hovered around its 12 year high, with nearly 1 in 4 Black teachers leaving annually.

The share of Black teachers rose 2% points in last 4 years, while Black student population has shrunk 4%. Due to a loss of Black students, a 5 point representation gap has become a 3-point gap since 2016

The Black teacher percentage has been inching up about 1% annually, hovering around 20% since 2014-15, while the Black student population has shrunk from 28% to 24%.

21%   24%

2017-18 percentage of Black teachers (21%) and students (24%).

Oakland

53%   13%

56

In 2018 52.9 of the students in Pittsburgh were Black compared to 13.4% of the teachers.

For charters it was 6.7% Black teachers to 62.7% Black students, a 56- point gap.

Data from 2012-13 showed that the percentage of teacher resignations at high minority, high low-income schools is twice that of teachers at other schools.

The district hires about 200 teachers a year. In 2014-15, all PA's ed schools only produced 158 Black grads.

Black women are 10% of the teaching force and 2.7% are black men.

Pittsburgh

De-skilled & Disconnected

Post-Katrina Hiring Patterns
Charter hiring results in a less-educated, less Black and less locally-educated teacher workforce

Before Katrina, the city's teachers had an average of **15** years of classroom experience. Now the majority of teachers have less than **5**.

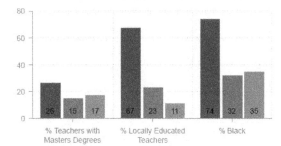

	% Teachers with Masters Degrees	% Locally Educated Teachers	% Black
Rehired Pre-Katrina Teachers 2007	26	67	74
New Hires 2007	15	23	32
New Hires 2013	17	11	35

74%
% Black teachers in 2003

49%
% Black teachers in 2013

89%
% Black students in 2013

#WeChoose
EDUCATION EQUITY, NOT THE ILLUSION OF "SCHOOL CHOICE"

Charter schools were more likely to hire from alternative certification programs than local universities, triggering shift to less experienced teachers and a smaller percentage of Black teachers.

Research suggests that post-Katrina hiring at charter schools is responsible for workforce composition shifts - not an exit of Black teachers.

Squandered Chances to Solve Problems of Cultural Mismatch

Opportunity Gaps

Just half the NOLA students identified for gifted & talented classes were Black, and Black students comprise 87% of the students at schools with no gifted programs.

Only about 40% of students in AP math or science courses were Black.

In high schools that don't offer calculus, 92% of students are Black. In HS that don't offer physics, 84% were Black.

- Black teachers are three times more likely to identify Black students as gifted in reading: 6.2 percent of the time. That's the same rate as for white students, no matter the race of their teacher.

- Non-black teachers of Black students have significantly lower expectations than do black teachers. Teachers' forecasts affect students' performance.

Attainment Gaps

80% of the NOLA students who were retained in 2015-16 were Black.

100% of the students retained in grades 4, 11 and 12 in 2015-16 were Black. In Louisiana, being retained in either fourth or eighth grade increased dropout rates by nearly 5 points.

The 2015-16 Black graduation rate was 71%, six points behind the state average.

- Having at least one black teacher in elementary school reduced Black students' probability of dropping out by 29 percent for low-income black students – and 39 percent for very low-income black boys.

Learn more at:
www.j4jalliance.com
www.stepuplouisiana.org

Discriminatory Discipline

89% of the NOLA students receiving in-school suspension in 2015 were Black.

87% of students punished with one out of school suspension were Black in 2015.

91% of students punished with more than one out of school suspension in 2015 were Black.

100% of the students expelled in 2015 and all those referred to law enforcement were Black

- Black teachers are less likely to refer Black students for disciplinary actions, especially in cases of perceived willful defiance and other subjective behaviors which drive disproportionality rates.

- The more times a black student is matched with a black teacher, the less likely that student is to be suspended.

Voices of Students

CHAPTER 23

They Don't Know the Half

By Kalani Rossman

Kalani Rossman wrote the following poem and delivered it during the 2020 Black Lives Matter at School Week of Action assembly at Seattle's Garfield High School.

Since we're seen as monkeys, it's only fair I address the elephant
It's the assumptions teachers hold about students with melanin
One that we're felons, and we're stupid, we're loud, and we're illiterate
But those are just preconceived assumptions produced by ignorance
Scariest thing about them is that those who have them are oblivious
Talking down to me slowly like I'm stupid
About work you've assigned as if I couldn't do it
If you leave me be, I could fly through it
Because I'm an intellectual, but I have to work two times as hard as my
    color-lacking classmates to prove it
All this teaching, you need to do some more learning, teach
Having trouble reading Davionte but can perfectly pronounce Bella's
    last name from Germany
I mean shoot, if you're asking me
You could read the names right if you had help from some African

American faculty
Black names would be given justice with a teacher of a color
A leader in our day-to-day lives who's also a sister or a brother
But instead we have an ignorant "teacher" with no racial bias training
    up there presenting
Who voted for an orange man who they feel represents them
and I feel resents me
Then they teach briefly about racism from our white textbooks like it
    isn't here too
And it isn't just our teachers—it's our classmates, "friends," and peers too
Doing little things you wouldn't notice unless you've been through it
Like "Can I touch your hair?" when you're already three knuckles into it
The "Why do y'all talk different with your Black friends then in class?"
The "Do you [insert stereotype]. I just had to ask"
The terrible racist jokes that fill the room with ignorant laughter
The "I don't get the movement, I say all lives matter"
Followed by "If we study Black lives, we'll have to study all groups after"
The using serious protests as an excuse to leave school
Listening to the music we produce, then asking for "the pass" to say
    that hateful word
just to feel cool
I generally don't understand some of the Caucasian youth obsession
    with that word of oppression
Like people who looked like them didn't use it to lessen those with a
    beautiful brown complexion back then and starting up once again
    with this last election
"Oh, it's in music," "Oh, it's in the text," "What's wrong if we say it out
    of context?"
But when the Black kid raises their hand to answer, you don't want to
    give any attention to the concept
But then some uneducated students are congratulated for listening to
    rap and being infatuated with Blackness
But the fact is they don't know the half of what's happened
They just know fry chicken, weaves, nappy hair, hip hop, rappin'
But not the fight, the struggle, the strength, the overcoming, the Black
    power,
Ugh the Black excellence, the Black intelligence

But it makes sense cause the media they consume has deemed those
things irrelevant
They social media, they one lesson on Black history, they textbook
The text and within these textbooks…now that's a whole different
topic
Writing only 'bout those who owned the fields and never those who
walked it
But it makes sense because the author looks like the oppressor
So of course he doesn't wanna talk about the experience of our ancestors
"It's Black History Month again, lets 'teach' them the same thing repeat-
edly"
When we're hungry for new knowledge, but it's the same old, same old
y'all "teachers" keep feeding
When we should learn about more Black leaders and scholars and
show little Black kids they free to be anything they want and not
the jail cell-filling, felon, ratchet hood rat, deadbeat dad, hashtag
the world repeatedly shows them they need to be
That's what Black Lives Matter at School means to me

CHAPTER 24

"Tearing It Down and Rebuilding"

An Interview with Student Activist Marshé Doss*

Jesse Hagopian: Hi, Marshé. I want to congratulate you for your great work in the struggle to defend students from over-policing in schools. Start by talking about what led you to want to get involved in the struggle to make Black student lives matter at school.

Marshé Doss: I started to get involved after I had been searched and the security who searched me confiscated my hand sanitizer and told me that I was going to sniff it and get high. It was a very emotional moment, it was very confusing, and I didn't really understand what was going on at the time.

Jesse: How did they pick you to be searched?

---

* Jesse Hagopian interviewed Marshé Doss, a 2019 graduate of Dorsey High School in Los Angeles. Here she tells the story of her involvement with the Students Deserve organization in Los Angeles—and a great victory for students that they fought for and won. Students Deserve is an organization of students, teachers, and parents working to stop the criminalization of students—especially Black, Muslim, undocumented, Indigenous, and queer youth in poor and working-class communities of color.

Marshé: They walk into a room and sometimes they'll knock, or if the door's open, they'll just walk in, or they might have the key and then they'll walk into the room and be like, "This is a random search. Everyone put your hands on the table." Then they'll count off one, two, three, four, one, two, three, four, one, two, three, four. And sometimes they intentionally have a list of people that they want to search so they'll rig the counting in a way where it'll get the people that they actually want to search and—

Jesse: Just dehumanizing.

Marshé: Yes! They'll pull you out into the hallway and they'll ask you to empty your bags, but moving too slow causes them to rush you and dump it all out on the floor anyway. And then sometimes they'll briefly check through it after they dump everything on the floor, and then they'll be like, "Okay, pack up your things and go back to class." And for me, after they'd dumped everything, they took my hand sanitizer, and they were like, "You're going to use it to get high and sniff it." But I only had it because LA's school district is so underfunded that we don't have soap in our bathroom sometimes, and just for cleanliness and protecting yourself from germs and sickness, it's necessary to have hand sanitizer. But they told me that I was going to use it to get high and that they "knew my type."

Jesse: They said they "knew your type"?

Marshé: Yes.

Jesse: That is really outrageous. What do you think they meant by that?

Marshé: Honestly, I don't know. I spent a lot of time questioning it, like, "Hey, what *is* my type? Is it because I'm low income? Is it because I'm Black?" There could be a number of things and only the person who searched me knows what they meant by that, and all I have to do is spend all this time wondering.

Jesse: I'm sorry that happened to you. So what did that feeling make you want to do about the situation?

Marshé: Well, at the time I didn't do anything about it because it hadn't happened to me since the sixth grade. I didn't actually get involved until I got to my history class and we had this debate about colonization—basically whose fault it was for Indigenous people being kicked off their land: Christopher Columbus, Christopher Columbus's men, or the king and queen of Spain.

Jesse: That's a powerful lesson!

Marshé: Yeah. So we just had this very passionate and fiery debate. I was one of the students who was really into it. So my history teacher called me and three other students outside of class and invited us all to a student meeting at lunch. During that meeting we all played this fact bingo game that included facts about random searches in school and we just learned so much. I learned that we spend $1 million every two years on random searches. And at the same time, we only have one college counselor. Our nurses aren't full time, our librarian isn't full time. I also learned there were only like 4 percent of schools in the United States that get searched, and those schools are predominantly Black and Brown schools.

Jesse: Wow, that's eye-opening.

Marshé: Yes.

Jesse: So once you learn those statistics, you realize that what had happened to you wasn't so random.

Marshé: Yeah. I realized that it was a way of the system setting me up for failure. I realized some basic things about the injustices of the educational system. It has some good things and some really bad things. What people need to know is that the system wasn't built at all for BIPOC. It made me realize that we need to reconstruct our education system to make it a place where Black lives matter, Brown lives matter, and Muslim lives matter, you know?

Jesse: For sure! So what did you do with this newfound understanding of the system?

Marshé: I was really upset about what I learned about this system, and I just kept going to chapter meetings of Students Deserve. Then I got invited to speak at a school board meeting. I was so nervous, but I got up the courage to speak in front of all the members of the school board. But the school board members weren't listening. They were doodling while another girl was talking, and they were having side conversations. They were just ignoring us, and it really sucked.

Jesse: That's painful to be bringing a concern about the well-being of you and your classmates forward to the people who are supposed to be providing for the well-being of students and they're doodling and distracted. You all could be punished for doing just that in class, and here are elected officials and they can't even listen to what the students need.

Marshé: Exactly.

Jesse: Wow. So that made you realize you had to keep organizing for what students deserve, I bet.

Marshé: Yeah, and I just stayed involved. I had a white teacher, Noah Lippe-Klein, who was very supportive of me in this movement. And there were many other teachers as well that supported us students. They used their voice to support us, help with speeches, help with practice. And sometimes we students would call each other and stay on the phone until one o'clock in the morning practicing our speeches and really trying to figure everything out.

Jesse: So then what were some of the main ways that you organized in this struggle?

Marshé: Well, we organized by word of mouth, we organized in social media, email, newsletters, people, and we did major events that pushed our movement forward. One of the key events we did was called "Making Black Lives Matter at School." The first one of these events happened in 2016. It was in Dorsey High School's auditorium. Some community members came, and there was a panel of students of color speaking about their experiences with random searches and explaining how they wanted community schools.

The second event had a panel full of women of color, and we also had the co-founder of Black Lives Matter, Patrisse Khan-Cullors, come talk to us about her experience being arrested at twelve years old, put in handcuffs, grabbed out of her classroom, and not even given an explanation of why it happened. That connected with me because it's so similar to what students today are facing. And students are finding creative ways to speak out about what's happening to them.

Jesse: Tell me more about that that second "Making Black Lives Matter at School" event and how it contributed to this struggle.

Marshé: It was amazing! We had over nine hundred people come to the event. And that wasn't something that had been experienced before. It was really big for us. It was a time where we really got people's attention—we had media there, and our event got put in newspapers. Before, when we did this first community forum, it was like maybe thirty people in the audience, so now we were really excited. We had booths from different community organizations as people entered, so people could learn more about issues impacting students.

And then once the panel started, we had all grades and ages speak from many different schools. One of the most important things that speakers talked about that day was community schools—a model of education that brings a lot of different supports to students. One panelist talked about school shootings and about how our hearts go out to the victims, but just because there was a school shooting does not mean that we should add more police on campus and reinforce all these new laws and regulations on Black students. That doesn't make us safer—especially for Black and Brown kids. We just wanted to let people know this isn't the time for people to be like, "Hey, put more police on campus," because that's actually not the solution. And they did have police on the campus at Parkland, and the shooting still happened.

Jesse: Absolutely. It sounds like a really powerful forum. I wish I'd been able to be there, with Patrisse Khan-Cullors and students from all over the district speaking about their experience. It must have had a big impact on you. I wonder what you think the significance of that forum was on helping the movement continue to grow.

Marshé: I think it had a big impact, which is why I said it was one of the significant events that had pushed our movement forward, because that was when we launched our second button campaign. In 2018, students designed a button at Dorsey to protest the random searches.

Jesse: So it sounds like you realized how big an opportunity you had, with so many people watching now, and that you had more support than you might've thought.

Marshé: Yeah. And just to see people actually come out and support it…

Jesse: That's beautiful. One of the things I really liked about the Students Deserve campaign was not only that you so wonderfully built resistance to these racist searches of students, but also that you had an alternative, and you guys talked about the power of community schools. Can you talk about what you all had as your vision for community schools?

Marshé: Our vision for community schools was about transforming regular schools into schools that provide full wraparound services. I haven't been to different high schools. I've only been to one, and I've been there for four years—Dorsey. So I can only really talk about Dorsey. And we have the safe passage program; we have parents come and volunteer, and they're on campus and things like that. And it's great. That's good to have community support in there. But on top of that, we also have a police officer literally stationed in the front of our school. We have cop cars stationed in the front of our school, and there's one outside; there are two in the front of the school; there might be some police in the back walking around. That's a lot of patrolling happening on our campus.

And that isn't what a community school is. In a community school, you have personal support workers and psychiatric social workers for people to talk to—a lot more mental health services, because we didn't have those at first at Dorsey. Community schools have full-time nurses and full-time librarians because it sucks when you have a paper to write, or you need to do some research, but you can't go to the library until the last class of the day.

And so when we talk about having community schools, we talk about having full access to social services to support students and families. Things like full-time nurses, full-time psychiatric workers, full-time social workers, full-time academic counselors, and not only full-time, but to have more counselors on campus because at Dorsey, we currently have only three academic counselors for over nine hundred students. And then one of the counselors, my last year, ended up retiring. So our college counselor became a ninth- and tenth-grade academic counselor and the college counselor. They had to just split her job in half, so it was harder for us to really be able to see her because she's also working with ninth graders.

Jesse: Right. Well, it was really amazing to follow your struggle growing in influence and power and also seeing the vision you have for the alternative to policing students. And it seems like you all got a really big boost of support when the Chicago Teachers Union went on strike and raised the demand that you guys had been advocating for some time in ending these so called "random searches." And I got a chance to go down to LA and speak with members of Students Deserve and feel all of your power.

Marshé: Yeah, that was great.

Jesse: That was really exciting for me to see a sea of red of sixty thousand people downtown rallying for the demands of the United Teachers Los Angeles (UTLA), which included a nurse in every school and an end to these searches of students. And getting to speak on that panel in the evening with students and parents and teachers who wanted to change those things was really eye-opening for me, and I thought you guys had a good chance of winning your struggle. Could you talk about what it meant to have the teachers union support and how you ultimately won an end to random searches?

Marshé: Yeah. So it was amazing having the teachers union's support in LA. And I was happy to see the strikes in Virginia, Chicago, Oakland, and everywhere else where teachers went on strike across the nation. And, honestly, to me it was so freaking liberating because a lot of people—I don't know if you heard—but a lot of people were saying during this event, "Oh, they're just trying to get better pay; they're only looking out for themselves. They don't care about the students. If they cared about the students, they would be in class teaching right now. They don't care. They shouldn't be teachers. They're making kids miss out on their education."

But what a lot of people don't actually know is that it wasn't about the pay. In LA, the teachers union had been offered money and a pay raise before they actually went on strike. So it wasn't about the money—it was about the students. So it felt very liberating to have the teachers on our side in the struggle against random searches.

Jesse: No doubt, no doubt. So talk about how you ultimately won this incredible victory against searches.

Marshé: So after the strike, the UTLA won many important victories for the schools—a nurse in every school, a librarian in every school, class size caps, and more. They also won getting rid of random searches in a few trial schools—with the idea that they could then expand that to all the schools. But then if anything went wrong the district could be like, "Hey, nope. Random searches are back on." So we students didn't stop organizing and pushing for the school board to get rid of the searches in every school. With this issue all in the news and with many of us speaking up, it pushed the school board to eventually put random searches up for a vote. And we all showed up for that school board meeting! Many of the board members were making long-winded speeches and we thought they were trying to stall and not have this voted on or passed, but eventually they voted. So Monica Garcia brought the motion forward and then four other members supported it and two others, I believe, strongly opposed. And with that vote we won an end to random searches!

Jesse: Amazing! Tell me more about the organizing it took to push the school board to agree to your demand.

Marshé: We had group meetings, we had individual meetings, we showed up to houses of public officials—and with all of that pressure on top of the pressure of the union, with over thirty thousand teachers, that is a lot of power. But I think we won because of the heartfelt stories we told. I know a lot of school board members at first were like, "Yeah, I'm so sorry that happened to you, but we still need this." But I think our humanity and our hearts won them over.

Marshé: And so when people are up there, students are literally sharing stories about how wearing the hijab results in them being searched or being called a terrorist or accused of having bombs in their backpack, about how sometimes they don't even want to come to school and how they just cry or feel super embarrassed. What's happening is not humane. Just hearing those stories, how could you not be moved and swayed?

Jesse: That's beautiful. My last question is where do you go from here? You have this incredible victory that could serve as an example to students and educators across the country for how to make change and what the priority should be in education. And I'm wondering how you build on that and where you go from here.

Marshé: So our next campaign is an end to police holding pepper spray on campus. It had already been banned in detention centers earlier this year—they're no longer able to carry pepper spray in a detention center, yet they're still allowed to carry pepper spray on Los Angeles Unified School District campuses. And there have been several incidents where school police have mindlessly sprayed students who've been in altercations. Instead of breaking up the fight with their hands, the police decided to pepper spray the students—even the students surrounding the altercation, the students walking to class, anybody passing by, and that has been caught on tape. It happened recently at Dorsey, and there was a big, big incident where the video went viral because all you see are police officers spraying out of control on all these Black and Brown children. There's people running around trying to pour milk into their eyes and people crying and just traumatized, and their friends are hurt and they don't know how to support them.

Some people are trying to pretend like it never happened because it's so traumatizing—they don't really want to face it. And it also happened at Fremont High School twice, once about three years ago and then again recently where they ended up calling the SWAT team, and they came with SWAT gear and surrounded campus—and they even ended up using pepper spray on children. And so with our next campaign, our whole goal is to make sure Black lives matter in schools by getting rid of pepper spray on campus. It doesn't happen at white schools; they don't spray mindlessly at white kids for getting into a fight. They only do that in Black and Brown schools.

Jesse: That's absolutely true. And I was pepper-sprayed in the face by a police officer without provocation at a Martin Luther King Jr. Day march back in 2015, and it was extremely painful. It's just outrageous that pepper spray can be brought into a place of learning. And you're absolutely right that this is treatment reserved for Black and Brown students by law enforcement. So I completely agree that pepper spray has got to go if Black lives are going to matter at school.

Marshé: Yes, and so much more has to happen! The whole point of Students Deserve is to make Black lives matter in schools. But how do you make Black lives matter in schools when the whole system wasn't even built for us? I'll tell you how. You tear it down and you build it into something that *is* made for us. And so that's what we're doing. Step by step, policy by policy, person by person, we're tearing it down and rebuilding it into a system that is meant to make sure that Black lives matter in schools.

CHAPTER 25

Minneapolis Public Schools Expel the Police!

An Interview with Student Leader Nathaniel Genene

On June 2, 2020, in the wake of the murder of George Floyd by a police officer, the Minneapolis Public Schools (MPS) board voted to terminate its contract with the Minneapolis Police Department (MPD), removing all police from their schools. The board also directed Superintendent Ed Graff to come up with a new plan for school safety by August 18, 2020, the date of the board's next meeting.

While the uprising in response to the murder of George Floyd was the immediate catalyst to the removal of police from MPS, many youth had been working toward this goal for years. A 2018–19 survey by MPS showed that school cops had more interactions with Black students than with their peers.[1] MPS will save $1.1 million annually by not contracting with the police department.[2]

On June 7, 2020, Jesse Hagopian interviewed student Nathaniel Genene about the uprising in Minneapolis against police violence and the movement to remove police from the schools. Nathaniel is currently the student representative on the Minneapolis Board of Education and an officer on the citywide Youth Leadership Council for Minneapolis Public Schools.

A version of this interview was originally published in *The Nation* magazine.

Jesse Hagopian: Thanks for taking the time to talk to me, Nathaniel. I know with the uprising at your doorstep, you have a lot going on. I want to talk with you about the dramatic victory to remove police from the Minneapolis schools. But before we get there, let's start with your experience as a Black student in the school system. Can you talk about how you have experienced racism at school?

Nathaniel Genene: We can start by looking at what happened even just two days after the murder of George Floyd—these are nights where I wasn't going to bed. I couldn't get my mind off his murder. And I had a teacher message me, the only Black man in class, "Nathaniel, if you are an IB [International Baccalaureate] diploma candidate, it is not reasonable to skip these exercises. I understand if you're struggling, but if it's simply because you have already passed, well…"

Instead of finding out how I was doing, he assumed I wasn't trying. But I was hurting. And I knew a lot of students of color were hurting as well. And that was definitely really frustrating. This kind of experience, of teachers not understanding the impact of racial violence on students or taking the time to really understand me, is not new for me or for Black students across the country. I did say something back to the teacher to let him know what I was going through, and he sent an apology out to the class. But that was really frustrating.

As far as encounters with school resource officers, I've never personally had an encounter with the school resource officer at my school [Washburn High School]. In fact, I never even got to know his name—which shows you that he certainly wasn't a helpful or supportive presence at our school. And I know many students who felt uncomfortable and intimidated by having him there. But especially now, I just can't imagine a climate or culture where MPD officers would be beneficial to a school's climate after the incidents that occurred last week, with students literally witnessing and recording a white officer putting his knee on an unarmed Black man's neck, students getting pepper-sprayed, teargassed, and shot with rubber bullets in the streets by MPD officers.

Jesse: I'm truly inspired by the bravery of the youth in Minneapolis who took to the streets and helped lead a movement against police terror. It would have been outrageous to have to return to school and have to walk by a cop in the hall who had assaulted you. Can you tell me about how you got involved in struggles to change education, and how you came to serve as the student representative on the school board?

Nathaniel: I have always believed in student voice and in amplifying and uplifting the voices of the most unheard students. I think that is really the most valuable thing a student rep can do. I started interning at an educational nonprofit last summer. Our goal was to redesign schools so that students lead lessons—and they're at the center of education. That made me think more deeply about how to engage students and what student voice really means. So going into the school year, I was thinking about: How do we engage students in their own education? And it's usually very tokenizing, or it's just about checking a box. I wanted to make sure that we did it differently this time. And I thought the easiest way to do that would be running to be the student rep on the school board. And here I am today.

Jesse: How did you come to see the video of George Floyd, and how you have been since then? How are you coping with the horror of the video? Have you been to the protests with your classmates?

Nathaniel: Tuesday morning I woke up to the video of George Floyd's murder, like a lot of people. I had a Zoom meeting that morning, but I literally couldn't get off Twitter. I couldn't get off the news. I literally just kept watching it. It got to be too much, so I just left the meeting. I actually drove down to Thirty-Eighth and Chicago where George Floyd was murdered. At that time there were only twenty-five or thirty people down there.

I actually never got out of the car. I just kind of went to see the scene and pay my respects and reflect. I'll be honest, I literally couldn't believe it, so I had to go down there and see that corner for myself to believe it. I have also gone to a couple of the demonstrations.

But to watch the struggle explode into what it has become across the city and across the country has been inspiring. It's been very motivating—but it's also been quite terrifying at times. There were days and nights last week where you go on social media and there were threats of white supremacists in my neighborhood. I have gone entire nights without sleeping. So, last week was really hard, but it was the first week in a while where I actually got to see and talk to my friends in person, and it did help a lot to reflect on all of this with friends.

Jesse: I am so glad you are finding ways to stay emotionally connected with your friends.

Nathaniel: For sure. I have also gone back to Thirty-Eighth and Chicago about four times to go see the memorial. I took my family, and I even got to take my little cousin. I also went with friends. I keep going down there thinking that it'll make me feel better, but it really hasn't. And I don't know if this feeling that I have right now will ever go away, but it still has been nice to go with family and friends and reconnect after being so isolated and disconnected the last couple of months.

Jesse: Let's talk about how the youth in Minneapolis organized this effort to get police out of schools. I understand that there's been a movement for some time to remove police from schools, that this didn't just start after George Floyd was killed.

Nathaniel: I think it's important to point out that this has been a generational struggle. We've had cops in schools since the '60s. So this movement definitely did not start last week. And groups today, such as Young People's Action Coalition (YPAC) and Our Turn, have been working on this issue for some time.

But watching the protests, I knew we had to make this struggle the number one priority. It was last Wednesday, one of those nights where I couldn't go to sleep, watching friends of mine get shot and teargassed, and I was thinking: There's no way that when we come back to school we can have those officers in our schools. This is not how we are going to want to set up our school climate.

So that's when we really got started talking. We had some very good leadership on this at MPS, and they actually decided to have a special session and to vote on this on June 2. We had to prepare for this important vote in a matter of days. So I sat down with a student from CityWide, our student leadership board in Minneapolis, and talked about how we could gather student testimonies, about their views on police in schools, in just a week. I knew I wouldn't be doing my due diligence just by telling students, "Go email your directors."

We decided we needed to make a survey form about police in schools and school safety—and we actually borrowed this idea from the teachers union. We reached out to students through many advocacy groups, such as Our Turn and YPAC, and through our citywide student government. And it ended up spreading a lot quicker than I had thought it would. We ended up getting over 1,800 responses, which is crazy, because that was in a matter of about three days.

We could have gotten even more responses if we had just made an online petition that anyone could respond to, but we really wanted to know what the students had to say. We asked students questions like, "If you had the funds to make changes, and if you had the funds to make yourself feel safe and secure, what would you use that money for?" And I think those received the most meaningful responses. So we made a summary of the responses and presented that to the board. Hopefully, as we start working on how to make sure that students feel safe next year, we can use those responses to help craft a plan.

Jesse: Actually asking students what they would need to feel safe and then funding it—that seems so straightforward, but it so rarely happens. Can you tell me about what happened during the vote to remove police from the Minneapolis Public Schools?

Nathaniel: On June 2, we held a virtual meeting because we're actually not allowed to meet in person yet. But there was a huge protest at the Davis Center, which is our headquarters at MPS. Our teachers union organized the rally, and Congresswoman Ilhan Omar was there. She spoke at the rally, and many students did too. In the end, the vote to remove all police from Minneapolis Public Schools went nine to zero. I think the vote going unanimous really sent a clear message to the MPD and to institutions across the country.

Jesse: As I'm sure you have seen in the days right after your vote, Portland also voted to remove police, and Denver is now considering it.[3] I am working with youth and other educators to remove the police from schools here in Seattle. There are also several important national organizations that have been working hard to remove police from schools, such as the Advancement Project, Dignity in Schools, and Black Lives Matter at School.

Nathaniel: Yes, and there was a student group, Students Deserve, that reached out to me from Los Angeles.

Jesse: I want to end with the vision of the students in the survey. What did they say about how police-free schools could make them safer, and what kind of alternative programs could be put in place to support students' overall well-being? What would it mean to make Black lives matter in school?

Nathaniel: Students came up with many important alternatives to police in schools, like increasing access to mental health services for Black, Indigenous, and other students of color; promoting restorative justice practices; hiring more social workers, counselors, and teachers of color; increasing the salaries of adults who already mitigate conflict, and security provided through community outlets.

In terms of making Black lives matter at school, I believe we need to hire more teachers of color. And we must make sure that we have a curriculum that reflects our students, especially our Black and Brown students. This uprising is showing us that we can make those changes— and so many more. We have to make these changes because our lives are at stake all around the country. If you think that the MPD just happens to be one bad apple, you're not that much different than the people who think that those four cops who murdered George Floyd were four bad apples. It's not just a Minnesota problem. It's a nationwide, systemic problem that people have been fighting against for years.

If there's one thing that I've learned in the last couple of weeks, it's that there are a lot of really good people who continue to hold up some really bad institutions and policies. And I think it's finally time for that to change.

CHAPTER 26

"Living in a Future of Success"

*An Interview with Student Activist Israel Presley
on Organizing for the Black Lives Matter at School Week of Action**

Jesse Hagopian: It's been amazing to watch all the powerful work you are doing in the community and in education. Talk about your experience in school. How was it for you as a young Black man in the school system?

Israel Presley: I felt like I didn't have access to truly learn what I could have been learning. I felt like there was a cap on my learning, essentially. I could only go so far.

Jesse: What was left out? What did they not teach?

Israel: They omitted so much about Black history and the histories of BIPOC communities. You've heard that phrase "lie by omission"? That was essentially my education—at least until I took a few classes in high

---

* A recent graduate of the Seattle Public Schools, Israel Presley attended Garfield High School and Rainier Beach High School. While attending Garfield, he was a student in Jesse Hagopian's world history and ethnic studies classes. Jesse interviewed Israel on May 15, 2020, about the miseducation of Black students, the struggle to make ethnic studies part of the curriculum, and the powerful student organizing in Seattle for the Black Lives Matter at School Week of Action.

school. They were lying by leaving out key parts of history that would have allowed me to gain knowledge of self. They were lying by leaving out concepts in literature that were developed by Black folks and then lying again about the African origins of science, and so much more—material that would have allowed Black students to connect to their learning environment. When you omit these topics, students won't really be able to grasp the whole story. That's like coming in halfway through a movie—you won't understand why a character is taking a certain action until you go back and see the whole movie from the start.

My experience was like that. I was ignorant because there was so much they were leaving out. I don't know if it was on purpose, but there were bridges of understanding that needed to be built and bridges of knowledge that were destroyed because of that education.

In middle school, we didn't even celebrate Black History Month. And that really shook me to my core. I didn't get the proper academic tools to defend myself. I had nothing—no way of actually building something for myself to give me some form of cover from racism.

Okay, sure, they might say, "Oh yeah, there were slaves." But I know that my people were more than slaves. Why don't you ever teach me about our history in Africa before we were enslaved? Why don't you teach about our resistance to slavery? Because I know my people are strong. But then you get history books given to kids in elementary school that leave out the many contributions to history by Africans and others. Or the textbooks that actually claim that Native Americans willingly gave up their land. Or history books, given to elementary students, talking about how the slave owners and slaves were friends.

I was honestly blessed to have a wonderful dad and mom who educated me and let me know that I came from important people. This was so important because I went through a lot of the struggles of being bullied because I looked different, because I was bigger than everybody. So people felt the need to test me, but the moment I raised my hand to defend myself, I was the bad guy. The villain. The angry kid who needed anger management. It's traumatizing to feel like that, to think, "If I defend myself, I'm the aggressor."

Jesse: I'm really sorry to hear about that. Can you say more about racist bullying at school?

Israel: Growing up, kids in school have said all kinds of things to me: "Why do you look like that?" or "You're Black, aren't you supposed to be able to shoot a basketball?" or "What's wrong with your hair?"

Well, the educators simply told me, "Kids are being kids. They're just poking fun" and that I needed to have thick skin since I was stronger than everybody. They were worried that I'd hurt a kid physically, but they weren't worried about the emotional and mental pain that they were dishing out. That's a whole different abuse and a kind they were too afraid to talk about.

Jesse: I'm disgusted that educators wouldn't stand up for you and take the opportunity to teach students about racist stereotypes and the beauty of Blackness. I'm sorry you had to go through that as a young student. Tell me about educational experiences that helped, as you said, "give cover" for racism.

Israel: My first experience was a class in my sophomore year of high school. It was the most liberating experience of my life, where I felt like I had freedom to really speak, and the teacher opened up all types of doors for my mind. It was a world history class at the time, and then eventually it got transformed into an ethnic studies class, taught by Jesse Hagopian.

Jesse: Oh yeah, I know that guy! [Laughs]

Israel: Wonderful person. [Laughs] But it really was one of the most liberating experiences of my life in the sense that I had the freedom to actually learn how defend myself from racism. Honestly, that was my biggest hurdle—feeling like if I fought back, if I defended myself, then I was the aggressor. Even during the times when I was verbally and mentally abused, somehow the people doing the abusing found a way to make it look like *they* were the victims.

Jesse: I can't even tell you how much my heart soars to hear that the class made a difference for you, Israel. That means so much to me. What were some of the things you learned that helped you feel liberated?

Israel: I learned that the people currently in power weren't always the people who were in power. I learned that power can change, and that power takes many forms. That was my big takeaway, that you don't have to be someone who's a colonizer to have power. You can be somebody who's educated and have power. That was something that really shook me. I remember one of the major activities we did was when you had the class get into your "time machine"—really just the projected image of one on the screen—and go back to different eras of Black history and "meet" the people that had been left out of the textbooks. One time we went back to the time of Mansa Musa, and we became different people who lived in Mali at the time—we were griots [storytellers and musicians], Muslim scholars, governors, and kings—and we learned about how Mansa legit broke the bank and caused inflation everywhere he went across the world because of all the money he gave away on his pilgrimage. And then to find out in the next class that, hey, some of the earliest forms of mathematics and astronomy were founded in Africa? That was mind-boggling! I was always told that we were dumb, that Black people can't do this or that. They throw a blanket over Africa and label it all as poor or undeveloped. So you get this mentality that, "Oh, someone needs to save it," when in actuality, Africans have been leading the world for a long time and, if they need anything, it's to be left alone from those with a colonizer's mentality.

Ethnic studies was important to me because I learned about the connections between BIPOC who have faced racism and colonization around the world. But I learned that we're not easily moved. I'm Black and Filipino and Native American. So it was very important to learn about the different ways racism impacts all those groups.

Jesse: No doubt. So talk to me about how you took what you were learning and became a student activist.

Israel: That was also a story built out of trauma. I remember waking up one morning and hearing about a bad thing that had happened to a woman in my community, that she was murdered by two officers who were called to help her.

Jesse: You're talking about Charleena Lyles.

Israel: Yes, sir. Charleena Lyles. I remember we got to talk about her death in your classroom that day and how it made us feel. Then we got a group of people together—me, Chardonnay, Kevon, Janelle—and we were the four founding members of the group we called "New Generation" at Garfield High School. We sat in your class and we said, "Hey, what are we going to do? Let's get a rally. Let's go rally in front of the school tomorrow." We gathered the students, and you gathered the teachers, and we had a rally the very next day to say that Charleena's life mattered.

For me, that was one of the most beautiful moments. It really gave me an opportunity to find my voice. Because at first, I wasn't going to speak. I hadn't ever spoken in front of that many people, and there were news cameras recording us, so I really didn't feel like I could say anything with that much pressure. But then my emotions took over and I spoke my mind. For me, that was a liberating experience. I can't really describe it as anything else. It was freeing to me to know that people actually cared to hear what someone like me had to say.

Jesse: Yes, that was a beautiful day. I remember it well, and it was amazing to see how you took what you were learning, brought it out, and really developed your voice to educate your peers and the public about what had happened to Charleena. That was powerful.

Israel: Yeah, that was a good day. It was sad, but it was also good.

Jesse: So talk about your work then with the Washington State NAACP Youth Council—or NYC, as it's called—and the organization's advocacy for ethnic studies.

Israel: We're a group that has formed to make demands of the Seattle school district to fully educate the students of color. One campaign we took on was demanding that they finally renovate Rainier Beach High School, where I went my senior year. It's the school in the area with the most Black students, and it's the only high school in Seattle that hasn't been renovated in a really long time. And, yes, your demand for ethnic studies has been one of our biggest campaigns, and we have had to build a movement to pressure the school board to implement ethnic studies.

It's scary for me that there are educators who are afraid that kids of color are actually going to learn about their own cultures and think for themselves. When you hear teachers say, "Well, how do you think our white students are going to feel?" that really shakes me up. I want to say, "Okay, and how do you think Black students have felt this whole time? And Asian students, Latinx students? Or how about Native students, sitting there listening to how Christopher Columbus was such a great guy? He exchanged gifts with Native Americans and then they gave him his land? Nope. Christopher Columbus came down, killed the people, stole their land, and literally committed a mass genocide. Americans still celebrate him. What a guy. He's swell.

But that's the thing. I remember one of the key points that I learned in the ethnic studies class was critical consciousness—we don't have to accept master narratives about history anymore. Before ethnic studies, thinking critically was something I never thought I could do in a classroom setting. That was really important to me. But then I found out we have to struggle with our own school district to get this education—it's kind of sad.

Jesse: You all in NYC have done such great work organizing and promoting ethnic studies. And I know that we wouldn't have it at all in Seattle schools if it wasn't for the work of many youth organizing and demanding that you get to learn about your own cultures and history. So I appreciate the work you've done on that.

Tell me about the Black Lives Matter at School movement and how the week of action fits into your work. I know you've been really involved in bringing that to the forefront in Seattle Public Schools.

Israel: Yes, we in NYC have been supporting Black Lives Matter at School from the beginning. I have gone to the Black Lives Matter at School planning meetings. This year, NYC organized the press conference and spoke to the media about how we need to change the school system. We have organized Black student talent showcases and rallies at the school board meetings.

We are building the Black Lives Matter at School movement, honestly, to achieve a better sense of community, a better sense of education within our community.

I had a mentor once who said something very profound to me: "By elevating Black people, you not only elevate them, but you elevate everybody else around them." When you raise the lowest of the low, everybody above them goes up too. Everybody rises.

And the demands of Black Lives Matter at School are so important to improving the lives of Black students. When you're talking about adding more counselors and not cops, using restorative justice, mandating ethnic studies, hiring more Black teachers—these are the things that can help students get a real education. These are the things that can help us achieve the saying of the Ashanti people of Ghana, "Boa me na me mmoa wo" (Help me and let me help you). I still live by that phrase that I learned in your ethnic studies class.

Jesse: That's right! So talk about your experience during the week of action.

Israel: During the week of action I learned that Blackness could be part of every subject in school. I was finally being taught things about myself. I learned about Black contributions to science in science class. I had a math teacher at Garfield who did excellent work, Ms. Dinh. She didn't use math to talk about the negative statistics about Black people. No, she used math to talk about the possibilities that we could achieve. It felt very powerful.

Also, during the week of action, NYC organized a rally at the school board meeting. And the turnout was amazing, man. We had elders. We had students, educators—all types of community. When you get a collective, a real community coming together to unite, man, that's something powerful. And I remember we were all chanting, and people, one after another, were grabbing the megaphone, speaking their minds, and demanding racial justice in the schools. And then to see us all united and standing in solidarity fighting for the Black Lives Matter at School demands? Fire. Then we all went into the school board meeting with our signs and our demands and testified about the changes we wanted to see.

For the last few years we have ended the week of action with a youth talent showcase. Last year we called it "Young, Gifted, and Black." This has been our opportunity to show people the power of Black education. Students dance, sing, give speeches, talk about their experience in school, and spit poems—I did a poem one year.

Black Lives Matter at School has showed us that our community can organize a fight and come together to celebrate ourselves and our accomplishments. We're no longer living in a history of defeat. We're living in a future of success.

CHAPTER 27

Students Deserve

The Organizing Work of a Grassroots Coalition*

What is Students Deserve?

We are students, teachers, and parents working for justice in and beyond schools. We are member-leaders who strategize, organize, set our own agendas, decide for ourselves, and grow this work. Students Deserve is Making Black Lives Matter in Schools. We want schools to divest from criminalization and policing. We want schools to invest in us as Black, Muslim, undocumented, Indigenous, and queer youth in poor and working-class communities of color.

What does Students Deserve do?

Our work has three main strands:

1. **Political education.** We name and challenge oppressive systems and the policies and practices that harm people at school and beyond. We learn and teach histories of dignity and resistance in oppressed communities. We build unity among people

---

* This statement of purpose appears on the website of Students Deserve, a student-led organization of parents, teachers, and students, based in Los Angeles.

255

for the sake of increasing justice. At our schools, this means supporting and protecting Black, Muslim, undocumented, and queer students who are vulnerable to being targeted.

2. **End policing and privatization.** We want an end to random searches, policing, charter school expansion, reconstitutions and all other practices that treat students, families, and teachers like problems rather than seeing us as human. We want public schools to be places that welcome and work with *everyone*. That's what makes public schools so powerful—they are for all of us.

3. **Fund community schools.** We want real support for students. This means schools with smaller class sizes and more arts, electives, college counselors, therapists, librarians, custodians, and healthcare services. We know that funding safe and high-quality schools is one important part of winning what students deserve. Investing in public schools is also part of challenging policing, privatization, charter school expansion, and reconstitutions or school closures and conversions. When our communities have well-funded and high-quality public schools, we don't need to turn to charter schools or rely on policing.

The heart of our work is our vision for what youth and communities deserve. But we know our schools and communities can't wait. We do the work to make that vision real *now*.

Vision for the schools LA students deserve

Youth, families, educators, and community members are coming together to build a new vision of education and schooling. We are working together because we know our communities have the power to transform our schools and our society. Our voices matter, and they need to be heard. We want students in LA to become literate, self-motivated critical thinkers who participate in our schools and communities. Students need to be able to build skills in a nourishing environment and be prepared for our lives when we leave school.

Unfortunately, we see that schools have historically not done this and that the current trends in education are still moving our schools in the wrong direction. We need to stop reforms that focus on testing, school closures, reconstitutions, pushing out more students, corporate charter companies running more schools, and cuts to vitals areas like arts, ethnic studies, libraries, counseling, adult education, and early childhood education. In addition, we need to change the culture and practices of our schools so that they truly support every young person. For example, we don't want to see some students branded as "good kids" and others as "bad kids." We don't want students to be pushed out of schools because they are being racially profiled, are low on credits, are gang affiliated, have special education needs, are facing homophobia, or have recently immigrated here.

We have a very different vision for the schools LA students deserve, and we are working together all across the city to make this vision a reality.

Goals for LA schools

1. Educate and care for the whole child

- Function as community centers with enough resources to serve the many needs of students, including physical, emotional, and mental health services.
- Support students' intellectual, emotional, cultural, creative, and logical and linguistic development.
- Help students identify as intellectuals, scholars, and responsible community members who understand their value, strengths, and areas for growth.

2. Ensure equity and access

- Schools should serve *all* students. End pushout and exclusion of all types. Public and charter schools need to stop the practice of pushing out or excluding students: English-language learners, Latino and Black students, transgender/bisexual/lesbian/gay students, students requiring special education services, and students with low test scores.

258 | Black Lives Matter at School

- Recognize that every person is capable of learning. There is no such thing as a "good kid" or a "bad kid"—all young people learn and can be supported to enjoy learning. Recognize that people learn in many ways and that art, music, physical movement, and other ways of learning are important. When schools eliminate athletics, arts, theater, music, and other programs, these cuts can also lead to pushout for many young people.

3. Provide full funding for services and resources

- Reduce class size and counselor loads to give students adequate time and attention.
- Improve school facilities (including technology, laboratories, and auditoriums).
- Ensure that every school has a fully staffed and open library, sufficient college and post-secondary counselors, psychiatrists, nurses, clerical, and custodial and cafeteria staff.
- Remove systemic funding inequalities that leave low-income schools of color behind.

4. Focus on student needs, not only on test scores

- Offer classes in diverse languages, arts, drama, dance, music, and health, as well as Black, Latino, Asian, Indigenous, lesbian/gay/bisexual/transgender/queer, ethnic, and women's studies.
- Expand learning outside the traditional classroom: community internships, field trips, and experiential opportunities to gain practical skills, learn from, and give back to the community.
- Create structures for students to voice their interests and reflect them in the curriculum.
- Ensure students have post-graduation plans supported by mentors and a college/career counselor. Students with low test scores are not pushed into the military or out of school.
- Teach critical thinking. Real learning and growth are not measured on standardized tests. Success on multiple choice tests and in classes focused on basic facts is not enough.
- Reduce unnecessary testing and detach high stakes from all

standardized testing. The purpose of tests should be to help students, families, and educators to figure out what students know, and how to move forward—*not* to punish students or schools.

5. Prioritize the community

- Break down barriers and improve relationships between parents, community, and school staff.
- Expand community outreach, community engagement, and community education.
- Provide professional development for schools staff that is created and led by community members in partnership with educators, students, and families.
- Increase staff diversity; recruit, support, and retain staff who come from the school community.
- Fully-resourced education at the adult education and early childhood education levels.
- Keep schools open beyond 3:00 p.m., with classes and workshops run by community members, families, students, and staff for community members, families, students, and staff.

6. Make real decisions for ourselves

- Democratically decide school policies and budgets by families, students, school staff, and community. Reconstitutions, school closures, school conversions, or other reform efforts should not be decided by a superintendent or school board.
- Ensure adequate funding so that we are not forced to make harmful decisions.

7. Develop safe, clean, and green spaces

- Support students and staff to use transformative or restorative justice practices, so that we can meet students' needs and move away from punishment and criminalization of young people.
- Redirect money from school police and law enforcement to-

ward counselors and peace builders.
- Systematically end bullying by students, staff, and school police.
- Ensure that each campus is clean, environmentally sustainable, and providing green jobs.

8. Promote economic and community health. Changes in schools require changes in the community so families and communities get what they deserve too. We must:

- Expand living-wage job development, affordable housing, recreational spaces, healthy food access, and public transportation in low-income communities of color.
- Redirect money from corporate tax breaks, military, police, and prison development to schools, youth programs, and living wage employment opportunities.
- Support unionization and fair working conditions for all school staff in all schools.
- Promote health and safety for youth/families by ensuring environmental justice and ending police violence.

CHAPTER 28

Montpelier High School Racial Justice Alliance *Statement to the School Board**

Dear Montpelier School Board,
Thank you for taking the time to meet with us this evening. With the support of our advisor, Mary Ellen Solon, and the school administration, we are here to encourage the school board to raise the Black Lives Matter flag at Montpelier High School. Raising the Black Lives Matter flag represents our school's affirmation that the experience of Black students has been and continues to be inequitable. This act demonstrates our shared commitment to improving our community through empowering and honoring all of our students.

Intentionally or not, many have benefited from and contributed to structural and institutional racism; part of the key to rebalancing lies

---

* On February 1, 2018, Montpelier High School, in Montpelier, Vermont, became the first high school in the nation to raise a Black Lives Matter flag on school grounds. The flag raising was the result of an organized campaign by the Montpelier High School Racial Justice Alliance. This is the statement written by members of the Racial Justice Alliance that was read to the school board by student leader Joelyn Mensah on January 17, 2018.

in open discussion and addressing the issues as they manifest within our school. For this reason, it is important to recognize that Montpelier High School is systemically racist by default.

Raising this flag is a part of a wider campaign to grow awareness and make changes in our curriculum, climate, and shared understanding of the need for racial justice. Over the past year, there have been many steps forward in our community, including some direct curricular choices, administrative trainings, faculty in-service, a schoolwide assembly, and the Race against Racism, presented by Montpelier High School. And yet, we need to do more to raise our predominantly white community's collective consciousness to better recognize white privilege and implicit bias. The Racial Justice Alliance believes putting up a Black Lives Matter flag is imperative for both demonstrating our school's fight for equitable education for our Black students and modeling a brave and appropriate challenge to the status quo impeding public institutions across the country.

While the protection of all students, including students in other minority groups, is equally important, there is a unique history of oppression and mistreatment of Black Americans that requires its own unique response. The justice and equity of Black Americans is dependent upon justice and equity for all Americans, just as justice and equity for all Montpelier public school students is dependent upon that of our Black students. We view the raising of this flag not as a culmination of our work but rather as a continuation of the work and learning together—a call for action.

We will raise the flag with love in our hearts and courage in our voices. We reject any purported connections to violence or hate that may or may not have occurred under the Black Lives Matter flag. We recognize that all lives do matter, but in this same spirit, not all lives are acknowledged for their equal importance until Black lives have been.

This evening, we urge you to join us in raising the Black Lives Matter flag and keeping it up on the pole until the American flag alone acknowledges the worth and dignity of Black lives. With this act you demonstrate your support in continuing the broader equity work being done in our community. Thank you for your time and for your continued dedication to all Montpelier public school students.

Sincerely,
The Montpelier High School Racial Justice Alliance

CHAPTER 29

"It Will Stay Up until Institutional Racism Is Over"

Raising the Black Lives Matter Flag at Montpelier High School

*An Interview with Student Activist Noel Riby-Williams**

Jesse Hagopian: Noel, you were a student at Montpelier High School when they were the first school in the nation to raise the Black Lives Matter flag. Tell me about your experiences in the K–12 school system that led you to know that we needed to raise the flag.

Noel Riby-Williams: I attended Montpelier school system from kindergarten to third grade, and I ended up moving out of the district because of

---

* Noel Riby-Williams is a student at the University of Vermont and a graduate of Montpelier High School. In 2018, while attending Montpelier High School, Noel helped to organize a victorious struggle to raise a Black Lives Matter flag in front of her school, making MHS the first public school in the country to fly the flag. At the time of this writing, eleven other schools in Vermont have joined the movement and raised Black Lives Matter flags. Jesse Hagopian interviewed Noel on May 21, 2020, about this victory for Black students.

racism. It started with kids picking on me at the bus stop in the morning. My dad had a really hard time dealing with those children and their parents. Because of the active racism I faced from these kids, I even moved to a different bus stop. But when I got on the bus, the racist bullying continued. They talked negatively about my skin color. I also had my hair in braids, and the kids would always touch my hair on the bus. I was scared to say anything.

And then I moved to the Barre school system in Barre, Vermont. I was still one of the only persons of color, but my experience was better than my kindergarten through third grade experience in Montpelier. And then I ended up moving back to Montpelier for high school. My experience got better in Montpelier when I moved back, but there is still so much to change.

I think my father, who was a gym teacher at the elementary school in the Montpelier school district, was the only Black male teacher in the district. I have never had a person of color or any Black teacher for any class. I have had some white teachers who made an important effort to be inclusive. For example, I had world history as a sophomore in high school, and we learned about apartheid in South Africa—that was important.

But oftentimes, the curriculum didn't support Black students. I took a US history class in high school that was just the basics of what everybody learns: white men and what they did.

Jesse: How did you begin to get together with other students to change these conditions? Where did your organizing start?

Noel: It started with my cousin Joelyn Mensah. We were at a talk by Major Jackson. He's a Black male poet in Vermont, and he was reading his poetry, and there were students behind us who were being disruptive and disrespectful to the poet. My cousin turns around, and she's like, "Can you please quiet down? You're being disrespectful." And the kids just said, "It's a free country." They were even saying the N-word.

Jesse: Sickening.

Noel: Joelyn said, "Can you stop it? I don't feel comfortable with you saying that, especially when there's a Black man reading his poetry," and they just repeated that it's a free country and they could say what they want. She got really upset and ended up leaving the poetry reading. So then Joelyn went to our school guidance counselor, Mary Ellen. Mary Ellen then helped create the diversity club that's now called Racial Justice Alliance. Joelyn became the president of RJA, and I was made the vice president. We got our friends together and started having weekly meetings on different issues about race along with a movie night to bring more people in.

Eventually, we came to the decision that in the upcoming month of February, we wanted to raise the Black Lives Matter flag. The month was followed by many activities, including a school-wide showing of the documentary *13th*, which was so powerful.

Jesse: How did you all decide to do that?

Noel: I went to my favorite English teacher, and she told me that University of Vermont, the college I go to now, had raised the BLM flag, but that it had been taken down. I thought, wouldn't that be interesting if we did that at our school? But I had my doubts. When I told my English teacher that I wasn't sure it would be possible, she was like, "No, you could do it." So I started thinking about it seriously. I talked to Joelyn and said, "Wouldn't it be cool if we raised the Black Lives Matter flag here at Montpelier?" And we both said, "Let's do it."

Jesse: That's an exciting moment, deciding to make a change! What happened next?

Noel: Yes! So next we needed to get support. RJA was behind it, and so now we were starting to work with supportive educators, like Mary Ellen Solon, who was also the RJA club advisor for the first year, and she was very encouraging. Also, our principal, Mike McRaith, was very supportive. I felt really lucky to have a principal who was completely supportive of our movement.

Jesse: That's great. So once you had your team together, tell me about the struggle you all organized to win permission to raise the flag.

Noel: Well, we had to take our case to the school district, and our superintendent was not on board for a long time.

Jesse: How did you organize to get the school district to agree to this?

Noel: We started with meetings with the superintendent as a club, but he was trying to explain why it couldn't work and why legally he couldn't allow it. He said, "Well, if I let you all raise the Black Lives Matter flag, I'm going to have to let everybody else raise any flag they want to raise." And he said something like, "God forbid that someone asks me, 'Can I raise a Confederate flag?' What would we do then? Where does it stop?"

Jesse: So, what did you say to that?

Noel: We responded that right now Black lives are under attack; our problems are real and they need to be heard. People are dying every day just for being Black. It's a movement that needs to be recognized right now. And, obviously, everyone's lives matter, but in this moment, we need to recognize that things are not equitable for everybody. And the reason is skin color. We said that the flag stands for lifting up Black people, but if you lift up one minority, you lift up everybody.

Jesse: Powerful argument. So what happened next in the struggle?

Noel: We went to the school board and Joelyn read the RJA statement about why we were demanding the Black Lives Matter flag be raised at our school. That was a big action. Fortunately, we had an ally on the school board, Becky Bowen. She has children who are Black, and her daughter is my best friend. That rally was a good day, and eventually the school board voted to allow us to raise the BLM flag.

Jesse: Amazing victory. So now tell me about what it was like the day you all stood in front of the school and raised the Black Lives Matter flag at a school for the first time in the United States.

Noel: We had a huge turnout. There were people from all over. Montpelier High School is right down the street from the state house, so we even had some legislators come. People from all of the three schools in town came, including kids and parents from the middle school and elementary school.

I remember Joelyn gave a really great speech. I read a quote by Martin Luther King Jr. And then we played the song, "Young, Gifted, and Black." It was so emotional. Every student of color that was there—whether they were in middle school or elementary school—were all able to help pull the flag up. So we got in a line, and we all pulled it up together. That was really beautiful. Our little brothers were there. And as we tugged at the rope, I started crying. At that moment I felt like I was doing this for my little brothers. They're Black young men, and it's hard to be Black in this world. But that day was overall just beautiful.

Jesse: That is really moving. Thanks for sharing that with me. So I know the struggle didn't stop with your school. What happened next?

Noel: From there we went to support other schools; any other school that raised a flag, we showed up to support them. So I went to U-32, a school about ten minutes away. The struggle there was different. Unlike our school, they had some backlash during the flag raising. They had people holding Confederate flags and signs while they raised the flag. It was shocking and heartbreaking to see, but I guess it just proved why we need our flag raised in the first place.

Jesse: That's really hard. But, you're right, bringing out the racist Confederate flag only proved your point. And I know that while you didn't get opposition at your flag-raising ceremony, later on there was a national backlash to you all raising the flag. Fox News came out against your action, and their news coverage led to people around the country attacking what you had done. Can you talk about that experience?

Noel: It was hard. But our principal, Mr. McRaith, dealt with it really, really graciously. He's amazing. I can't say enough good words about him. A lot of the backlash was directed at him personally. He got flooded with voicemails from people all over the country who disapproved of what our school was doing, calling him a bad principal, a bad person. He took so much abuse, but he never backed down.

Other messages were directed at our group, RJA. So yes, we got hate mail. But then we sat down and looked at the amount of hate mail versus the support we got. And we could clearly see that we had a lot more supporters than the people who sent the hate mail. That made it easier to ignore the haters.

Jesse: You didn't back down in the face of that racist hate, and you found support and solidarity with each other. What did raising the BLM flag mean to you?

Noel: It meant a lot. People said to us, "Why do you need to raise another flag? Doesn't the American flag represent you?" And I said, no, it doesn't. Not when our country is still allowing unarmed Black people to be killed and nothing is being done about it. Like Joelyn said during the flag-raising ceremony, the Black Lives Matter flag is going to stay up at Montpelier High School until institutional racism is over, until people can go to school and feel represented and like they're learning about themselves in all aspects of the curriculum and have teachers of color that look like them and support them.

Jesse: What would you say to students around the country who are considering raising a Black Lives Matter flag at their school?

Noel: It's 100 percent worth it. It's definitely not easy, and it takes time and patience, but I couldn't imagine my life without having had that moment. That's a moment I'll forever carry in my heart. I even take my family there to look at it. Every time I drive by the flag, I just smile. It gives me pride and hope for the future.

CHAPTER 30

Black Lives Matter Student Creative Challenge 2020 Submissions

B eginning in 2018, the national BLM steering committee organized a Student Creative Challenge. The committee settles on a prompt and asks students to respond by creating a piece of art or creative writing. For the 2020 week of action, the prompt posed this question: "What do the 'mirrors, windows, and sliding glass doors' look like when we create a world where Black Lives Matter at school?" Featured below are the flyer for the 2020 challenge and several entries.

Flyer promoting the 2020 Student Creative Challenge. Image first appeared on the Black Lives Matter at School website.

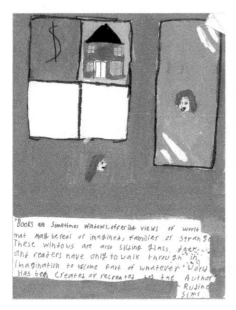

"Books are sometimes windows, offering views of world
that may be real or imagined, familiar or strange.
These windows are also sliding glass doors...
and readers have only to walk through in
imagination to become part of whatever "world
Has been Created or recreated by the Author
— Rudine
Sims

Andera Becerril, San Jose, CA

Grace Slayton, San Jose, CA

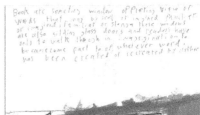

Joham Amerzcua, San Jose, CA

Keyla Garcia

William Ong, San Jose, CA

Mia Moreno, San Jose, CA

Ivon Calle, San Jose, CA

Epilogue

Inequity and COVID-19

By Jesse Hagopian

The global COVID-19 pandemic has devastated Black communities and had a dramatic impact on public education. As of May 2020, Black people are dying of COVID-19 at three times the rate of white people. As the *Guardian* reported in May 2020:

> Across the country, African Americans have died at a rate of 50.3 per 100,000 people, compared with 20.7 for whites, 22.9 for Latinos and 22.7 for Asian Americans. More than 20,000 African Americans— about one in 2,000 of the entire black population in the US—have died from the disease. At the level of individual states, the statistics are all the more shocking. Bottom of the league table in terms of racial disparities is Kansas, where black residents are dying at seven times the rate of whites.[1]

These disparities are the result of the many manifestations of institutional racism. There is growing evidence that Black people are disadvantaged in terms of access to diagnostic testing and treatment for the disease.[2] Black people are more likely to have preexisting health conditions. As Dr. Rashawn Ray wrote in April 2020 for the Brookings Institution:

274

Blacks, relative to Whites, are more likely to live in neighborhoods with a lack of healthy food options, green spaces, recreational facilities, lighting, and safety. These subpar neighborhoods are rooted in the historical legacy of redlining. Additionally, Blacks are more likely to live in densely populated areas, further heightening their potential contact with other people. They represent about one-quarter of all public transit users. Blacks are also less likely to have equitable healthcare access—meaning hospitals are farther away and pharmacies are subpar, leading to more days waiting for urgent prescriptions. So, health problems in the Black community manifest not because Blacks do not take care of themselves but because healthcare resources are criminally inadequate in their neighborhoods.[3]

Additionally, Black people are more likely to be employed in workplaces deemed essential during the COVID-19 pandemic. For example, Black people represent nearly 30 percent of bus drivers and nearly 20 percent of all food service workers, janitors, cashiers, and stockers.[4]

As I write these words, COVID-19 is becoming a defining crisis that will create new challenges for the Black Lives Matter at School movement. With nearly all the public schools in the United States closed at the time of this writing, our movement will have to find ways to organize remotely. It is quite possible that schools will still be shut down during the first week of February 2021, and we will have to find ways to organize a remote week of action.

One of the primary challenges the Black Lives Matter at School movement now faces is organizing a struggle to ensure that Black students' physical, social, and emotional needs are prioritized by the school system during the time they are out of school.

COVID-19 has exposed the crucial role that schools play in the lives of low-income, disproportionately BIPOC families and communities. Schools often provide two meals, special education services, trauma counseling, showers, laundry for homeless students, and other resources and services. For this reason, the shut down of schools from COVID-19 has had a disproportionate impact on Black students. As crucial as schools can be to the support of Black students, the Black Lives Matter at School movement will also likely have to resist pressure from politicians to prematurely open schools in a way that could put children and their teachers at risk for contracting COVID-19.

Additionally, Black Lives Matter at School will have to join in co-alition with others to resist a "shock doctrine" approach to education in which corporations seek to profit off of the disaster. Already educational technology companies are salivating at the opportunity to pillage tax-payer monies by selling their software products to school systems that have moved online for the long term.

Finally, BLM at School will need to be part of a great uprising to reimagine what schools need to become when they do reopen. To that end, BLM at School voted in May 2020 to endorse the nine demands of the organization Journey for Justice to oppose the worst impacts of the COVID-19 crisis on our schools:

The impact of COVID-19:
Nine demands from Journey for Justice

1. No child can fail or be suspended this year. All children must be held harmless from a D or an F or punitive discipline policies as a direct result of the interruption of their education process, the trauma of living through COVID-19, *and* inequity of access to technology and internet. In addition, we call for:
2. Stimulus funding to ensure that every child that needs one has a computer and access to the internet. COVID-19 has revealed that access to technology is not a luxury but is essential to student success. We insist on a comprehensive demand to elim-inate the digital divide that languishes between Black, Brown, Indigenous, and white children.
3. Federal mandate to stop school boards from closing schools and approving new charter or voucher initiatives and a nation-al moratorium on new charter schools. We are calling for a federal ban on online learning / charters as a replacement for brick-and-mortar buildings as centers for public education.
4. Elimination of punitive standardized tests for at least the next two years. Student assessments will be based on multiple mea-sures such as portfolios, oral assessments, project-based assess-ments, and tests that are only used to evaluate student needs. The NAEP should be the only test administered next year, as

a formative assessment, to gauge student needs, not to punish students, teachers, or schools.

5. Full funding of Title 1 and the Individuals with Disabilities Act to double the number of special ed instructors and resources available to children with special needs. Funding to increase the number of counselors for students (dramatically reduce counselor/student ratio) and wraparound supports for every student.

6. Stimulus investment of $75 billion for community schools, which will allow all schools with at least 70 percent free and reduced lunch to become sustainable community schools, an evidenced-based model of equitable school improvement. This must happen in conjunction with a federal moratorium on charter expansion.

7. Elimination of voter suppression through mayoral control and state takeovers, and support for local, publicly elected school boards. This support must be a comprehensive plan that provides equitable school board race financing, training, and on-the-job technical assistance for school board members.

8. We demand the immediate decriminalization of students of color and school cultures. We insist upon the immediate implementation of true restorative justice, language justice, and wellness training for implementation and culture with the necessary resources (human, medical, and financial) to sustain this culture in all schools. We believe a comprehensive plan to transform racist cultures that criminalize Black, Brown, and Indigenous children is necessary, which includes more Black, Brown, and Indigenous teachers, mandatory restorative justice and racial justice training for all administrators and school staff, and federal penalties for districts that continue with zero tolerance and other inequitable discipline and instruction cultures.

9. We are suggesting that J4J and the federal government partner to form an Education Equity Task Force that monitors inequity and brings recommendations to the US Department of Education and Congress.

About the Editors

Denisha Jones is the director of the Art of Teaching Program at Sarah Lawrence College. After earning her bachelor's degree in early childhood education from the University of the District of Columbia, Dr. Jones worked as a kindergarten and preschool teacher, and a preschool director. She earned her PhD in curriculum and instruction from Indiana University in 2013. In 2018, she earned her JD from the David A. Clarke School of Law at the University of the District of Columbia.

Dr. Jones is an education justice advocate and activist. She serves as the director of Early Childhood Organizing for Defending the Early Years, Inc., and is the interim assistant executive director for the Badass Teachers Association. Since 2017, she served on the steering committee for the national Black Lives Matter at School Week of Action. In 2019, Dr. Jones joined the Anji Play Study Fellowship program, where she will learn about true play based out of the Anji province in China and become an Anji play ambassador.

Jesse Hagopian teaches ethnic studies at Seattle's Garfield High School and is a member of the national Black Lives Matter at School steering committee. Jesse is an editor for the magazine *Rethinking Schools*, the co-editor of the book *Teaching for Black Lives*, and the editor of the book *More Than a Score: The New Uprising against High-Stakes Testing*. Jesse is a recipient of the 2013 national Secondary School Teacher of the Year award and the Special Achievement "Courageous Leadership" award from the Academy of Education Arts and Sciences. In 2019 Jesse received the Racial Justice Teacher of the Year award from the NAACP Youth Council and the Social Justice Teacher of the Year award from Seattle Public School's Department of Racial Equity. Jesse serves as the director of the Black Education Matters Student Activist Award, which he created from a settlement he reached with the City of Seattle after having been pepper-sprayed in the face by a police officer without provocation at Seattle's 2015 Martin Luther King Jr. Day rally. Jesse blogs at his website, IAmAnEducator.com.

About the Contributors

Tamara Anderson is an advocate for children and teens, an antiracist trainer, a professional artist, an editor, a freelance journalist, and a blogger with over twenty years of experience as an educator. She supervises middle and high school pre-service teachers at La Salle University and serves as an adjunct at Harcum College. Her work with juvenile justice led to her being the recipient of the Leeway Foundation Art and Change Grant. Tamara provides workshops in effective therapeutic strategies that combine music and theater with human services, social work, juvenile justice, and education. She is one of the founding steering committee members of the national Black Lives Matter at School Week of Action, a member of the Racial Justice Organizing Committee of the Caucus of Working Educators (Black Lives Matter at School Week Philly), a previous steering committee member of WE (four years), and a core member of the Melanated Educators Collective.

Tamara received her bachelor's degree in secondary education from the University of Illinois at Urbana–Champaign and her master's degree in curriculum and instruction from National Louis University. Tamara holds teaching certificates in English and theater from three different states, including Pennsylvania. She continues to organize in partnership with other grassroots organizations in Philadelphia in pursuit of racial justice.

Awo Okaikor Aryee-Price is a former classroom teacher, antiracist organizer, core trainer with the People's Institute for Survival and Beyond, teacher educator, and a steering committee member for the national Black Lives Matter at School coalition. Most importantly, Okaikor is mom to Saige Ayikailey and Kaeden Nii Ayikundzra, and a partner to Keith Price.

Wayne Au is a former public high school teacher and currently a professor in the School of Educational Studies at the University of Washington Bothell. He is a longtime Rethinking Schools editor, and he has edited or co-edited several Rethinking Schools books, including *Rethinking Ethnic Studies, Teaching for Black Lives*, and *Rethinking Multicultural Education*. As an academic and an activist, he remains involved in local and national struggles over racial justice in schools. His most recent scholarly book is *A Marxist Education: Learning to Change the World.*

Takiema Bunche-Smith has worked for over two decades in support of children, families, and educational programs and systems through her work as a teacher, teacher educator, curriculum director, parent activist, and executive leader. Her life's work has been guided by a deep commitment to racial equity, social justice, and a belief that centering the histories and perspectives of marginalized people can support individuals, institutions, and systems to become more equitable for all. Her work lives at the intersection of theory, policy, and practice, and she uses a culturally responsive and anti-oppression lens to reframe and reimagine what educational experiences could look like for children, adults, families, and communities.

In 2014, Takiema became a part of a multiracial group of parent leaders in the NYC Opt Out (standardized test refusal) movement and has spoken out in various venues against the harm of high-stakes standardized tests, particularly as they impact the lives of the youngest Black and Brown children, children with special needs, and children from under-resourced communities. She has presented on education-related topics to a variety of audiences across New York, the United States, and Sweden, and has published articles and op-eds in venues such as *Childhood Education Innovations*, NAEYC's *Young Children*, *Al Jazeera*, and the *Washington Post*. She is also a doula, and is passionate about creating a culture of self-care, particularly as it relates to professional environments.

Takiema holds master's degrees in early childhood and elementary education from Bank Street College of Education, urban education policy from the CUNY Graduate Center, and from NYU Wagner's School of Public Service.

Erika Strauss Chavarria teaches high school Spanish in Howard County, Maryland. An advocate for racial and social justice, she became a practitioner and trainer of restorative justice in an effort to end the school-to-prison pipeline. She currently keeps a classroom grounded in restorative justices principles and work. Additionally, she served on the National Education Association Task Force on the school-to-prison pipeline and school discipline and is now an NEA director representing Maryland, a director for the Maryland State Education Association, and a board member of the organization *Racial Justice NOW!*

Rosy Clark is a pre-K teacher at a public school in Brooklyn, New York. She has been organizing with Black Lives Matter at School for two years. She is a member of the Movement of Rank and File Educators (MORE), the social justice caucus of the United Federation of Teachers; and a member of the Labor Branch of the Democratic Socialists of America.

Anthony Dandridge is a visiting lecturer in the Black Studies Department at the State University New York at New Paltz, the second-oldest department in the nation. An Afrocentric philosopher educated in Philadelphia at Temple University, he prioritizes the agency of people of African descent as he seeks to positively impact the current social, political, economic, and environmental conditions that limit the lives of Black people and others in our society. Much of his work establishes new ways of understanding our world and those fundamental relationships within it toward a more liberating understanding of ourselves and others. From the incarcerated to the educated, he engages a broad spectrum of communities to bridge gaps between theory and praxis, college and community, Blacks and others, in a tragically anti-Black world. Follow him on Instagram at @kepra1.

Marshé Doss was born and raised in South Los Angeles. She is a recent graduate from Dorsey High School in South Los Angeles. Marshé is an organizer and leader in the student-led movement Students Deserve. She leads the Making Black Lives Matter in Schools effort in LA, which tackles the school-to-prison pipeline and over-policing of schools in Black communities. She is a nationally recognized speaker, organizer, and activist, known for direct actions and addressing crowds of over fifty thousand people. She can be reached on Instagram at @its.marshe.

Maria C. Fernandez is the senior campaign strategist at the Advancement Project's national office. With over fifteen years of youth organizing and education justice experience, Maria's work focuses on supporting Black youth and students of color across the country as they develop local and national campaigns to dismantle the school-to-prison pipeline and demand #PoliceFreeSchools. A Bronx-raised New Yorker, she now lives in Washington, DC, with her partner, Jonathan Stith.

Brian Ford is a high school history teacher and social justice educator in New Jersey. He has served on national, state, and local organizing committees for the Black Lives Matter at School Week of Action. Brian is a member of a local antiracist group, Teachers Undoing Racism Now (TURN), and is a doctoral candidate researching social justice education.

Rosie Frascella has taught high school English and history for the past thirteen years in the New York City neighborhoods of Washington Heights and Crown Heights. She was trained as an English as a New Language (ENL) teacher through the Peace Corps Fellows Program at Teachers College, Columbia University. Before becoming a teacher, Rosie was a labor union organizer and cut her activist teeth as a queer student activist in college. Currently, Rosie is a core leader for the New York Collective of Radical Educators (NY-CoRE) and a member of the Movement of Rank and File Educators (MORE), the social justice caucus of the United Federations of Teachers.

Laleña Garcia is a kindergarten teacher hailing from Brooklyn. After receiving her BA in history from Yale University in 1998, Laleña worked with high school students in New Haven, Connecticut, long enough to realize her love is early childhood education. After receiving the Minority Fellowship from Bank Street College of Education, she began teaching in New York City in 2000, graduating from Bank Street in 2002 with an MS in early childhood and elementary education. Laleña has worked with three- through eight-year-olds, and is currently teaching five- to six-year-olds (kindergarten) at Manhattan Country School. In 2018, Laleña helped organize New York City's first year of participation in the Black Lives Matter at School Week of Action, and created a document translating the thirteen principles of the Movement for Black Lives into child-friendly language, in order to support classroom teachers beginning this work. She has brought this work to local schools and community organizations, as well as to national conferences. Laleña also works for the Early Childhood Professional Development Institute as a gender and sexuality trainer, working with early childhood professionals and families to create expansive and supportive understandings of gender, sexuality, and family structure.

Beth Glenn is a visiting scholar at the NYU Metropolitan Center for Research on Equity and the Transformation of Schools and consultant for a range of education justice organizing groups. She is the former director of the Education Justice Network, and former national education director for the NAACP. In a career spanning journalism, civil rights organizing, and policy advocacy, Beth has been a fierce champion for social, racial, and education justice; serving variously as a policy analyst, hill staffer, and reporter and editorial writer for newspapers. She earned her Master's Degree in policy analysis at the New School in New York and a Bachelors in journalism from UNC Chapel Hill. The daughter of an educator who spent more than twenty years in North Carolina public schools, Beth is an enthusiastic collector of African art, an avid reader, eager traveler, and novice scuba diver.

Nathaniel Genene is a rising senior at Washburn High School in South Minneapolis. He serves as the student representative to the Minneapolis Board of Education and the at-large member on the City-Wide Youth Leadership Council. He also works with ThriveEd, a nonprofit working to build an educational paradigm shaped by innovation and joy for learners and educators, and Our Turn, an advocacy organization fighting to mobilize young people in the fight for educational justice.

Kiersten Greene is an associate professor for literacy education at the State University of New York at New Paltz in the Department of Teaching and Learning. She teaches aspiring teachers how to teach reading, writing, and multimodal text production, and her scholarship critically examines the disconnect between policy and practice in twenty-first-century schooling. She has been an antiracist educator and union activist for the past twenty years, and prior to pursuing a career in higher education, taught elementary school and was a literacy coach in New York City. When she's not teaching, reading, or sharing her research, you can find her chasing her son (who can't wait to start kindergarten next year!). Visit kierstengreene.net for more information.

Angela Harris is a first-grade leader at Dr. Martin Luther King Jr. Elementary School, the African American immersion school in Milwaukee. She is also an active member of the Milwaukee Teachers' Education Association, chair of the Black Educators Caucus MKE, and a member of the national Black Lives Matter at School steering committee. As a Black liberatory educator, she has been able to combine the mission of her school and the Black Lives Matter at School Week of Action into a district and community week of action in Milwaukee. She has often remarked in her school, "It is Black Lives Matter every day." Her hope is that this will become the reality for all students everywhere.

Raquel James-Goodman is a middle school teacher leader and advocate in Bergen County, New Jersey. She is a mom to Myles, Drew, Aes, and partner to Andrew Goodman.

Jennifer Johnson taught high school history in Chicago Public Schools for ten years before joining the staff of the Chicago Teachers Union (CTU) in 2013. She has a BS from Northwestern University in secondary education and an MA from Northeastern Illinois University in community and teacher leadership. She is currently the CTU chief of staff and believes that teachers union activism for public schools and the teaching profession is part of a larger struggle for social and racial justice, which connects educators with students, parents, and communities.

Brian Jones is an educator, activist, and writer in New York and the associate director of education at the Schomburg Center for Research in Black Culture.

Dedicated Los Angeles Unified School District (LAUSD) elementary teacher and civil rights advocate, **Erika Jones** serves on the board of California Teachers Association, representing members of United Teachers Los Angeles (UTLA). She has taught for fourteen years, teaching kindergarten through fifth grade. Within that time, she has been part of multiple school plan writing teams, and a national professional development trainer specializing in classroom management, culturally responsive teaching, racial equity, and supporting school communities. She also co-chairs UTLA's Racial Justice Taskforce, collaborating with community organizations, students, parents, and educators.

Born in New York and raised in Kentucky, Jones has lived in California since 1990. For two years before her teaching career began, she worked in public relations and coordinated a school assembly program focused on educating children about being environmentally conscious.

"As a social justice advocate, I was drawn to the classroom," Jones says. "I haven't looked back since and truly feel educators can and will change the world for the better."

She holds a bachelor's degree in international business from Mount St. Mary's University, Los Angeles, and earned her teaching credential and a master's degree in curriculum and instruction from California State University, Northridge. She also holds a credential in administration. She has completed the Harvard Kennedy School Executive Education program Leadership, Organizing, and Action: Leading Change, and was a member of Governor Gavin Newsom's task force on charter schools.

B. Kaiser is an antiracist white educator. She teaches art in Brooklyn with a focus on contemporary artists and social justice. She has been helping organize the Black Lives Matter Week of Action in New York City for three years.

Makai Kellogg is an antibias early educator and equity and diversity coordinator at School for Friends in Washington, DC. Makai creates age-appropriate curriculum on social justice for her students to explore equity issues. Makai leads programming throughout the year that allows parents to address their biases in order to be proactive as their children learn about the world around them. Makai facilitates trainings and opportunities for her colleagues to engage in identity work and discussions on equity and antibias education in the classroom. Through her work with young children and their families, she is creating an inclusive community of critical thinkers and change makers. Makai works closely with Teaching for Change and its initiative, the DC Area Educators for Social Justice, as an advisory board member. She is also part of the leadership team for the Anti-bias Early Childhood Educator Working Group. She attended Trinity Washington University for undergraduate study of history and education and completed a master of arts in teaching in early childhood education.

Bettina L. Love is an award-winning author and the Athletic Association Endowed Professor at the University of Georgia. Her writing, research, teaching, and activism meet at the intersection of race, education, abolition, and Black joy. She is the author of the books *We Want to Do More Than Survive: Abolitionist Teaching and the Pursuit of Educational Freedom* and *Hip Hop's Li'l Sistas Speak: Negotiating Hip Hop Identities and Politics in the New South.*

Dana Morrison is an assistant professor in the Department of Educational Foundations and Policy Studies at West Chester University of Pennsylvania. Her research focuses on educational grassroots organizing, teacher unionism, and critical practices in teacher education. She has participated in organizing for the national Black Lives Matter at School Week of Action in higher education since 2018.

Cecily Myart-Cruz is a teacher, activist, and the vice president of the United Teachers Los Angeles / NEA. She has taught for twenty-four years, at both the elementary and middle school levels, most recently at Angeles Mesa Elementary. She has been recognized for her work in the classroom, including as UTLA/NEA WHO award winner, and she is trained in the American Federation of Teachers' Education Research and Dissemination framework. She has helped shape racial justice within the work of the union through critical dialogue, forums, all the while making sure student voices are front and center. Lastly, Cecily has continued to build strength and power for UTLA through a strong relationship with the state and national affiliates. She is also a member of Black Lives Matter Los Angeles.

Dermott Myrie (preferably called Myrie and known by the pronouns he/him/his) has taught social studies for thirteen years in the Bronx. Currently, Myrie teaches at MS 391 in District 10. He has been the United Federation of Teachers (UFT) chapter leader at his school for the past three years. Before he became a chapter leader, he spent three years as a delegate. He is a member of the Movement of Rank and File Educators (MORE), the social justice caucus of the UFT. He has been actively involved in the group's efforts to stand up to UFT leadership on many issues, including fighting for a fair contract. He has opposed psych evaluations for new employees, testing tied to evaluations, and school closings and mergers. In addition, he has worked to secure restorative coordinators in schools and demanded that the union mobilize its members to endorse Black Lives Matter at School collectively, even as the union has pushed back. Myrie has worked with many groups all over New York City, including Teachers Unite, Coalition for Education Justice, Alliance for Quality Education, and Educators against Displacement. Myrie fights constantly for racial justice, housing justice, economic justice, and educational justice.

Israel Presley is a student at South Seattle College and a former student of Garfield High School and Rainer Beach High School. Israel is a member of the NAACP Youth Council and an advocate for social justice.

Marynoel (Noel) Naa Lamiley Riby-Williams is a Ghanaian woman who grew up in Montpelier, VT, and graduated from Montpelier Highschool in 2018. She now attends The University of Vermont and is studying health science and hopes to become a pediatrician. She is a devoted activist and works hard to make changes within her community.

Christopher Rogers (he/him/his) was born and raised in Chester, Pennsylvania, and is now a PhD student within the Reading/Writing/Literacy program at the University of Pennsylvania Graduate School of Education. Chris is a core member of Teacher Action Group Philadelphia and public programs director for the Paul Robeson House and Museum in West Philadelphia. He serves as curriculum committee coordinator for the national Black Lives Matter at School Week of Action. His current research interrogates the intersections of race, space, and place in community literacy efforts, negotiating how intergenerational place stories relate to the necessity for community preservation and social action.

Kalani Rossman is a poet and a high school student in Seattle.

Jeff Stone is a longtime public school employee and a doctoral student seeking to work in solidarity with Black, Indigenous, Latinx, Asian, Pacific Islander, and 2SLGBTQ+ communities to disrupt racism and other intersecting forms of oppression in schools and society. Jeff's current efforts focus on collaborating with students to implement ethnic studies in K–12 school systems.

Notes

Foreword

1. Matt Barnum and Alex Zimmerman, "Stop-and-Frisk under Michael Bloomberg Led More Black Students to Drop Out, Study Shows," *Chalkbeat*, February 18, 2020.
2. The Advancement Project, https://advancementproject.org/wecametolearn; "Counselors Not Cops: Ending the Regular Presence of Law Enforcement in Schools," Dignity in Schools, www.dignityinschools.org; Students Deserve, https://www.schoolslastudentsdeserve.com.

Chapter 1: Making Black Lives Matter at School

1. The thirteen principles of the Black Lives Matter movement are Collective Value, Restorative Justice, Black Women, Queer Affirming, Black Families, Empathy, Globalism, Transgender Affirming, Diversity, Intergenerational, Loving Engagement, Unapologetically Black, and Black Villages. The principles are an adaptable set of concepts and their precise wording and framing tend to vary by organization and audience. See, for example, Laleña Garcia's feature in this book, "How to Talk to Young Children about the Black Lives Matter Guiding Principles."
2. Jamiles Lartey, "'We've Ignited a New Generation': Patrisse Khan-Cullors on the Resurgence of Black Activism," *Guardian*, January 28, 2018.
3. Barbara Ransby, *Making All Black Lives Matter: Reimagining Freedom in the Twenty-First Century* (Oakland, CA: University of California Press, 2018), 3.
4. African American Policy Forum, *Say Her Name: Resisting Police Brutality against Black Women* (New York: AAPF, 2015).
5. Mark Berman, John Sullivan, Julie Tate, and Jennifer Jenkins, "Protests Spread over Police Shootings. Police Promised Reforms. Every Year They Still Shoot and Kill Nearly 1,000," *Washington Post*, June 8, 2020; Tucker

Higgins and John W. Schoen, "These Four Charts Describe Police Violence in America," *CNBC*, June 1, 2020.

6. Laura Putnam, Erica Chenoweth, and Jeremy Pressman, "The Floyd Protests Are the Broadest in US History—and Are Spreading to White, Small-Town America," *Washington Post*, June 6, 2020.

7. Jack Arnholz, Ivan Pereira, and Christina Carrega, "US Protests Map Shows Where Curfews and National Guard Are Active," *ABC News*, June 4, 2020.

8. Anya Kamenetz, "Why There's a Push to Get Police out of Schools," *NPR*, June 23, 2020; Michael Sainato, "'They Set Us Up': US Police Arrested Over 10,000 Protesters, Many Non-Violent," *Guardian*, June 8, 2020; "How Police Departments Can Identify and Oust Killer Cops," *The Conversation*, June 10, 2020.

9. Mariame Kamba, "Yes, We Mean Literally Abolish the Police," *New York Times*, June 12, 2002.

10. "Aaron Ross Coleman, "Minneapolis May Be the First City to Dismantle the Police," *Vox*, June 8, 2020.

11. James Rainey, Dakota Smith, and Cindy Chang, "Growing the LAPD Was Gospel at City Hall. George Floyd Changed That," *Los Angeles Times*, June 5, 2020.

12. Daniel Beekman, "Seattle City Council Bans Police Use of Tear Gas and Chokeholds as Protests for Black Lives Continue," *Seattle Times*, June 15, 2020.

13. David Kroman, "King County Labor Council Expels Seattle Police Union," *Crosscut*, June 17, 2020.

14. Adam K. Raymond, "Here's How the George Floyd Protests Have Already Changed the Country," *Intelligencer,* June 9, 2020.

15. "Thomas Jefferson Statue Toppled at North Portland's Jefferson High School," *KGW8*, June 15, 2020; Henry Wiencek, "The Dark Side of Thomas Jefferson," *Smithsonian Magazine*, October 2020.

16. Peter Myers, "How Black Lives Matter Is Moving into the Schools," *New York Post*, August 29, 2019.

17. Adeel Hassan, "Hate-Crime Violence Hits 16-Year High, FBI Reports," *New York Times*, November 12, 2019.

18. Ali Vitali, Kasie Hunt, and Frank Thorp V., "Trump Referred to Haiti and African Nations as 'Shithole' Countries," *NBC*, January 11, 2018.

19. Rosie Gray, "Trump Defends White-Nationalist Protesters: 'Some Very Fine People on Both Sides,'" *Atlantic*, August 15, 2017.

20. Zeke Miller, "Trump Tweets Video with 'White Power' Chant, Then Deletes It," *AP News*, June 28, 2020.

21. Teaching Tolerance, *Special Report: Hate at School*, May 2, 2019, https://www.splcenter.org/sites/default/files/tt_2019_hate_at_school_report_final_0.pdf.

22. "Boy, 10, Charged with Aggravated Assault during Dodgeball-like Game," *ABC News*, July 31, 2019.
23. Leslie Postal, "Six-Year-Old Boy with Dreadlocks Banned from Private School in Orange County," *Orlando Sentinel,* August 14, 2018; Janelle Griffith, "Second Black Teen Told by School to Cut Dreadlocks, according to His Mom," *NBC*, January 4, 2020; Lateshia Beacham, "Student Will Be Barred from Graduation Unless He Cuts His Dreadlocks, School Says," *Washington Post*, January 24, 2020; Jacob Bogage, Eli Rosenberg, and Alex Horton, "A White Referee Told a High School Wrestler to Cut His Dreadlocks or Forfeit. He took the Cut," *Washington Post*, December 22, 2018.
24. Rebecca Klein, "The Other Side of School Safety: Students Are Getting Tasered and Beaten by Police," *HuffPost*, September 8, 2018.
25. P. R. Lockhart, "Police Officer Resigns after Video Shows Him Using Excessive Force on an 11-Year-Old Girl," *Vox*, October 24, 2019.
26. Cynthia Greenlee, "How History Textbooks Reflect America's Refusal to Reckon with Slavery," *Vox*, August 26, 2019.
27. "Black Lives Matter at School: From the Week of Action to Year-Round Anti-racist Pedagogy and Protest," *Rethinking Schools*, https://rethinkingschools.org/articles/black-lives-matter-at-school-from-the-week-of-action-to-year-round-anti-racist-pedagogy-and-protest/.
28. Alex Paterson, "Laura Ingraham Lies That Affirming Trans Students Is 'Child Abuse,' Will Lead to Lower Age of Consent," *Media Matters America*, February 6, 2020.
29. Opal Tometi, "Black Future Month: Examining the Current State of Black Lives and Envisioning Where We Go from Here," *Oakland Post,* February 11, 2015.
30. Jody Sokolower, "Schools and the New Jim Crow: An interview with Michelle Alexander," *Rethinking Schools* 26, no. 2 (2011/12).
31. Nick Morrison, "Black Students 'Face Racial Bias,' in School Discipline," *Forbes*, April 5, 2019.
32. Monique Morris, *Pushout: The Criminalization of Black Girls in Schools* (New York: New Press, 2016), 3.
33. Wayne Au, "Racial Justice Is Not a Choice," *Rethinking Schools* 33, no. 4 (Summer 2019).
34. Au, "Racial Justice."
35. Au, "Racial Justice."
36. Melinda A. Anderson, "Why Schools Need More Teachers of Color—For White Students," *Atlantic,* August 6, 2015.
37. Kristina Rizga, "Black Teachers Matter," *Mother Jones*, September/October 2016.
38. Andrea Parker and Jim Staros, "Black Teachers Matter," *CTU Speaks!*,

podcast, January 18, 2020.

39. Anya Kamenetz, "Having Just One Black Teacher Can Keep Black Kids in School," *NPR*, April 10, 2017.

40. "I Know My People Are Strong," Black Lives Matter at School video, 2:18, January 29, 2019, https://blacklivesmatteratschool.com/2019/01/30 /video-black-lives-matter-at-school-i-know-my-people-are-strong/.

41. Thomas Dee and Emily Penner, "The Causal Effects of Cultural Relevance: Evidence from an Ethnic Studies Curriculum," CEPA Working Paper, Stanford Center for Education Policy Analysis, https://cepa.stanford.edu/sites/default/files/wp16-01-v201601.pdf.

42. Kenrya Rankin, "Study: Nation's Largest Public Schools Have More Police Than Counselors," *Colorlines,* March 29, 2016.

43. American Civil Liberties Union, *Cops and No Counselors: How the Lack of School Mental Health Staff Is Harming Students,* March 2019, https://www.aclu.org/report/cops-and-no-counselors.

44. "More than 14 Million Kids Go to a Public School with Police but no Mental Health Staff. That's Bad, ACLU Says," *CNN,* March 12, 2019.

45. American Civil Liberties Union of Washington, *Students Not Suspects: The Need to Reform School Policing in Washington State,* April 18, 2017, www.aclu-wa.org/docs/students-not-suspects-need-reform-school -policing-washington-state.

46. ACLU of Washington, *Students Not Suspects.*

47. ACLU of Washington, *Students Not Suspects.*

48. Dignity in Schools, *Police in Schools Are Not the Answer to School Shootings,* March 2018, https://dignityinschools.org/resources/police-i n-schools-are-not-the-answer-to-school-shootings/.

49. Anya Kamenetz, "DeVos to Rescind Obama-Era Guidance on School Discipline," *NPR*, December 18, 2018

50. ACLU of Washington, *Students Not Suspects.*

51. ACLU of Washington, *Students Not Suspects.*

52. Heather Long and Andrew Van Dam, "US Employment Rate Soars to 14.7 Percent, the Worst Since the Depression Era," *Washington Post,* May 8, 2020.

53. Naomi Klein, *The Shock Doctrine* (New York: Picador, 2007).

54. "Frederick Douglass, 'If There Is No Struggle, There Is No Progress' (1857)," BlackPast.org, January 25, 2007.

Chapter 2: Black Lives Matter at School: Historical Perspectives

1. I summarized this history in "The Struggle for Black Education," in *Education and Capitalism: Struggles for Learning and Liberation,* Jeff Bale and Sarah Knopp, eds. (Chicago: Haymarket Books, 2012), 41–69.

2. See, for example, Ibram Rogers, *The Black Campus Movement: Black Stu-*

dents and the Racial Reconstitution of Higher Education, 1965–1972 (New York: Palgrave, 2012); and Martha Biondi, *The Black Revolution on Campus* (Berkeley: University of California Press, 2012).

3. Katherine Mellen Charron, *Freedom's Teacher: The Life of Septima Clark* (Chapel Hill: University of North Carolina Press, 2009).

4. Daniel Perlstein, "Minds Stayed on Freedom: Politics and Pedagogy in the African-American Freedom Struggle," *American Educational Research Journal* 39, no. 2 (Summer 2002): 249–277.

5. Russell Rickford, *We Are an African People: Independent Education, Black Power, and the Radical Imagination* (New York: Oxford University Press, 2016).

6. Quoted in Robert Robinson, "Until the Revolution: Analyzing the Politics, Pedagogy, and Curriculum of the Oakland Community School," *Espacio, Tiempo y Educación* 7, no. 1 (2020): 196.

7. See Pero G. Dagbovie, *The Early Black History Movement, Carter G. Woodson and Lorenzo Johnston Greene* (Champaign: University of Illinois Press, 2007); and Jeffrey Snyder, *Making Black History: The Color Line, Culture, and Race in the Age of Jim Crow* (Athens: University of Georgia Press, 2018).

8. "History Is Truth," *Negro History Bulletin* 1, no. 5 (February 1938): 9.

9. Imani Perry, *May We Forever Stand: A History of the Black National Anthem* (Chapel Hill: University of North Carolina Press, 2018); see especially Chapter 3, "School Bell Song."

10. Heather Andrea Williams, *Self-Taught: African American Education in Slavery and Freedom* (Chapel Hill: University of North Carolina Press, 2005).

11. Ronald E. Butchart, "Race, Social Studies, and Culturally Relevant Curriculum in Social Studies' Prehistory: A Cautionary Meditation," in *Histories of Social Studies and Race: 1865–2000*, Christine Woyshner and Chara Haeessler Bohan, eds. (New York: Palgrave, 2012), 19.

12. Ronald E. Butchart, *Schooling the Freed People: Teaching, Learning, and the Struggle for Black Freedom, 1861–1876* (Chapel Hill: University of North Carolina Press, 2010), 126.

13. *Freedman's Torchlight* 1, no. 1 (December 1866): 1.

14. See Williams, *Self-Taught,* Chapter 8.

15. Butchart, *Schooling the Freed People,* 134. See also Williams, *Self-Taught,* Chapter 8.

16. Systemic racism and civil rights activism in northern and western cities (and in schools) is well documented. See, for example, Jeanne Theoharis and Komozi Woodard, eds., *Freedom North: Black Freedom Struggles Outside the South, 1940–1980* (New York: Palgrave, 2003); and Brian Purnell and Jeanne Theoharis, with Komozi Woodard, eds., *The Strange Careers of Jim Crow North: Segregation and Struggle Outside of the South* (New York: New York University Press, 2019).

17. Clarence Taylor, "Harlem Schools and the New York City Teachers'

Union," in *Educating Harlem: A Century of Schooling and Resistance in a Black Community*, Ansley T. Erickson and Ernest Morrell, eds. (New York: Columbia University Press, 2019), 142.

18. Clarence Taylor tells the story of the rise and fall of the teachers union in *Reds at the Blackboard: Communism, Civil Rights, and the New York City Teachers Union* (New York: Columbia University Press, 2011).

19. See, for example, Jerald E. Podair's discussion of the controversy over the union's contractual "disruptive child" clause: *The Strike That Changed New York: Blacks, Whites, and the Ocean Hill–Brownsville Crisis* (New Haven: Yale University Press, 2002).

20. Advancement Project and Alliance for Educational Justice, *We Came to Learn: A Call to Action for Police-Free Schools* (Washington, DC: Advancement Project), 2018, 17, https://advancementproject.org/wecametolearn/.

21. See Kathleen Nolan, *Police in the Hallways: Discipline in an Urban High School* (Minneapolis: University of Minnesota Press, 2011). In particular, see Chapter 1, "How the Police Took Over School Discipline: From Policies of Inclusion to Punishment and Exclusion."

22. New York Civil Liberties Union, *A Look at School Safety: School to Prison Pipeline*, https://www.nyclu.org/en/look-school-safety.

23. Wendy Parker, "Desegregating Teachers," *Washington University Law Review* 86, no. 1 (2008): 1–52.

24. Quoted in Vanessa Siddle Walker, *The Lost Education of Horace Tate: Uncovering the Hidden Heroes Who Fought for Justice in Schools* (New York: New Press, 2018), 19–20.

25. On the neoliberal attack on public education, see Noliwe Rooks, *Cutting School: The Segrenomics of American Education* (New York: New Press, 2017).

26. Brian Jones, "Keys to the Schoolhouse: Black Teachers, Education Reform, and the Growing Teacher Rebellion," in *What's Race Got to Do With It? How Current School Reform Policy Maintains Racial and Economic Inequality*, Edwin Mayorga, Ujju Aggarwal, and Bree Picower, eds., 2nd ed. (New York: Peter Lang, 2020), 63–86.

Feature: How One Elementary School Sparked a Movement to Make Black Students' Lives Matter

1. Janet Kim, "Black Lives Matter at Schools Rally Draws Hundreds, Including SeaHawks DE Michael Bennett," *Q13 Fox News*, October 19, 2016.

Chapter 3: From Philly with Love

1. Greg Windle, "This Is Black Lives Matter Week in Schools," *Philadelphia Public School Notebook*, February 4, 2019.

Chapter 4: Organizing the National Curriculum

1. Black Lives Matter, "What We Believe," https://blacklivesmatter.com/what-we-believe/.

2. Until We Are Free, "Art + Culture Resources," http://www.untilweareallfree.com/#art-culture-resources.

3. Barbara Ransby, *Making All Black Lives Matter: Reimagining Freedom in the Twenty-first Century* (Oakland: University of California Press, 2018).

4. Django Paris and H. Samy Alim, eds., *Culturally Sustaining Pedagogies: Teaching and Learning for Justice in a Changing World* (New York: Teachers College Press, 2017).

5. Noah De Lissovoy, Alexander J. Means, and Kenneth J. Saltman, *Toward a New Common School Movement* (New York: Routledge, 2015).

6. Grace Lee Boggs, "Reimagine Everything," *Race, Poverty and the Environment* 19, no. 2 (2012): 44–45.

7. Ashon Crawley, "Otherwise Movements," *New Inquiry*, January 19, 2015.

8. Assata Shakur, *Assata: An Autobiography* (London: Zed Books, 2016).

9. "The Ferguson Syllabus: A Teacher on Teaching about Race in America," *Lenny*, September 14, 2016.

10. Keisha N. Blain, "#Charlestonsyllabus," African American Intellectual History Society, https://www.aaihs.org/resources/charlestonsyllabus/.

11. "Prison Abolition Syllabus," *Black Perspectives*, published by the African American Intellectual History Society, September 8, 2018, https://www.aaihs.org/prison-abolition-syllabus-2-0/.

12. Vanessa Siddle Walker, *The Lost Education of Horace Tate: Uncovering the Hidden Heroes Who Fought for Justice in Schools* (New York: New Press, 2018); Heather Andrea Williams, *Self-Taught: African American Education in Slavery and Freedom* (Chapel Hill: University of North Carolina Press, 2009); Jarvis R. Givens, "'He Was, Undoubtedly, a Wonderful Character': Black Teachers' Representations of Nat Turner during Jim Crow," *Souls* 18, nos. 2–4 (2016): 215–234.

13. Angela Ryan, "Counter College: Third World Students Reimagine Public Higher Education," *History of Education Quarterly* 55, no. 4 (2015): 413–440.

14. Proposal for a Third World College, 1969, CES ARC 2015/2, Location 2:7, twLF, Box 1, Folder 7, Ethnic Studies Library, University of California, Berkeley.

15. Robin D. G. Kelley, "Black Study, Black Struggle," *Ufahamu: A Journal of African Studies* 40, no. 2 (2018): 157.

16. Fred Moten and Stefano Harney, *The Undercommons: Fugitive Planning and Black Study* (New York: Minor Compositions, 2013).

17. Eli Meyerhoff, *Beyond Education: Radical Studying for Another World* (Minneapolis: University of Minnesota Press, 2019).

18. NoViolet Bulawayo, "Migrant Rights Meets Racial Justice: Declaration of Unity," Until We Are All Free, http://www.untilweareallfree.com/declaration

-of-unity-english.

Chapter 5: MapSO Freedom School and the Statewide and National Black Lives Matter at School Week of Action Organizing

1. See Christina Sharpe, *In the Wake: On Blackness and Being* (Duke University Press, 2016), which examines Black precarity within the context of what Sharpe calls "slavery and its afterlives" (12).
2. Advancement Project and Alliance for Educational Justice, *We Came to Learn: A Call to Action for Police-Free Schools* (Washington, DC: Advancement Project), 2018, 17, https://advancementproject.org/wecametolearn/.
3. bell hooks, *The Will to Change: Men, Masculinity, and Love* (New York: Atria Books, 2004), 17.

Chapter 10: Seattle Educators' Lesson Plan for City Officials

1. Michelle Alexander, "America, This Is Your Chance," *New York Times*, June 8, 2020.
2. A youth-sponsored petition calling on Seattle Public Schools to sever ties with the Seattle Police Department is available at https://tinyurl.com/ybsvn5uw.
3. The BIPOC union members' petition to remove the Seattle Police Officers Guild from the Martin Luther King Jr. Labor Council is available at https://tinyurl.com/yas9p4e6.
4. The sign-on endorsing the call to defund the Seattle Police Department is available at https://tinyurl.com/yd4br5me.
5. Yawu Miller, "Boston Teacher's Black Lives Matter Initiative Draws Fire from Police Union," *Bay State Banner*, February 6, 2020.
6. American Civil Liberties Union, *Cops and No Counselors: How the Lack of School Mental Health Staff Is Harming Students*, March 2019, https://www.aclu.org/report/cops-and-no-counselors.
7. Amir Vera, "ACLU Says Schools Need More Mental Health Professionals, Not Police," *CNN*, March 12, 2019.
8. Alliance to Reclaim Our Schools, *Confronting the Education Debt: We Owe Billions to Black, Brown, and Low-Income Students and Their Schools*, http://educationdebt.reclaimourschools.org/wp-content/uploads/2018/08/Confronting-the-Education-Debt_FullReport.pdf.
9. "Disparities Persist in School Discipline, Says Government Watchdog," *NPR*, April 4, 2018.

Chapter 13: Bringing the Team Along: When Solidarity Leads to Progress

1. Bettina L. Love, *We Want to Do More Than Survive: Abolitionist Teaching and the Pursuit of Educational Freedom* (Boston: Beacon Press, 2019), 112.
2. Beverly Daniel Tatum, *Why Are All the Black Kids Sitting Together in the Cafeteria?: And Other Conversations about Race* (New York: Basic Books, 2017), 117.

Chapter 14: Centering the Youngest Black Children

1. Michael J. Dumas and Joseph Derrick Nelson, "(Re)Imagining Black Boyhood: Toward a Critical Framework for Educational Research," *Harvard Educational Review* 86, no. 1 (Spring 2016): 27–47.

Chapter 15: Organizing the Black Lives Matter at School Week of Action in New Jersey

1. The term "anti-police" is often weaponized against the Movement for Black Lives and other racial justice activists and organizers who resist and organize against the carceral and police state of the United States, which allows police to control, surveil, and kill Black, Indigenous, and other people of color (BIPOC), (dis)abled people, poor and working-class people, and queer and trans people, with impunity. Through manipulative messaging, to be "anti-police" is to seek death and violence against individual members of the police force. However, for abolitionists, the elimination of the police state means an end to policing, surveillance, prisons, the carceral state, and the far-reaching tentacles of a racist, capitalist system, while creating more humanistic and caring alternatives to this penal system.

Chapter 16: This Is My Education: Bringing the Black Lives Matter at School Week of Action to an African American Immersion School in Milwaukee

1. Diane Pollard and Cheryl Ajirotu, *African-Centered Schooling in Theory and Practice* (Westport, CT: Greenwood Publishing Group, 2000), 7.

Chapter 17: Higher Education Organizing for the Week of Action

1. More details about the Black Lives Matter at School events held at SUNY New Paltz can be found at https://hawksites.newpaltz.edu/blmatschool/schedule/.

Feature: Solidarity with Migrant Families at the Border

1. "Families Sue Gov't over Family Separation Policy," *Democracy Now!,*

February 13, 2019.

2. Shaila Dewan, "Family Separation: It's a Problem for US Citizens, Too," *New York Times,* June 22, 2018.

3. Dewan, "Family Separation."

4. Teachers Against Child Detention, https://www.teachersagainstchilddetention.org.

Chapter 20: The Black Lives Matter at School Pedagogy

1. Gloria Ladson-Billings, "Toward a Theory of Culturally Relevant Pedagogy," *American Educational Research Journal* 32, no. 3 (Autumn 1995): 465–491; and Geneva Gay, *Culturally Responsive Teaching: Theory, Research, and Practice* (New York: Teachers College Press, 2000).

2. Christopher Emdin, *For White Folks Who Teach in the Hood...And the Rest of Y'all Too: Reality Pedagogy and Urban Education* (Boston: Beacon Press, 2016).

3. Bettina L. Love, *We Want to Do More Than Survive: Abolitionist Teaching and the Pursuit of Educational Freedom* (Boston: Beacon Press, 2019), 112.

4. Jamila Lyiscott, *Black Appetite. White Food. Issues of Race, Voice, and Justice within and beyond the Classroom* (New York: Routledge, 2019).

5. Dyan Watson, Jesse Hagopian, Wayne Au, eds., *Teaching for Black Lives* (Milwaukee: Rethinking Schools, 2018), 12.

6. Denisha Jones, review of *Teaching for Black Lives, Oregon Journal of the Social Studies* 7, no. 1 (2019): 110–112.

7. Daniel A. Laitsch, Elizabeth E. Heilman, and Paul Shaker, "Teacher Education, Pro-market Policy, and Advocacy Research," *Teaching Education* 13, no. 3 (2002): 251–271.

8. See Violet Harris, "In Praise of a Scholarly Force: Rudine Sims Bishop," *Language Arts* 85, no. 2 (2007): 153–159.

Chapter 21: Not Just in February!

1. "Abolishing Prisons with Mariame Kaba," *Why Is This Happening? With Chris Hayes* (podcast), April 10, 2019.

2. Nicole Lee, "Healing-Centered Youth Organizing: A Framework for Youth Leadership in the Twenty-first Century," Urban Peace Movement, 2014, urbanpeacement.org.

Chapter 22: Hire More Black Teachers Now

1. Albert Shanker Institute, *The State of Teacher Diversity in American Education,* https://www.shankerinstitute.org/event/teacherdiversity; US Department of Education, Civil Rights Data Collection, https://ocrdata.ed.gov/Home.

Chapter 25: Minneapolis Public Schools Expel the Police!

1. Emily Bloch, "Minneapolis City Schools Are Cutting Ties with Local Police after Death of George Floyd," *Teen Vogue,* June 3, 2020.
2. Ryan Faircloth, "Minneapolis Public Schools Terminates Contract with Police Department over George Floyd's Death," *Minnesota Star Tribune,* June 2, 2020.
3. "School Resource Officers Will No Longer Patrol Portland Schools," *KGW8,* June 4, 2020; Matt Sebastian and Tiney Ricciardi, "DPS Board Members Seek Removal of Denver Police Officers from Schools by 2021," *Denver Post,* June 5, 2020.

Inequity and COVID-19

1. Ed Pilkington, "Black Americans Dying of Covid-19 at Three Times the Rate of White People," *Guardian,* May 20, 2020.
2. John Eligon and Audra D. S. Burch, "Questions of Bias in Covid-19 Treatment Add to the Mourning of Black Families," *New York Times,* May 10, 2020.
3. Rashawn Ray, "Why Are Blacks Dying at Higher Rates from COVID-19?" Brookings Institution, April 9, 2020.
4. Ray, "Why Are Blacks Dying?"

Index

About Haymarket Books

Haymarket Books is a radical, independent, nonprofit book publisher based in Chicago.

Our mission is to publish books that contribute to struggles for social and economic justice. We strive to make our books a vibrant and organic part of social movements and the education and development of a critical, engaged, international left.

We take inspiration and courage from our namesakes, the Haymarket martyrs, who gave their lives fighting for a better world. Their 1886 struggle for the eight-hour day—which gave us May Day, the international workers' holiday—reminds workers around the world that ordinary people can organize and struggle for their own liberation. These struggles continue today across the globe—struggles against oppression, exploitation, poverty, and war.

Since our founding in 2001, Haymarket Books has published more than five hundred titles. Radically independent, we seek to drive a wedge into the risk-averse world of corporate book publishing. Our authors include Noam Chomsky, Arundhati Roy, Rebecca Solnit, Angela Y. Davis, Howard Zinn, Amy Goodman, Wallace Shawn, Mike Davis, Winona LaDuke, Ilan Pappé, Richard Wolff, Dave Zirin, Keeanga-Yamahtta Taylor, Nick Turse, Dahr Jamail, David Barsamian, Elizabeth Laird, Amira Hass, Mark Steel, Avi Lewis, Naomi Klein, and Neil Davidson. We are also the trade publishers of the acclaimed Historical Materialism Book Series and of Dispatch Books.

Also Available
from Haymarket Books

Badass Teachers Unite!: Writing on Education, History, and Youth Activism
Mark Naison

Education and Capitalism: Struggles for Learning and Liberation
Edited by Jeff Bale and Sarah Knopp

Freedom Is a Constant Struggle
Ferguson, Palestine, and the Foundations of a Movement
Angela Y. Davis, edited by Frank Barat, preface by Cornel West

From #BlackLivesMatter to Black Liberation
Keeanga-Yamahtta Taylor, with a foreword by Angela Y. Davis

A Marxist Education
Wayne Au

More Than a Score: The New Uprising Against High-Stakes Testing
Edited by Jesse Hagopian, foreword by Alfie Kohn,
preface by Diane Ravitch

#SayHerName: Black Women's Stories of State Violence and Public Silence
African American Policy Forum, edited by Kimberlé Crenshaw

Schooling In Capitalist America
Educational Reform and the Contradictions of Economic Life
Samuel Bowles and Herbert Gintis

This Is Not A Test: A New Narrative on Race, Class, and Education
José Luis Vilson, foreword by Karen Lewis, afterword by Pedro Noguera

We Still Here: Pandemic, Policing, Protest, and Possibility
Marc Lamont Hill, edited by Frank Barat,
foreword by Keeanga-Yamahtta Taylor

CPSIA information can be obtained
at www.ICGtesting.com
Printed in the USA
BVHW051916260821
615341BV00002B/45

9 781642 593891